"This volume brings theological, multicultural, [and] psychospiritual insights to bear on the multifac[eted ... what] does it take to become and remain a happy, healtny, and holy priest.... [Exploring the] inner life of the priest in search of those dimensions of 'affective maturity'—the *sine qua non* of priestly ministry today—McGlone and Sperry offer no facile, one-size-fits-all, cookie-cutter answers. I encourage seminarians, priests, and all who are entrusted with seminary formation and the ongoing formation of priests to take to heart the wisdom found in these pages."

—The Most Reverend Gerald R. Barnes,
bishop of San Bernardino, California

"McGlone and Sperry are both clinical professionals with many years of experience in priestly formation. Their book explores the ways that good clinical practice and good formation work together to produce and support happy, healthy, holy priests. Every formation director, seminary rector, vocation director, and vicar for clergy should have *The Inner Life of Priests* on his reference shelf."

—Mary L. Gautier, PhD, senior research associate,
Center for Applied Research in the Apostolate
(CARA), Georgetown University

"*In The Inner Life of Priests* Jesuit father and psychologist Jerry McGlone and Catholic psychiatrist Len Sperry offer a thoughtful, articulate, and evidence-based reflection on the multifaceted inner life of Catholic priests today. During a time when priestly life has come into question and sometimes scandalized, this much-needed book provides an insightful and reasoned discussion that cuts through the myths and misinformation about this important and still noble vocation. It is a must read for everyone who wears a Roman collar, for the layperson in the pews, and anyone interested in the inner life of Catholic priests today."

—Thomas G. Plante, PhD, ABPP, professor of
psychology and director of Spirituality and Health
Institute at Santa Clara University

"At last a book about American priests, neither anecdotal nor "a priori" but data-based and well analyzed."

—Rev. Robert Curry, SJ, chaplain, Saint John Vianney
Center; former pastor and superior in the Maryland
Province of the Jesuits

"This carefully researched collection of articles makes important distinctions based on observation of various aspects of the lives and personalities of priests. It offers new categories for thinking about the priestly and religious life based on recent trends in American society, such as the cultural diversity of the Catholic population in general as well as the new seminarians and international missionaries to America. The historical perspective on the development of the role of psychology in evaluating priests and seminarians is a very helpful context in the life of the church and society. The book also provides very helpful tools for dealing with the priestly sexual abuse scandal by presenting solid data about the abusers and the effects of the scandal on other priests.

While *The Inner Life of Priests* is a well-informed analysis of psychological, social, and physical dimensions of priestly and seminary life, it carefully and boldly incorporates the theological and spiritual dimensions into the discussion as completely normal and necessary. The insights derived from this more holistic approach to the needs of seminarians and priests stem from the careful integration of all these aspects. Faith is treated as a normal and necessary dimension—faith in God and his gracious call, faith in the need for the church, and faith in an authentically Catholic anthropology. This faith is presented as a natural ally of the psychological, social, physical, and cultural dimensions of priestly and seminarian life.

This collection of articles is not only closely in tune with the most recent developments in the situation of American priest and seminary life but it also extracts from these situations some of the trends for the future. It makes important recommendations for correcting gaps in already existing psychological, professional, and cultural analyses of priests and seminarians. This book will be very useful to seminary staff, diocesan bishops, religious superiors, vocation directors, and anyone else involved in the promotion of vocations to the priesthood. Furthermore, the average priest can read this book with great benefit to help him examine factors in his own personality and social relationships with a refinement based on the excellent research done by these authors."

—Rev. Mitchell C. Pacwa, SJ, PhD, television host,
EWTN

"*The Inner Life of Priests* is a timely and important review of issues confronting the selection, formation, and ministry of those called to the priesthood. It provides a comprehensive review along with the developing issues that need to be considered and confronted for improving the life and mission of priests."

—Ronald J. Karney, PhD, senior psychologist,
Catholic Clinical Consultants, Philadelphia

"Not since the bygone days of Kennedy and Greeley has there been a serious attempt to contextualize the psychological and spiritual landscape of American priests. This attempt is not rosy or sugarcoated, but it does present a comprehensive portrait and offers a great deal to think about. A welcome addition to the literature."

> —Rev. John Allan Loftus, SJ, PhD, former executive director of the Southdown Treatment Center in Ontario; former president of Regis College at the University of Toronto

"A much-needed appeal to seminaries, religious communities, and dioceses to be true spaces of ongoing human formation. This book not only calls attention to the proper role of psychology, it provides a road map to wholeness and holiness for those called to ministry in the church."

> —Rev. Alejandro Crosthwaite, OP, faculty of Social Sciences, Pontifical University of St. Thomas Aquinas (Rome)

"This study on the inner life of priests marries richly researched knowledge with encouraging yet hard-won insights about how priesthood in the Roman Catholic communion of faith might be lived healthfully and integrally in the increasingly multicultural reality of North American life. The text contributes immensely to essential information for all those seeking to foster and develop vocations to the priesthood in wholesome ways."

> —Rev. John Pavlik, OFM Cap, executive director, Conference of Major Superiors of Men (CMSM)

"*The Inner Life of Priests* is a practical presentation, grounded in research and clinical pastoral experience that serves as a helpful resource for those who are involved in the work of formation for priestly ministry in the church. The use of data and case studies provides meaningful insights into the joys and challenges of living authentically and faithfully the call to holiness, and to following Christ in serving the people of God as a priest."

> —Rev. John P. McGarry, SJ, rector, Jesuit School of Theology of Santa Clara University; former provincial, California Province of the Society of Jesus

"Father McGlone and Dr. Sperry have explored and described the complex psychologies of men called to the celibate priesthood with an eye for accuracy and depth. This timely book serves as an excellent and necessary resource for those providing psychological services to priests, as well as spiritual directors and those in the work of formation of priests."

—Jeffrey Feathergill, PsyD, psychological consultant to dioceses and religious orders

"With honesty, insight, and respect, this book offers a long, loving look at the priesthood of Jesus Christ. This is a must read for those engaged in formation and anyone engaged in work within the life of the Catholic Church."

—Rev. Thomas M. Dragga, DMin, president-rector, Borromeo Seminary, Cleveland

"Few times have I read a book that both impressed and encouraged me. This book by Fr. McGlone and Dr. Sperry was impressive in its use of research and hopeful in providing us with solutions to our problems."

—The Most Reverend Joseph C. Bambera, DD, JCL, bishop of Scranton, Pennsylvania

"This book is the necessary conversation by psychologists and those in seminary formation. It will be a great resource for seminary admission committees, vocation directors, and bishops as it provides a contemporary portrait of priestly life from the perspective of psychological and sociological research that is grounded in the theological anthropology of the Roman Catholic tradition."

—Rev. Mark A. Latcovich, PhD, vice-rector and academic dean, Saint Mary Seminary & Graduate School of Theology

"Father McGlone, SJ, Len Sperry, and others address the inner life of the priest in a very insightful and helpful way. They use spirituality and psychology in a way that enables the priest to come to a deeper understanding of himself and his vocation."

—The Most Reverend Gregory Aymond, archbishop of New Orleans

The Inner Life of Priests

Gerard J. McGlone, SJ, and Len Sperry

LITURGICAL PRESS
Collegeville, Minnesota

www.litpress.org

Cover design by Ann Blattner. Photo: iStockphoto/Thinkstock.

Excerpts from documents of the Second Vatican Council are from *Vatican Council II: The Basic Sixteen Documents*, by Austin Flannery, OP, © 1996 (Costello Publishing Company, Inc.). Used with permission.

Excerpts from Guidelines for the Use of Psychology in the Admission and Formation of Candidates for the Priesthood, by the Congregation for Catholic Education, © 2008 Libreria Editrice Vaticana. Used with permission.

Scripture texts, prefaces, introductions, footnotes and cross references used in this work are taken from the *New American Bible, revised edition* © 2010, 1991, 1986, 1970 Confraternity of Christian Doctrine, Inc., Washington, DC. All Rights Reserved. No part of this work may be reproduced or transmitted in any form or by any means, electronic or mechanical, including photocopying, recording, or by any information storage and retrieval system, without permission in writing from the copyright owner.

1   2   3   4   5   6   7   8

Library of Congress Cataloging-in-Publication Data

The inner life of priests / edited by Gerard J. McGlone and Len Sperry.
     p.   cm.
  Includes bibliographical references and index.
  ISBN 978-0-8146-3438-7—ISBN 978-0-8146-3439-4 (e-book)
  1. Catholic Church—Clergy—Psychology. 2. Catholic Church—Clergy—Religious life. 3. Priests. I. McGlone, Gerard J. II. Sperry, Len.

BX1912.7.I56   2012
262'.142—dc23   2012009888

In loving memory of my deceased parents
Mary and Steve McGlone, and to my sister Kathleen;
and
to Patti, the love of my life,
and our children Christen, Tim, Jon, and Steve;
and
to those who have served, will serve, and currently serve
the church we love.

Thank you!

Contents

Preface

Presiding at the Eucharist, hearing confessions, giving homilies, visiting the sick, speaking words of advice and encouragement, attending and chairing meetings—these and much more represent the outer life of priests. These responsibilities amount to eight or ten hours a day of visible and public ministry, the outer life of priests. But what about the rest? What about those hours when the priest is out of the public eye, offstage, and by himself? This is the invisible and private ministry—this is the inner life of priests.

So what is this inner life? Is it all psychological? Is it the unconscious? Is it dominated by unfinished business and regrets from roads not taken? Is it (or much of it) spiritual and grace-filled? Is it different than the inner life of laypersons? Is it similar to or different from the inner life of religious sisters and brothers? Just what is the inner life of priests really like?

For many laypeople, there is an air of mystery about priests who are set apart by their lifestyle and perhaps even their clothing. This mystery evokes a curiosity about their private lives, their prayer lives, their aspirations, and their longings. The reality is that most priests seldom—if ever—talk about these matters with fellow priests, except possibly for their spiritual directors. Until now there has been no book, article, or website to turn to for answers.

This book lays the foundations for how a man enters and understands that inner world more fully and honestly. The reader will be challenged by the research and data, yet also humbled by spiritual profundity. Few resources exist that give the historical and current integrated perspectives through which one can judge (and be judged) more accurately and profoundly. This book first plots the unique maps of the church and the arena of psychology. It then leads us through the necessary views about God, self, and others that allow us to view our Catholic tradition in a healthy and holy manner.

This book details ways the two worlds of theology and psychology might converge and diverge. Each area clearly has its special claim and authority, but new forms of dialogue and respect emerge here. The explanations of each expertise is simultaneously differentiated and integrated.

This book provides the priest and those who care about him the ability to contextualize and better understand him as a man and as a priest. It also allows those who are to direct, form, and guide that man the necessary language and skills to serve the community to which this man is called. It allows the layperson a focused lens through which she or he may see the man who both mystifies and leads others to holiness on a regular basis.

The priest in modern society is seen quite differently than in years past. Of course the priest is not alone in this regard; many public figures have "fallen from grace." But when a priest or minister falls, the implications and the repercussions seem to be far more challenging. The public arena is often full of contradictions, controversies, and conundrums. Such complexity must find resolution somewhere. This book begins to place the reader within that world more fully. It challenges the priest himself to search that world.

Priests must face that interior dimension of a celibate world within a new cultural and societal challenge. The many facets of this celibate world are explored in both their beauty and their darkness. Few books detail the challenge and grace in celibacy and the skills necessary to live such a life well.

Essential to this book is a new model of what the inner life can be, needs to be, and indeed ought to be. It is timely written for the Church and her present and future needs. What became clear in writing this book was that the life of the priest today is one of hope.

It is both mystery and clearly seen. It is both pure grace and sinful. It is communal and yet very solitary. It is both deeply intimate and yet starkly lonely. It is sometimes filled with promise and pathology. It is both transcendent and immanent. It is profoundly complex and yet utterly simple. It is a pure gift and a learned process. It is both known and utterly unknowable. It is very human and clearly called into the divine. It is the inner life of priests.

This book is our gift to the Church. We hope that diocesan, provincial, and seminary personnel will appreciate the insights contained herein, in addition to seminarians and those considering religious and priestly vocations. And, most of all, we hope it will be of inestimable value to priests themselves.

Gerard J. McGlone & Len Sperry
Easter Triduum 2012

Acknowledgments

We wish to express our heartfelt appreciation to all who have made this book possible:

To our loved ones, friends, and colleagues who by their encouragement and example have directly and indirectly influenced our personal and professional lives—including this book.

To J. Michael Miller, CSB, archbishop of Vancouver; Fernando Ortiz, PhD; Katarina Schuth, OSF; Msgr. Jeremiah J. McCarthy; Jan Slattery; and Allan Figueroa Deck, SJ, for their wise contributions and timely commentaries, which have elevated the conversation regarding inner lives to a level that will undoubtedly influence the formation of seminarians and the continuing formation of priests for the better.

To the staff at Liturgical Press: thanks for everything! Peter Dwyer, director, immediately recognized the value and importance of this book in the lives of priests, and Trish Vanni, publisher, seamlessly operationalized the process of getting the book to press in record time. This was made possible by the expertise of Colleen Stiller, J. Andrew Edwards, Monica Schulzetenberg, and Stephanie Lancour.

Finally, to all those from the Saint John Vianney Center and Saint Charles Borromeo Seminary who participated in the groundbreaking Joint Conference: A Necessary Conversation, held in Philadelphia in June 2010. We express our deep gratitude for joining us on this inner journey for which this book has been our inspiration.

The Inner Life of Priests:
Introduction and Overview

Gerard J. McGlone, SJ, and Len Sperry

Introduction

Recently, when at a priests' convocation, I asked each individual priest, four to five in one row and section and four to five in another row and section of the hall, "Are you happy with yourself, your work, your parish, and your ministry? Is your morale high?" The individual responses were clear, unambiguous, emphatic, and a resounding *yes*! Then, I asked a group of priests in one row a very different question: "Are you all happy with where you are as priests today? Where the church is today, where you are as men, with the demands placed upon you, with your sense of meaning and mission? How you are viewed in society?" The group of priests in the row and the priests in the hall also had a resounding answer: "*No*!" It was quite clear and quite emphatic. This example highlights the limitation and downright naiveté of asking individuals about their morale, well-being, and happiness and does not take into account the power and influence of the situation. Social and organizational psychology has been critiquing such an approach for almost forty years. The jury is not out anymore, the research is clear and overwhelming in this regard. Any such research is simply not valid nor is it descriptive of the true reality and situations facing clergy today. Hence, the rationale for this book is to place the life of priests in a more appropriate and fuller context. *The Inner Life of Priests* is about the full reality facing today's church.

The inner life of priests is an intriguing, complex, multifaceted, and important topic. Recently, when at this same gathering of priests at their

annual convocation, the men and their struggles touched me deeply. It became clear to me that I, as a religious priest, and we missed something in our
formation and human development. Our documents, *Pastores Dabo Vobis*
(PDV), the Vatican statement Guidelines for the Use of Psychology in the
Admission and Formation of Candidates for the Priesthood (Guidelines),
and the Program of Priestly Formation, fifth edition (PPF), all speak of an
interiority expressed in a term called "affective maturity." The documents
are exquisite and inspiring. In this book, two leading experts will give their
views on the role that the church and psychology have played and can play
in this regard in both chapters 3 and 4. These insights provide you with an
important historical context through which you can view the fuller and more
complex ecclesial and psychological lenses through which we can view and
discuss the inner life of priests today. They also detail some concerns, cautions, and important ways that these two fields of expertise can collaborate
in the future life of priests and the church.

The practical manifestations and the practical manner within which these
church documents are embodied is, unfortunately, another story. In reality,
most of us in religious and diocesan life have not been taught to develop
our emotions, our affects, and we downright avoid them and maybe some
of us actually fear them. Affective maturity is not only a recent term and
concept in these documents but it also was not specifically taught as a skill
set in formational programming in seminaries and religious houses of formation. This fact poses significant problems. Most priests never heard of the
term affective maturity and therefore have not been taught the reality, and,
though more recent priests have heard the term and can cite all the four pillars (human, spiritual, intellectual, and pastoral) of formation in PDV, they
cannot detail how they were taught to manage their emotions. They took
no classes on emotional intelligence, no seminars on pastoral maturity, and
no classes on affective and normal development. Unfortunately, it has been
assumed as one of those skills that you "just learn" in the real world. All
research to the contrary with business executives and professionals being
brushed aside (Goleman, 2006; 2007), most seminary curriculum is superb
on the pastoral, intellectual, and spiritual pillars but lacking on the human
pillar most concerned with affective development.

This lack of training also has a cumulative, disturbing, and more recent
effect. An example of this is the startling data that is seen across the country
in almost every diocese in that priests overwhelmingly want to live alone in
rectories built for four to eight priests and yet yearn to connect with their
brothers in a new fraternity and a "brotherhood of brothers" as imagined in

John Paul II's PDV. Rectory living is not being seen by many as interpersonally life-giving. They desire celibate intimacy yet do not know how to achieve it. They do not know what it looks like and how to attain it in their daily lives. These lives are experienced more and more often in solitary, sometimes isolating, and often lonely internal struggles. They often eat alone and yet "break bread" in communal sacramental settings with their parishes or communities regularly. This disconnect and dissonance is startlingly unhealthy and yet more common than previously imagined. It strikes at the very heart of the inner life of priests. How can I be a man of *communio* (Latin for "communion") if I live, eat, pray, and drink alone regularly? In survey after survey, isolation and loneliness are themes about which priests consistently request knowledge and information. Struggles, conflicts, divisions, and strategies in communication amongst and between groups of priests who differ in their ecclesiologies are avoided. Such communication and confrontation skills are fundamental to their well-being as individuals, as presbyterates, and as religious communities. Yet, they feel paralyzed and often fearful to achieve this connection and level of intimacy, and to manage these conflicts.

In survey after survey conducted at all of these convocations across the country, the constant source of stress most often cited by priests is their "spiritual" stress. It is not that they are overworked, feeling sad or anxious, or overwhelmed with cognitive or intellectual worries. They publicly represent something or someone with whom they do not spend time, with whom they lack intimacy and yet yearn to love more, with whom they want to communicate, with whom they long to see and know better—God! Like many males in our American society, priests are abandoning their religious intimacy in the same way that some men are abandoning and running from their essential emotional-affective bonds of relational, spousal, and familial intimacy. Fear of the unknown is at the root cause of this abandonment. This fear is not irrational. It is built upon the fact that with little training in these emotional and spiritual realms, as males, they flee from what they *feel* they can't do. Males are doers, action-oriented creatures; our well-being is most often associated with our "doing." If as male, I do not feel competent in an action, I avoid it. It is the basic type of information and learning one sees in a developmental psychology 101 class.

The Current Pastoral Context

This interiority issue is a major concern that tends to express itself in the life of priests and it's linked to an essential spiritual vacuum or lack of faith development. Most often, priests are extraordinary workers in the vineyards (Center for Applied Research in the Apostolate [CARA], 2010). Generally, "they priest well." There are always exceptions to this rule but usually, priests are good "workaholics." Most often priests work hard in their communities, their schools, or parishes with an amazing amount of dedication and devotion. If anything, there is too much dedication and devotion that is directed externally. The pastoral realities often consume these men to such an extent that they neglect themselves and their well-being. Research has indicated that they adapt well, if not too well. They adapt too much to the situation so that the inner sense of self is diminished, if not neglected totally. This lack of understanding and training in the power and demands within the pastoral situation often expresses itself in a cadre of unhealthy adaptations. These will be explored further in this book. Suffice it to say, though they "priest" others well, most often they fail to "priest" themselves and their fellow priests or religious. This creates both personal and situational problems; the pastoral context is in crisis.

At the root of these problems is an essential lack of training and a fear. The complex life of managing emotions well is not an easy task or discipline nor is it for the fainthearted (Goleman, 2006). The consistent lack of formation in the basics of this aspect of our emotional life and well-being has several implications (Schuth, 1999; 2006). The first is an inability to know and manage what one experiences on a regular and consistent basis. This lack of training and knowledge is the context within which most priests function today. Second, it also shows itself in the current sexual abuse crisis affecting the church as will be discussed in chapter 7. Priests fear the pastoral situation, as never before. They too, like the people in the pew, are victims of secondary trauma. Pastoral collaboration and cooperation is viewed with suspicion and a great deal of trepidation. The current sexual abuse crisis stirs enormous emotions of fear, paralysis, and confusion with little expertise, knowledge, or training in how to manage such complicated, nuanced, and traumatized emotions. The biggest emotion felt in priests is that of fear, the fear to be intimate and the fear that their own failings in sexual intimacy would be known by others, as their brother priests' secrets have become known in the media. Lack of knowledge about sexual intimacy and the many fears in this issue cloud and distort the pastoral context.

Ronald Rolheiser (2002), in his article "On Carrying the Sexual Abuse Scandal Biblically," aptly describes how the current place of the church might be best viewed as being set at the "foot of the cross." This is a difficult place for any person or collective body to be and to remain. There is precedence and many apostolic models have been given to us in this regard. But, it is the unspoken part of the scandal that we run from and into which God is calling us. Most of the apostles did run, and they ran for a reason: fear.

Difficult challenges and emotions require an essential training in the basics of how to identify, acknowledge, and manage what is present affectively. To manage this task well requires training that is given for "ministerial" or "pastoral" capacities. Most priests face these situations quite well when they minister to others. They confront the buryings, the anointings, and the deaths and dying of so many, so often. They all too often forget that they too might have losses, deaths, and grieving that need the same attentive time, processing, and care they give to others. They often forget to "priest" themselves. Additionally, they do not "priest" each other. They, like the apostles, do what most men do: they run from their fear, their pain, and their grief.

The dilemma, indeed crisis, facing the church and the clergy today is a problem with this type of spirituality. If I am trained to be superficially and externally proficient in all matters clerical and ecclesial, that is where I will work, stay, and thrive. The current crisis and situational factors demand a new and yet more traditional spiritual, internal capacity and prowess. This prowess is a mystical skill and discipline. It is not a "white-knuckling" mysticism. One can't just "pray it away," as many have falsely attempted to do with their sexuality and their losses. Feelings once felt need expression. It is a standing within the moment. It demands a "standing at the foot of the cross" capacity as Rolheiser aptly describes. It demands facing our darkest fears, failings, and difficult feelings with courage, consistency, and persistence. The mystics have written extensively of this skill. So too have the new schools of psychology who see the connections of mental and psychical well-being and the proper role of a healthy spirituality. The current situation demands a new mysticism that we will speak of throughout this book and especially in chapter 7.

The Historical Context

Throughout this book, one will see the role of psychology and its relationship with the church. This history is central to our discussion. As mentioned in the beginning of this chapter, it is essential to consider the actual living situation and environment of most priests. Until recently, most priests have lived with many other priests in rectories built for two, four, or eight, and sometimes more. Priests were typically formed in huge monastic-like seminaries, expected to conform to authority from the central office, and sent to live in rectories. In these rectories, they were expected to live a "priestly" life in the parish or school within which they were to serve or teach. Though not ideal, most often the camaraderie and the support necessary to live the priestly life was more easily accomplished, easily known and seen. There was an inherent relational accountability. Oftentimes, there was little to say if the pastor did not want it said. In healthier situations there was a good communal sharing and fraternity; the opposite was also likely and true in the more unhealthy rectories. These situations created an unhealthy dependency (McGlone, 2001). The monastic-like structures of the seminary and the hierarchical structure of the diocese and rectory had created adolescent-like maturity and often dependent responses, which can be seen in the data from the John Jay study (Terry, 2010). The situation in both seminary training, dioceses, religious institutes, and in the rectories created situational unhealthy living (Schuth, 1999; 2006).

This situational reality has changed dramatically and is changing quickly in most religious orders and dioceses (CARA, 2010). Because of the priest shortage, it is more and more rare to have priests actually residing in the same rectory or community. This new pastoral living situation is both challenging and forcing new skills that have not been considered in priests' formation. There is less and less relational accountability and less and less opportunity for celibate intimacy. There is a situational setup for even less relational and celibate accountability. The situational pressures of today have the possibility for creating new, even more isolating, dependency-building, and insulating lives for the priests of tomorrow. These factors often form the basis for more sexual misconduct problems and addictive disorders, and more problems in anger management conflicts, authority issues, and conflict resolution. These situations challenge the priest at his core and in his essential character as priest. The challenge and the opportunity is an essential new understanding of the power of the situation, a new and healthier spirituality rooted in a healthier sense of self and others.

Theological Perspective

There are two theological considerations that greatly influence the inner life of each priest on a daily basis. They are the priest's anthropology and his theology of ministry.

Anthropology

Every priest has a theory or framework for understanding what it means to be a human person, how sin occurs, and how restoration results. For some, this theory is *implicit*, meaning that it has not been consciously and logically articulated, while for others it is *explicit*. This theory is referred to as an anthropology, and it can profoundly influence one's attitudes, decisions, and actions. When it is compatible with the Catholic vision, it is a Catholic anthropology. Whether explicit or implicit, this anthropology guides the priest's inner life.

Central to a healthy Catholic anthropology is the belief that all individuals are made in the image of God and can respond to grace, and that human nature is viewed as good, albeit tainted by original sin. However, there can be a disconnect between knowing this and acting in light of it because negative early life experiences, including trauma and deprivation, can distort or override an individual's formal learning and religious beliefs. In such an anthropology, there is redemption; life has a transcendent purpose; and healing, spiritual growth, and living life to the full are considered normative (Brugger, 2009).

There are also unhealthy Catholic anthropologies. Common to these is the view that human nature is basically bad and that individuals are too damaged or conflicted to effectively cooperate with grace. Negative early experiences, cravings and compulsions, or other factors are understood as accounting for one's problems with little expectation for transformation or growth, except for mere adjustment to life circumstances. Such a sense of spiritual futility is inconsistent with the Catholic vision, and adversely affects the priest's personal and spiritual well-being. These beliefs are more consistent with "cultural Calvinism" than with a Catholic anthropology. Priests whose outer life and inner life are guided by such a view of human nature will perform priestly functions of preaching, confession, teaching, moral guidance, or spiritual direction quite differently than a priest with a healthier anthropology. Not surprisingly, they often fail to develop emotionally and spiritually. Chapter 10 further discusses anthropologies.

Theology of Ministry

Just as a priest's anthropology reflects his core convictions about self, the world, and human nature, so does his theology of ministry. Basically, there are two distinctively different theologies of ministry: effortful and effortless. In the more effortful view, ministry is understood as a personal responsibility in which the priest focuses his talent and energy on serving others. The focus is on action and results, and the "doing" pole of existence. Compulsiveness and perfectionistic tendencies are not uncommon, and delegation is difficult (Sperry, 2003). Loneliness, burnout, and compassion fatigue are also associated with this view of ministry.

In the more effortless view, ministry is understood as being in God's hands and that everything also works out. "Being" is favored over planning and focused efforts at implementation. Shared leadership is valued and is seldom problematic as long as parishioners or other stakeholders are ready for mutual collaboration and the priest sufficiently leads. Instead of burnout and compassion fatigue, priests with this theology are more likely to "rust out" and be viewed as procrastinators, lazy, under involved, or emphasizing faith over works.

A more balanced theology of ministry is midway between these two extremes: an individual that is focused and effective who can practice a ministry of presence. Doing springs from the "being" pole of existence, and action flows from contemplation rather than compulsiveness. Achieving such balance may require considerable experience and some transformation of personality. Moderating compulsive and perfectionistic dynamics are necessary for priests with a more effortful theology of ministry, just as dealing with the tendency to procrastinate for priests with a more effortless theology of ministry. Chapter 8 provides an extended discussion of theology of ministry.

Psychological and Psychospiritual Perspectives

Psychological Perspective

Psychological factors can and do impact the inner life of priests. Of all these factors one stands out as one of the two best predictors of positive outcomes in life, which includes inner life, and that is self-control (Baumeister and Tierney, 2011). The other is intelligence. Unlike intelligence, which cannot be permanently improved, it is possible to improve self-control. Self-control is the capacity to control one's emotions, behaviors, desires, and impulses to achieve long-term goals. In the past self-control was known as willpower. A high level of self-control is associated with good physical health, emotional maturity, goal attainment, career success, and effective interpersonal relationships. In contrast a low level of self-control is associated with all behavioral and impulse-control problems, including overeating, alcohol and drug abuse, smoking, and sexually impulsive behavior, as well as emotional problems, underachievement, and various failures at task performance. It is also linked to relationship difficulties and dissolution (Baumeister, Vohs, and Tice, 2007). Needless to say, the inner life is significantly impacted by levels of self-control.

Psychospiritual Perspective

Related to the psychological perspective is the psychospiritual perspective, which focuses on the relationship of the psychological to the spiritual. In terms of the inner life of priests, the psychospiritual is reflected in the relationship of emotional maturity and spiritual maturity. While there is a difference between emotional and spiritual maturity, the two are interrelated. Emotional maturity is reflected in the quality of our relationships with others, and spiritual maturity is reflected in the quality of our relationship with God. Scripture points to this interrelationship: "You shall love the Lord, your God, with all your heart, with all your soul, and with all your mind. This is the greatest and the first commandment. The second is like it: You shall love your neighbor as yourself" (Matt 22:37-38). Research also suggests that emotional maturity interacts with and influences spiritual development and maturity (Tischler, Biberman, and McKeage, 2002). In short, self-control is a vital strength and virtue and is central to an emotionally and spiritually mature inner life. Chapter 9 continues the discussion of psychological factors influencing a priest's inner life.

Cultural Perspective

The American Catholic Church has always been a diverse church but until very recently, cultural competence among ministry personnel was optional, which is to say that some priests would volunteer or be "volunteered" for ethnic parishes or to mission assignments, while the majority were "safe" and relatively immune from the requirements of cultural competence. Today, however, the broadening scope of diversity is requiring higher levels of cultural competence from a greater percentage of ministry personnel than ever before. It is hard to imagine that many, if any, priests will remain immune from this requisite in the near future. This is not to suggest that most priests and ministry personnel totally lack cultural competence. Not at all. In fact, most have some level of cultural competence, but these levels are insufficient in light of what is and will be needed.

Cultural sensitivity is the capacity to anticipate likely consequences of a particular cultural problem or issue and to respond empathetically (Sperry, 2011a). Cultural competence is the capacity to effectively draw upon cultural knowledge, awareness, sensitivity, and skillful actions in order to relate appropriately and work or minister effectively with others from different cultural backgrounds.

The challenge of increasing the level of cultural competence in priests, religious, and other ministry personnel is immense. To deal with this challenge, changes in the education and formation of seminarians and religious, as well as continuing education for priests and other ministry personnel, will be inevitable. Changes will also be required in the organizational dynamics of diocesan and religious life, as well as parish life. The measure by which such changes will be evaluated as successful is the extent to which ministry personnel are able to recognize cultural factors and to respond appropriately and effectively to them. Chapters 5 and 6 provide an extended discussion of cultural sensitivity and competence.

This book invites you, the reader, to explore the various aspects that might encompass the inner life of priests. Chapter 2 will provide you with a new model of conceiving this inner world both in formation programs in seminaries and in the ongoing formation programs of priests. Chapters 3 and 4 provide you with the necessary historical context within which this can be understood today. Chapters 5 and 6 allow you to enter the growing world of cultural diversity in the church today and the nuances within intercultural competency for priests and religious. The other chapters allow you to see the world of sexuality and the person from new and important perspectives. In chapter 11, we conclude with an important look at priests throughout the life span in light of the current sexual abuse scandal. Finally, we have gathered experts from across various disciplines and a broad spectrum to give you their perspectives on the inner life of priests.

The Inner Life of Priests:
A Model in the Journey of Holiness
and Wholeness

Fernando A. Ortiz and Gerard J. McGlone, SJ

The ability to know the capacity of a man to enter religious life or the seminary is essential to both understand and assess. In a very real sense it is trying to formulate a way to understand the "inner world" and experiences of this candidate. The vocational experiences of applicants to Catholic seminaries and religious orders and of ordinands completing the seminary program are widely diverse. According to the Center for Applied Research in the Apostolate (CARA, 2011b), there are about 39,466 total priests in the United States. About 26,837 of these are diocesan and 12,629 religious. The ordinands of the 2011 ordination class had an average age of thirty-four. Though this is slightly younger than in 2010, this age average follows the pattern in recent years of average age at ordination in the mid-thirties. Seven in ten responding ordinands (69 percent) reported their primary race or ethnicity as Caucasian/European American or white. Almost one-third of ordinands were born outside the United States, with the largest numbers coming from Columbia, Mexico, the Philippines, Poland, and Vietnam. On average, responding ordinands who were born in another country have lived in the United States for thirteen years. Most ordinands have been Catholic since birth, although one in ten (8 percent) became Catholic later in life. Before entering the seminary, three in five ordinands completed college (60 percent). On average, responding ordinands reported that they were about sixteen when they first considered a vocation to the priesthood. Psychologists evaluating vocational examinees with such heterogeneity often grapple with enormous conceptual and practical challenges.

In a recent national survey of psychologists and seminary formators (McGlone, Ortiz, and Karney, 2010), psychologists reported that there is the need for (a) uniformity and consistency in the psychological evaluation of applicants to the seminary, (b) clear expectations and guidelines from the Catholic Church regarding the evaluation of the complex vocational experience, (c) psychological mindedness of the vocation admissions committee, (d) ecclesiastical and religious mindedness of psychologists, (e) courtesy to evaluated candidates to the seminary, (f) ongoing assessment of seminarians in formation, and (g) development of solid norms for the evaluation of candidates to the seminary. Part of these difficulties experienced by both psychologists and formators may be attributed "to the different professional worldviews and expectations, which may be expressed and articulated in different languages (e.g., ecclesiastical vs. psychological)" (p. 531). It is very important that these needs be systematically addressed because "the psychological assessment of candidates to the priesthood, religious life, and ministry should be accurate, thorough and, most importantly, ethically informed, culturally sensitive, and theologically sound" (Ortiz and McGlone, 2010, p. 25). Moreover, experts conducting psychological assessments must be inspired by an anthropology that openly shares the Christian vision about the human person. These criteria are implicitly and explicitly delineated in the Vatican-issued document Guidelines for the Use of Psychology in the Admission and Formation of Candidates for the Priesthood (McGlone, Ortiz, and Viglione, 2009). It is in this context of increasing vocational complexity in the Catholic Church and of emerging conceptual and professional practice needs among psychologists that the following multidimensional model of vocation was developed. The model is presented in figure 2.1.

As the figure shows, there are three phases at which the multidimensional model has been conceptualized: the *alpha dimension* comprising the foundational components of the vocational experience (i.e., biological, psychological, theological, sociological, and ecological), the *beta dimension* including the formative pillars of seminary training (i.e., human, spiritual, intellectual, pastoral), and the *omega dimension* representing potential outcome integrative experiences (i.e., holiness and wholeness versus sin and pathology). The purpose of this model is to integrate a number of theological and psychological perspectives and articulate a comprehensive framework that is readily accessible to both practitioners (evaluating psychologists) and seminary formators. In so doing, it attempts to bridge a gap between diverse dimensions of voca-

Figure 2.1. Multi-dimensional model of vocation

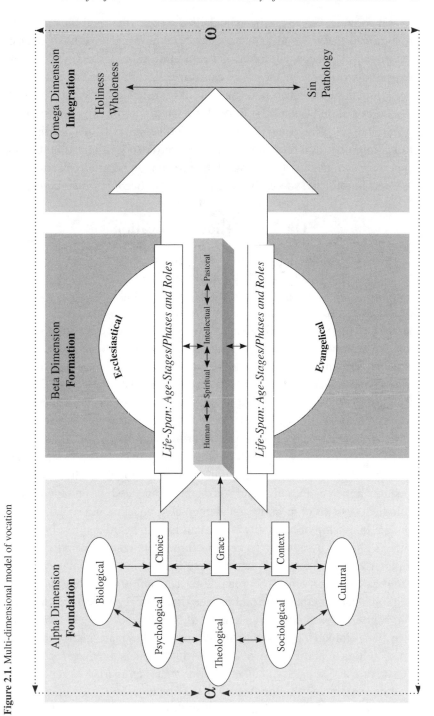

tional theorizing, on the one hand, and, on the other, the need for vocational professionals to use a model that bridges worldviews and hopefully enhances the evaluation, conceptualization, and communication of the vocational experience. As will be seen, the model can also be incorporated into a stepwise, decision-making flowchart potentially used by evaluating psychologists interested in a sound Catholic anthropology when interpreting their psychological findings. When both psychologists and seminary formators/directors of ongoing formation programs use an integrative model, interventions and support for seminarians and priests in their formation programs can likely be more meaningful and successful. The *inner world* becomes more knowable.

The Foundation of Vocation

The term "vocation" derives from the Latin *vocare* (and its Greek equivalent *kalein*) meaning "to call." In the Bible, the Hebrew verb "to call" (*qārā*) is one of the more frequently occurring words in the Old Testament. It is often closely associated with "election" (*bāḥār*), as in Isaiah 41:8-9 (Schuurman, 2003, p. 18). This call refers to a personal or collective summons by God, whereas election is the deliberate act of God in choosing someone to share in his saving purposes. In the New Testament, the Greek verb "to call" (*kalein*) appears frequently too, often associated with the call to Christ's discipleship (Badcock, 1998). As a summons, vocation is an invitation to a particular way of life (Billett, 2011). It refers to the specific call that God places in our minds and in our hearts. Everyone has a vocation. On the most basic level we each have a primary call to faith. We are called to respond to the love and grace of God, revealed in the life of Christ. As such, vocation does not happen in a vacuum and it is deeply embedded in sociological and ecological systems of meaning. Fundamentally, vocation is a social interaction, a relationship of mutuality where call is both heard and responded to. Voice is elicited by another voice. Vocation, then, results from the perennial interface between God's self-communication and our human response to that call through grace (Giordan, 2007). A multidimensional model of vocation must integrate these biblical and theological perspectives on vocation. Namely, that the transcendental call to follow Christ and to become Christlike is initiated by God and this summons takes place in the ecological and sociological particularity of an individual. This is the first step into the very private and yet graced "inner" world of the seminarian or candidate.

When psychology defines vocation, the emphasis is usually on *personal choice* and *agency*. According to the vocational theorist John Holland, for example, an individual's vocational choice is the result of the combined influence of inheritance, civilization, culture, guardians, peer group, elders, family's socioeconomic level, and physical environment. First, the individual knows his or her vocational skills, talents, abilities, and values. This self-knowledge then leads to vocational choice. The individual examines at least six vocational environments (intellectual, aesthetic, conventional, realistic, enterprising, and social) and, based on this self-knowledge, the person then chooses one of these vocational settings as long as there is a goodness-of-fit between the individual's vocational self-concept and the characteristics of the vocational milieu (Kinra, 2008, p. 114). Whereas these positivistic vocational paradigms heuristically offer applicable insights to an understanding of vocation, a Catholic conceptualization of vocation suitably reorders the definition of vocation and places a proper emphasis on the calling as being graced and fundamentally theological in character. God initiates the summons and the human person responds in a context of grace. The multidimensional model has the theological foundation as a core and centrally located dimension mediated by grace, thus moving the individual toward a formative period of growth. The other dimensions (biological, psychological, sociological, and ecological) are peripheral to the theological domain.

Human behavior has biological underpinnings and therefore it is important to consider the biological dimensions of vocational behavior. An era of breakthroughs in genetics, brain science, and in health has contributed significantly important scientific and empirical findings for a better understanding of the development and functioning of the human person. Genetic influences on personality structure and the aging process has helped us understand and measure genetic predispositions to illnesses and disease processes that affect many individuals. The increasing complexity in our knowledge of neurotransmitters and the role they play in mood disorders is an example of how brain structures are intrinsically related to emotional functioning. It is important that this scientific knowledge is properly utilized to better understand vocational behavior. Candidates to the priesthood's sexual development, diet, and health status are experiences that can be better defined, measured, and understood if evaluators incorporate rigorous scientific findings in their evaluations.

A person's choice to respond to God's summons springs forth from a unique psychological makeup. This particularity in cognition, emotion, perception, personality, and development is positively correlated with the person's level of maturity at the time of the choice. A person responding at the age of twenty most likely will differ from an individual responding at the age of forty on the strength, depth, and decisiveness of their fundamental choice to discern his vocation. Therefore, the psychological character of vocation needs to be evaluated in the context of the other dimensions outlined in this model. Vocational maturity can be tentatively described as the individual's balanced integration of these foundations aimed at the ultimate *telos*, the transformation of the person into a Christlike identity through a process of rigorous formation. Evaluating psychologists should assess the person's vocational experience in a holistic manner while avoiding reductionistic frames of reference. The multidimensional model includes two-pointed arrows to illustrate the dynamic relationship existing between biological and theological dimensions. It is not just the person's individualistic choice to respond to a divine call, but rather a transcendental option that implicates psychic structures and functions where God's grace and human choice are dynamically operative.

A globalized and multiculturally interconnected and interactive world provides the context for very diverse vocational identities. The Catholic Church in the United States, for example, continues to welcome applicants to the seminary and clergy from very different sociological worldviews and countries. Individuals in these societies have been formed and conditioned under specific cultural orientations, which may include culture-specific gender roles, indigenous notions of femininity and masculinity, non-Western conceptions of power and hierarchy, and other more specific belief and value systems. A sociology of vocation is also needed in any multidimensional model that purports to accurately define and measure vocational foundations. An applicant to the seminary emigrating from a war-torn country and from a culture that is very different from the "American culture" will most likely have a different vocational experience from one whose country is relatively stable and linguistically and culturally comparable to the United States. Like Abraham, God calls individuals out of particular sociological contexts and "sends them forth" on their unique vocational pathways. Evaluating psychologists pay particular attention to the sociological context and attempt to evaluate how these ecosystemic experiences may have negatively or positively affected the person's sense of vocation.

Ultimately, a person's vocation unfolds in an ecological niche that comprises immediate, extended, and transgenerational family structures, schools, churches, communities, and global systems. Urie Bronfenbrenner's Ecological Systems Theory includes five environmental systems that influence human development: (1) microsystem (person's family, peers, school, and neighborhood), (2) mesosystem, (3) exosystem, (4) macrosystem, and (5) chronosystem. The various interactions between the microsystemic entities are defined as the mesosystem in this model. One's family's attitudes toward the vocational experience may correspond to the person's own vocational identity. This is one example of the interaction between family and self. Also, the faith identity of the family or of the school may have facilitated the expression of one's vocational experience. The exosystem refers to ecosystems where the individual does not necessarily have an active role but that indirectly still have an effect on the person's vocational discernment. Global, sociopolitical, and historical influences are related to macrosystemic factors informing one's vocation. Vocations from formerly soviet countries or from African countries evangelized by European and predominantly Catholic countries will most likely exhibit the effects of sociopolitical and historical conditionings. The patterning of environmental events and transitions over the life course may have direct and indirect influences on the vocational experience. The vocational experience of baby boomers may be different and similar in many ways depending on their generational preferences. This constitutes chronosystemic factors conditioning the onset and expression of one's vocational choice.

The Formation of Vocation

An individual with a specific theological, biological, psychological, sociological, and ecological background enters seminary formation and it is within the church that his vocation is ultimately formed. In this ecclesiastical context the person responds to the radical evangelical call to follow Christ. It underscores the reality that while deeply personal, vocation is intrinsically relational and communal. Community is a sine qua non of seminary formation. The seminarian will be able to successfully develop humanly, spiritually, intellectually, and pastorally to the extent that he develops all of these dimensions in a holistic and developmentally appropriate manner. The multidimensional model adds a life-span continuum comprising age stages or phases and formation roles. A seminarian who is relatively young and therefore within a specific developmental age will have a qualitatively different level of human, spiritual, intellectual, and pastoral experience of integration than someone who is relatively older. Moreover, the person's roles may determine the level of integration. A seminarian in an educational setting and therefore in the role of student will have a relatively different level of integration than a seminarian in the role of educator. Social, occupational, academic, and pastoral roles play a pivotal role in influencing how the human, intellectual, spiritual, and pastoral pillars of formation are expressed and developed by the seminarian. An optimal level of exposure to these roles should be considered because they offer contextual influences that may facilitate seminary formation. As an example, a seminarian who has an academic opportunity of teaching or intellectual involvement in some fashion will likely exhibit a greater awareness and stronger sense of intellectual formation.

The Integration of Vocation

One's vocation is a call to wholeness and holiness. The correlation between the seminarian's vocational foundations and formative experiences is very important because this relationship ultimately is conducive to optimal integration. Therefore, a seminarian with significant deficits at the foundational level very likely will struggle being formed along one of the pillars of seminary formation and "miss the mark" (omega point in multidimensional model) of integration. The model references pathology or sin as two vocational outcomes suggesting maladaptive or unachieved integration status. This status is not terminal or hopeless, however, and the model includes a recursive line that perpetually returns to the central foundation of vocation—that is, the theological dimension. Integration is not a static or point in the continuum of formation that one day is achieved and declared finalized. The recursive line brings the discerning person back to the originating summons (alpha point) to reconsider his vocational foundations and to be moved into the formative dynamic in an ever-developing fashion. It is worth noting that the two vocational outcomes (wholeness/holiness and pathology/sin) are not dichotomous or mutually exclusive.

The Evaluation of Vocation

The complexity of one's vocation demands an equally complex and systematic process to accurately and reliably evaluate the vocational experience. As an art and a science, the evaluation flowchart included in this multidimensional model requires creativity and method. While respecting every psychologist's approach to evaluation based on professional expertise, the multidimensional model herein proposes several phases for a multifaceted evaluation of vocation: (1) *Pre-Data Collection*, (2) *Initial Data Collection*, (3) *Development of Inferences*, (4) *Iterations*, (5) *Integration of Hypotheses*, (6) *Conceptualization*, (7) *Consideration of Situational Variables*, (8) *Completion of Report*, and (9) *Feedback*. These phases are analogous to the scientific method whereby a problem is identified, data collected is obtained and analyzed, hypotheses are formulated to conceptualize, analyze, and resolve the problem, and ultimately data is subjected to a rigorous process of testing and experimentation. These powerful analytical tools and standards can be creatively and methodologically applied to the assessment of vocation.

Figure 2.2. Systematic and collaborative methodology of vocational assessment

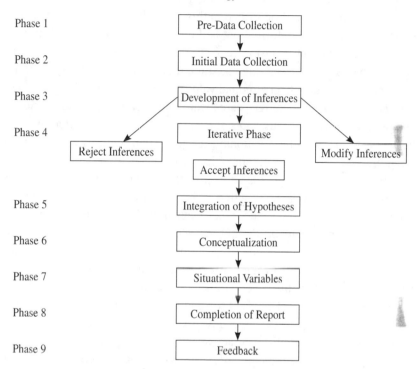

Pre-Data Collection

Psychological evaluations can be highly impersonal, bureaucratic, and anxiety-provoking experiences. Some examinees may be wary that the psychologist will probe their innermost sense of self and deeply personal experiences. Studies have shown that social desirability, which motivates examinees to intentionally portray themselves in an overly virtuous way during the assessment process, may invalidate or at least diminish the validity, reliability, and predictive value of psychological findings. Consequently, it is recommended that the psychologist make an effort to establish appropriate rapport prior to the evaluation and before any formal data collection. Seminary formation is a culture in itself with a set of shared meanings and practices. Psychologists demonstrate intercultural competence by demonstrating awareness, some level of knowledge, and familiarity with seminary culture.

As it is customary with any psychological evaluation, a referral source provides the psychologist with clearly stated referral questions to be addressed in the psychological report. Psychologists then interact with the vocational referral sources to clarify and fully agree on what the evaluation expectations are. Psychologists also understand the multidimensional aspects of the vocational experience as described in this multiphase model in its tripartite structure of foundation, formation, and integration. It would be simplistic, for instance, if a psychologist were to see the assessment primarily as evaluative of the person's psychological suitability for mere admission into the seminary and as lacking longitudinal value that may apply to a long seminary formative period. Psychologists are aware that even the most sophisticated and psychometrically robust tools of evaluation may in some circumstances be unable to measure the vocational experience in its entirety and recognize the limitations of the data obtained during the evaluation.

The evaluation of candidates to priestly formation implies the use of professional standards and practices. The evaluating psychologists understand their scopes of competence when evaluating these candidates and make an effort to monitor any biases and remove misconceptions they may have about the Catholic priesthood. They discuss confidentiality with seminary formators and the limits of the consent by the candidate. In the context of a collaborative effort, the psychologist and the seminary personnel discuss the scope of internal and external forums and the sharing of psychological evaluation information. To dispel any anxiety on the part of the examinee, the evaluating psychologist uses active and empathic listening to clarify the understanding of the candidate about the psychological process and seminary expectations, and an effort is made to clarify areas of concern with the utmost respect for the free consent and dignity of the seminary applicant. At a fundamental level, the candidate is entrusted to the caring and respectful expertise of a professional with the purpose of sharing the deeply meaningful religious experience of being called by God.

Fostering an active and conscious participation of the candidate in the assessment process by respectfully listening to the candidate's expectations, apprehensions, and anxieties is consistent with a Catholic anthropology of vocation. The personhood implicated in the calling is treated with dignity and never as simply a datum for psychological scrutiny. Some candidates, for example, from countries where psychology is negatively stigmatized may approach the assessment experience with some apprehension. It is important to know the candidate's perceptions of the psychologist and of the use of psychological evaluation.

Initial Data Collection

Once the referral questions have been obtained by the psychologist and clearly understood, the psychologist proceeds to select the assessment instruments to be used for the assessment. An effort is made to use evaluation tools with relatively high indexes of reliability, validity, and cultural sensitivity. An optimal psychological battery contains both performance-based ("projective") and objective tests. The psychologist reviews the referral questions and explains to the candidate the assessment process and how the assessment findings will be used during the admission to the seminary. The psychologist also reviews the candidate's previous history and any additional collateral data obtained by the seminary. Ideally, the preliminary data obtained from the seminary is objective and the impressions are mainly behavioral. The psychologist looks beyond the referral questions and determines the basis for the referral questions in their widest scope. It is important to understand the complexity of the seminary setting including the relationship with authority, and implications of internal and external fora.

Most psychological evaluations obtain data on the examinee's identity (demographics), dates of evaluation, reason for referral questions, assessment procedures, and extensive background information regarding family, academic and employment history, seminary and vocational experience, psychosexual development, health status, behavioral observations and mental status examination, psychological test results (interpersonal, cognitive, emotional functioning), diagnosis, and summary and recommendations. Identity data may include the applicant's self-identified sexual orientation and family and personal religious affiliation. In obtaining vocational experience, the candidate is asked to describe the development of his vocational aspirations. Based on the theological foundations outlined in the multidimensional model, the candidate can be asked to describe his relationship with God and how he has experienced the grace of God as it relates to his calling. The psychologist can use the other foundations listed under the alpha section to obtain data regarding the applicant's biology (health status, dietary behavior, allergies, sleep hygiene, use of alcohol and drugs, etc.), sociology, and ecology.

To help both the seminary referral source and the psychologist organize the referral questions in a systematic manner, we introduce a framework we have tentatively labeled the *vocational hexagon*. The Program of Priestly Formation (PPF) has outlined specific personality traits or character dispositions that comprise the human dimension of the candidate. These are core personality characteristics predictive of human functioning in the seminary and thus important for psychologists to evaluate. However, these traits are not organized in any systematic way in the PPF document. We have embedded the personality characteristics into a scientific personality model proposed by psychologists Kibeom Lee and Michael C. Ashton (Lee and Ashton, 2010). They propose that most personality traits can be evaluated along six major dimensions of personality: (1) Honesty-Humility, (2) Emotionality, (3) eXtraversion, (4) Agreeableness, (5) Conscientiousness, and (6) Openness. This personality configuration (i.e., HEXACO©) has been empirically tested and replicated in extensive, cross-cultural personality assessment studies. The theoretical basis for the HEXACO© is similar to another psychological model, the Big Five, which posits that certain basic personality tendencies (Openness to Experience, Conscientiousness, Extraversion, Agreeableness, and Neuroticism) are universal and measurable. See figure 2.3 for additional details on the dimensions and facets of the vocational hexagon.

Figure 2.3. Vocational hexagon

Adapted from Michael Ashton and Kibeom Lee (2007). "Empirical, Theoretical, and Practical Advantages of the HEXACO Model of Personality Structure." *Personality and Social Psychology Review* 11, 150–66.

Table 2.1. Sample of referral questions, evaluative and predictive of human formation

HEXACO Dimensions	Human Seminary Formation Dimension (PPF, 76 and 89)	Referral Questions
Honesty-Humility	"A man who demonstrates the human virtues of prudence, fortitude, temperance, justice, humility, constancy, sincerity, patience, good manners, truthfulness, and keeping his word."	How sincere is his motivation to enter the seminary and undergo the seminary formation program? What is the evidence suggesting that he will be able to grow in the virtues of humility, sincerity, patience and honesty?
Emotionality	"A person of affective maturity: someone whose life of feelings is in balance and integrated into thought and values."	Is there any evidence of a mood disorder or a history of emotional problems?
	"A man of communion . . . should be one of inner joy and inner peace."	What is his tolerance for stress? How does he emotionally cope under difficult situations?
eXtraversion	"A man of communion: a person who has real and deep relational capacities, someone who can enter into genuine dialogue and friendship."	How interpersonally engaging and pleasant is he? Is there evidence suggesting that he is a good communicator, or has the potential to be a good listener? How does he cope with, or is he able to engage in public speaking?
	"A good communicator: someone who listens well, is articulate, and has the skills of effective communication."	
Agreeableness	"A person open to others and available to them with a generosity of spirit."	How well will he relate to other seminarians? Is there any history of interpersonal difficulties? Is there any evidence of personality disorders such as narcissism, psychopathy, and eccentric traits? How willing is he to cooperate and compromise with others?
	"A person of true empathy who can understand and know other persons."	
Conscientiousness	"A prudent and discerning man: someone who demonstrates a 'capacity for critical observation so that [he] can discern true and false values."	Is there any history of impulsive, unconscionable, unethical, or illegal behavior?
	"A person who respects, cares for, and has vigilance over his body: a person who pays appropriate attention to his physical well-being."	What is the evidence suggesting that he is a person who deliberates carefully and inhibits impulses? Is he thorough, dutiful, organized, and concerned with details?
	"A good steward of material possessions."	
Openness	"A free person: a person who is free to be who he is in God's design."	How motivated is he to embrace a celibate lifestyle? How does he deal with ambiguity, different opinions and change? How inquisitive and intellectually curious is he?
	"Candidates have the potential to move from self-preoccupation to an openness to transcendent values."	

We have drawn a direct correspondence between the vocational hexagon and the Program of Priestly Formation personality traits. We have included these sample questions as an aid in the referral process and to provide psychologists with a mnemonic and practical device (HEXACO©).

Development of Inferences

The evaluating psychologist uses clinical inference at this phase, which is the use of human judgment and reasoning to interpret the data gathered during the previous two phases. In generating a series of hypotheses about the data, the psychologist uses the principles of formal logic to draw conclusions: that is, to arrive at a set of diagnostic statements descriptive of the candidate's current psychological functioning, as well as prognostic statements about the candidate's future functioning in the formation setting. Two types of reasoning are at the basis of formal logic: inductive and deductive. Induction is the process of reasoning from the particular to the general, drawing general conclusions after examining specific aspects of the candidate's profile. Deduction is the process of reasoning from the general to the particular, in which the conclusion is drawing that a particular datum is a verified example of a known general principle or premise. It is the former, inductive logic, that is used by examiners evaluating the vocational experience of a candidate while formulating hypotheses about the meaning of the psychological findings.

During the process of inductive reasoning the examiner will critically and thoroughly examine all of the *particular* data obtained about and from the vocational candidate to make *general* conclusions and recommendations. Specific aspects of the test findings, observations, interview data, and records are combined to provide support for specific hypotheses or inferences about the candidate's personality and behaviors. The psychologist is aware that the information available is partial and that it is only a tiny sample of all of the behaviors in the candidate's life. The assumption is made that the limited sample of data obtained is representative of the candidate's typical way of behaving, thinking, and feeling (Dorfman and Hersen, 2001). It is one piece in the growing puzzle of information that forms the composite structure of the known aspects in this "inner" world.

If two psychologists were to argue over differing evaluations of a vocational examinee, each would probably cite those behaviors or data supporting his or her conclusions. Each might have chosen a different group of behaviors to interpret. But they might cite the same behavior or data sets as pointing to divergent conclusions. The locus of disagreement would then appear to

Table 2.2. Vocational assessment biases

Type	Definition and Example	Corrective and Remedial Steps
Fundamental Attribution Error	This happens when the psychologist may overestimate the candidate's internal causes of his behavior while omitting or underestimating contextual or external behavioral explanations.	✓ Look for external contributing factors to the candidate's behaviors. ✓ Ask yourself: What factors in this candidate's situation might lead to his behavior?
Halo Effect	This bias surfaces when the psychologist evaluates the candidate on several traits or dimensions. If the psychologist is overly impressed by the favorability of one dimension and lets this favorable impression (halo) bias the evaluation and interpretation of the other dimensions or traits, the multidimensional assessment results may be inaccurate.	✓ Be mindful to assess both strengths and deficits. ✓ Monitor subjective and evaluative judgments based on personal or impressionistic reactions.
Confirmatory Bias	This occurs when the evaluating psychologist is motivated by the desire to bolster a favored hypothesis or impression about the candidate to the seminary and engages in selective or skewed interpretation of the data and thus produces a distorted picture of the candidate.	✓ Consider discrepant assessment findings. ✓ Include disconfirming and contradictory results with explanation of why this data emerged.
Hindsight Bias	This happens when the outcome of the psychological report influences the judgments the psychologist makes on previously formed behavioral impressions of the candidate. For instance, if the psychological report suggests that the candidate experienced a panic attack just a few days prior or during the actual assessment, a psychologist may erroneously conclude that "I knew it all along based on the seminary collateral data." Most likely, the psychologist's interpretation of the current panic attack is influenced by hindsight bias as he/she retrieves and interprets past data.	✓ Consider behavioral data in their proper timeframe. ✓ Accurately note the onset, development, and duration of behaviors and symptoms. ✓ Differentiate past-oriented, present, and future-oriented expressions of psychopathology.
Illusory Correlation	This biased assessment approach occurs when the psychologist erroneously concludes that two behaviors, symptoms, or events in the life of the candidate are correlated or causally linked when in reality they are not. The perceived relationship may be due to limited data, a flawed assessment methodology, an erroneous Catholic anthropology, or professional assessment incompetence.	✓ Monitor premature conclusions about co-occurring behaviors and events. ✓ Obtain additional information that may clarify causation and correlation of behaviors, symptoms and events. ✓ Consider using model in figures 2.1 and 2.2 for sound anthropology and rigorous methodology.
Ethnocentric, mono-cultural, and racial biases	This occurs primarily in assessment situations when the evaluating psychologist and the candidate may be from ethnically, racially, and culturally dissimilar backgrounds. The psychologist, for example, may over-pathologize or mis-interpret the candidate's behaviors, personality, attitudes, values, and beliefs if these are culturally different or unfamiliar to the psychologist. The psychologist may be culturally encapsulated and use a non-cultural interpretative lens during the application, interpretation, and integration of assessment results.	✓ Be aware and monitor preconceived and prejudicial views. ✓ Develop multicultural competencies. ✓ Become familiar with and appreciate cultural and ethnic differences and their impact on the assessment process.

be in the process of inference leading from the data to the psychologists' conclusions. This suggests that the inferential process may be fraught with biases and reasoning errors (Myerson-O'Neill, 1968). Therefore, psychologists strive to avoid cognitive biases during the inferential task and these may include the halo effect, the confirmatory and hindsight bias, illusory correlations, and ethnocentric and monocultural biases in the case of ethnically or racially different candidates (Dana, 2005; Groth-Marnat, 2009).

Iterative Phase (Rejection, Modification, and Acceptance of Inferences)

The psychologist makes an effort to counter the fundamental attribution error, which refers to the tendency to overemphasize personality-based explanations for the candidate's behaviors while contextual factors contributing to behavior are unconsciously or intentionally undervalued (Ross, 1977). The psychologist is encouraged to look for unseen behavioral causes and to use a disconfirmation strategy while looking for information that might disprove incorrect or unfirmed hypotheses. Accuracy may be improved by delaying the decision-making process while the assessment is being conducted. In the analysis of behavioral and test data, the psychologist systematically considers alternatives and does not rush to interpretative judgments or conclusions. Interpretative descriptions continue to be generated and an effort is made to avoid interpretations biased by early impressions. Given the varied sources and forms of data being obtained, the psychologist avoids using a "shotgun" or unspecified approach to the assessment process without an adequate focus.

Integration of Hypotheses

The psychologist elaborates on each formulated inference and those do not merely describe the candidate's behavior in a piecemeal or disjointed manner but the assessment descriptions attempt to capture behavioral trends or patterns. The interpretative descriptions are specific, accurate, objective, and behavioral in order to maximize their use during the seminary admission and formation process.

Conceptualization within Dynamic and Relational Anthropology

The interpretation of psychological and vocational data obtained from a candidate responding to God's calling presupposes a Catholic theological anthropology. The scientific methodology used during the inferential, interpretative, and integrative assessment phases is cognizant of the candidate's dynamic and relational vocational experience. A merely secular, scientist, reductionistic, atomistic interpretation of the candidate's vocational data may be countered and avoided by a Catholic, theologically sound, integrative, and personalist anthropology. The psychologist may use figure 2.1 during the conceptualization and interpretation of behavioral and test-derived data.

Situational Variables

To avoid a purely individualistic and dispositional interpretation (based primarily on personality traits versus contextual and situational factors) of the candidate's data, the psychologist considers the context of the candidate's behavior. For example, precipitating and perpetuating factors are considered and this may include interpersonal stress and other environmental triggers. Personality traits are interpreted in reference to their manifestation and expression in specific contexts (e.g., narcissistic traits and fantasies for power, prestige, and status as activated in contexts conducive to the expression of these personality characteristics).

Completion of the Report

The psychologist completes the comprehensive psychological report and submits it to the referral source. The evaluation statements avoid being merely speculations that may lead the seminary team to develop incorrect conclusions about the candidate. Also, the report conclusions should not be phrased in an overly authoritative and dogmatic manner. Misinterpretations may result from vague and ambiguously worded sentences that place incorrect or misleading emphasis on the candidate's behavior. For example, if the report were to include a statement such as "Sam lacks social skills," one could argue that Sam must have some social skills, although these skills may be inadequate. Therefore, the statement is technically incorrect. A more correct description would be to state that Sam's social skills are "poorly developed" or "below average." This phrasing adds specificity and behavioral accuracy. A statement such as "Sam uses socially inappropriate behavior" may be subject to many interpretations by the seminary formation team. This report assertion could be improved by including more behaviorally oriented descriptions, such as "frequently interrupts in classes or meetings."

The report contains relevant, clear explanations that meet needs of the formation team while addressing the specific referral questions. The language used links behaviors and therapeutic issues and needs. When the conclusions are presented, it is helpful to indicate the psychologist's relative degree of certainty. The report also indicates whether the interpretation is based on objective data or facts or if it is based on speculative and inferential extrapolations from the clinical interview. The psychologist is also sensitive to content overload. If the report contains too many details, it begins to become poorly defined and vague and thus lacking impact of usefulness. An example of an overloaded statement might be "Sam's relative strengths are in abstract reasoning, general fund of knowledge, short-term memory, attention span, and mathematical computation." A more accurate and readable report would adequately develop each of the various points and focus instead on the areas that are more relevant to the purpose of the report. Most reports include detailed vocational and spiritual history that places the data obtained in the form of a seamless life narrative.

Feedback

Even the most psychologically confident candidate might easily feel uncomfortable knowing that a report with highly personal information might be circulated and used by persons in power to make decisions about his admission and formation. In providing feedback to normalize the anxiety experienced, the psychologist may paraphrase, elaborate on, and explain select portions of the report. The rationale of the assessment can be briefly explained to the candidate and any misconceptions the candidate may have can be corrected. Some candidates can mistakenly fear that the purpose of the assessment is to evaluate their sanity. Using his or her professional and clinical judgment, the psychologist can select the most essential information from the report and provide the candidate with constructive and informative feedback. The psychologist is also considerate of the candidate's ego strength, life situation, emotional stability, and receptiveness to the psychological assessment findings. The psychological material may be negatively interpreted or detrimental to the candidate.

Seminary Formation:
Application of Psychological Assessment Findings

The seminary formation team will use the most appropriate and seminary-specific interventions first. For example, spiritual direction could be given a priority and this can be concurrent with supervision and regular communication and ongoing meetings. An effort is made to be creative in looking for simple, specific, and situational interventions so that improper emphasis on personality areas of growth is not prematurely addressed. Seminary policies and procedures are not a surprise to the candidate during the implementation of assessment recommendations. If counseling is recommended, the seminary personnel and the counselor consider the candidate's concerns about the use of counseling or psychotherapy. Educating the candidate about the usefulness of counseling increases the probability of therapeutic success.

The seminary personnel are cognizant of the various phases when the psychological findings can be utilized and applied during the seminary formation. For example, some psychological data will be more applicable to the preadmission selection process. Some other psychological recommendations will be applicable at a later time during the various formation stages (use figure 2.1 to see developmental application of psychological data). The psychological report may also anticipate crisis moments and provide recommendations for dealing with psychological crises (e.g., bipolar disorder acute crisis). Other issues that require not only descriptive but prescriptive recommendations include addictions, problems with sexuality, celibate lifestyle, struggles with authority, anger management, rigid and dogmatic cognitive style, moral character (honesty, authenticity), clericalism, and burnout.

Conclusion

This heuristic model represents a general model that may be adapted and used according to local, religious, and seminary-specific circumstances. The application of these best practices occurs in the context of relational trust and partnership among the professionals involved. Regular meetings between seminary personnel and evaluating psychologists are encouraged. A feedback loop can be helpful with regular progress reports on the collaborative relationship. The use of constructive feedback will improve the interface between the seminary and the psychologists. This will, in summary, provide for a new way to access and know the inner life of seminarians, candidates to religious life, and priests more accurately and more collaboratively.

3

Psychology's Contribution to the Church

Len Sperry

Psychology can and does influence the inner lives of priests. It is hard to imagine that any priest living in the United States for any length of time is not impacted by psychology. Whether its influence is direct or indirect and subtle, psychology impacts all phases of priestly formation from seminary through retirement. Even the Guidelines for the Use of Psychology in the Admission and Formation of Candidates for the Priesthood from the Vatican Congregation for Catholic Education (2008) presumes this influence. The Guidelines have evoked varying responses ranging from wariness to optimism about psychology's influence and role in priestly formation (McGlone, Ortiz, and Viglione, 2009). In fact, psychology's influence has been controversial for a long time, with some claiming its influence and contributions have been significant and positive, while others insist that the influence has been largely negative. Over the years, wariness and suspicion about psychology have been expressed by some Vatican officials, seminary administrators and faculty, seminarians, and even seminary candidates. In order to better understand and appreciate psychology's influence and contributions to the inner life of priests, it is essential to understand the contextual factors that have influenced priestly formation, as well as how psychology has changed and evolved during this period.

This chapter endeavors to provide a broad context for understanding psychology's contributions in light of the various contextual influences on priestly formation, particularly the history of psychology's involvement and contributions in American seminaries. In emphasizing the past sixty-five years the reader can better appreciate both views of psychology's contribution. Most of these contributions were from clinical psychology, particularly assessment of seminary candidates and psychological treatment and consultation. Then, the chapter describes psychology's potential contributions. There is a wide panorama of what the psychological sciences can offer to the assessment process as well as the formation process above and beyond the clinical realm. More specifically, the potential contributions of philosophical psychology, vocational psychology, social psychology, and organizational psychology will be briefly discussed.

Contextual Influences

Understanding context is useful in evaluating any phenomenon and this section reviews some of the major social, cultural, political, and theological-psychological considerations that have influenced seminaries and priestly formation as well as psychology itself. These considerations include shifts in seminary enrollment, changes in Catholic identity, educational achievement, and economic prosperity. Vietnam, equality, Vatican II, and the American Catholic Psychological Association were also key considerations. To complicate matters, these changes occurred while psychology was undergoing its own evolution from a branch of philosophy to a science.

According to data from the Center for Applied Research in the Apostolate (CARA), seminary enrollment rose every year since World War II, peaking at 48,000 seminarians in 1965 and decreasing afterwards. From the 1940s through the 1960s, there were often more candidates than seminarians and houses of formation could accept. Reflecting on this spike in applicants to the priesthood and religious life, Thomas Merton notes in his autobiography, the *Seven Storey Mountain*, that a constant stream of men sought admission to the contemplative life at the Gethsemani Abbey following World War II and the Korean conflict. In contrast, seminary enrollment today is less than 10 percent of that peak. It is ironic that during the period of unlimited numbers of seminary applicants, there were very limited tools for effective assessment. Today, however, there are extraordinarily sophisticated assessment methods and considerable experience using them, but there are fewer candidates to assess.

An explanation of the precipitous drop in seminary enrollment is arguably multifactorial. Among the many factors are the change in Catholic identity and the meaning of a priestly vocation among Catholic families. During the 1950s and 60s American Catholics emerged from the fortress or ghetto mentality that had forged the Catholic identity in America for seventy or more years. This fortress identity provided a safe subculture and supported and assisted generations of Catholics in their parishes. Because many Catholics had been immigrants who experienced religious discrimination, it is not surprising that the Catholic parish and a Catholic identity became the center of their lives. Having a unique set of religious beliefs, practices, and forms of piety made Catholics different from other Christians in their commonness. This long-standing identity would change dramatically in the 1960s.

Economically, Catholics moved from the bottom among the major religious groups in America to first place among all Christian denominations in the late 1960s and early 1970s. The reason is that educational achievement among Catholics increased dramatically and with it increased income. In the years following World War II, the Servicemen's Readjustment Act, better known as the GI Bill, had a significant influence in expanding the middle class by increasing education levels. Particularly for Catholics, the GI Bill made college education a reality for an entire generation of returning Catholic servicemen. Access to and attainment of a college education, previously unaccessible for many Catholics, led to managerial jobs and professional positions. This resulted in a dramatic shift upward in socioeconomic status for a large segment of the Catholic community. It involved a shift from being laborers and craftsmen to becoming executives, physicians, lawyers, and academics, in numbers that were previously unimaginable.

As Catholics were transitioning into the middle class, major changes in American core values were occurring. During the late 1960s America shifted from a nation characterized by duty, a high work ethic, and the capacity to delay gratification, to a nation of individuals characterized by pleasure, a reduced work ethic, and immediate gratification. These changes occurred as the Vietnam War continued and the war protest movement intensified. A number of social movements that championed the cause of social equality and equity were also prominent in those days. These included the civil rights movement, various human rights movements, the woman's movement, and the so-called sexual revolution. Because "doing your own thing" and equality was associated with the sexual revolution and humanistic psychology, those who were wary of psychology had even more reason to be skeptical.

Vatican II occurred in the midst of these changes. The first Vatican document on the dogmatic constitution of the church radically redefined the Catholic identity and the priesthood. The role of the laity shifted from its previous role of "pray, pay, and obey" to sharers in the "royal priesthood." As the "baptized priesthood," laity were now charged with transforming the world, an equal but different role from priest or the "ordained priesthood." It is noteworthy that this changed role for laity occurred simultaneously with the steep decline in seminary enrollment.

Finally, the emergence of the baby boom generation is noted. Made up of the sons and daughters of returning servicemen, approximately 70 million, these individuals greatly influenced most aspects of American life. For instance, some communities witnessed a 50 percent increase in the number of schools, social agencies, and new hospitals. Occurring almost simultaneously, American Catholics experienced a new Catholic identity because of Vatican II changes, and gains in educational achievement and economic prosperity. Of interest is that David Leege, director of an ongoing national study on Catholic family life in America, noted that while Vatican II had a significant influence on the changes in the church, the GI Bill was even more influential.

Taken together, a highly educated Catholic community and a shift in understanding of Catholic identity and vocation combined to significantly change American Catholicism. Prior to the 1960s, it was not uncommon for a working class family with five or six children to send a child to the seminary or religious life. Often, such a family vocational "sacrifice" would result in the family being recognized and esteemed by the Catholic community while their priest-to-be received a college education. But as families moved into the middle class and the laity's sense of unity and common vision began to fade, Catholics became increasingly heterogeneous and college educations could be acquired without entering a seminary. This heterogeneity would be reflected in all indicators of religiosity, ranging from theological beliefs to level of parish involvement and participation to views of the priesthood. It also led to the demise of the "fortress" mentality that had provided a subculture that supported and assisted generations of Catholics.

American Catholic Psychological Association

To more fully appreciate psychology's role in American Catholic seminaries, as well as the ambivalence and wariness of Catholics toward psychology, it is necessary to understand the history and impact of the American Catholic Psychological Association (ACPA). During its existence, from 1948 to 1968, this professional organization left an indelible imprint on psychology in seminary admissions and seminary formations. It also had a role in reducing the ambivalence, wariness, and suspicion of Catholics toward psychology.

It is important to understand that ACPA was founded during the time psychology underwent a transition from being a branch of philosophy—

specifically, moral philosophy—to becoming a natural science. Gordon Allport, the legendary Harvard University psychologist, was considerably instrumental in this transition. He understood that for psychology to become a science, it had to formally and decisively divorce itself from philosophy. To accomplish this, psychology had to stop equating personality (in its scientific sense) with character (in its moral sense) and relinquish its claim to being value-based. So, Allport and others endeavored to make psychology a value-free science that studied personality empirically. With the rise of scientific psychology came the expected death of virtue as a focus of psychology. Fortunately, virtue has recently been rediscovered by the positive psychology researchers (Seligman et al., 2005).

William Bier, SJ, was a pioneer in several areas of psychology. These included clinical psychology, the psychology of religion, and particularly the psychological assessment of seminary candidates (Bier, 1970). Bier is also noted for his efforts in establishing clinical psychology doctoral programs and clinical psychology internship sites. He was also the founder of ACPA. Before he finished a PhD at Catholic University in 1948, Bier exerted considerable leadership as a graduate student, which led to the founding of ACPA. At the 1946 American Psychological Association meeting he met with about fifteen professors and other psychologists affiliated with the three main doctoral institutions and Catholic circles at the time, which were Loyola University of Chicago, Catholic University of America, and Fordham University. Subsequently, Bier sent out a letter to about four hundred psychologists with some affiliation with Catholicism or a Catholic institution and invited them to meet at the 1947 APA meeting to discuss the formation of an organization of Catholic psychologists. In 1948 ACPA became a reality. It began with 220 members and at its peak in 1965 had 840 members.

The organization had two specific purposes or goals. The first was to increase participation of Catholics in scientific psychology, not philosophical psychology. Achieving this goal regarded the expansion of undergraduate and graduate psychology programs in Catholic colleges and universities. It also meant the development of placement service. Equally important was the development and advocacy of psychological assessment in seminary and religious life. This would become the most important legacy of the ACPA. The second purpose or goal was to bring the Catholic perspective to bear on the emerging field of scientific psychology.

In 1968 ACPA concluded that its primary purpose had been achieved and that ACPA should reconfigure itself into an organization that was open to other denominations and other world religions. Accordingly, in 1970 ACPA became known as Psychologists Interested in Religious Issues (PIRI). Later, in 1975, PIRI evolved into the Division of Psychology and Religion of the American Psychological Association, also known as Division 36 of the American Psychological Association. At the first meeting of Division 36, Eugene Kennedy was elected president of the organization. In his inaugural address, he reviewed the historical roots of the new division and jubilantly announced that the ACPA had achieved its goals. In actuality, it had met its first goal. In hindsight, it may have been somewhat grandiose to expect that any organization could actually bring a lasting Catholic perspective to psychology in a mere twenty years. However, the dream of achieving this second goal has never really died.

Philosophical Psychology

Philosophical psychology studies the philosophical issues and underlying assumptions about the nature of the human person. Neoscholastic psychology was a form of philosophical psychology derived from neoscholasticism that influenced Catholicism and priestly formation for nearly a century.

Neoscholastic Psychology

For decades, neoscholastic psychology became the intellectual substrate for priestly formation. In 1879 Pope Leo XIII issued the encyclical *Aeternis Patris*, which introduced neoscholasticism and neoscholastic psychology into seminary formation. The pope appointed Mercier, who would soon become a cardinal, to spearhead the shift in the way psychology was to be viewed. Cardinal Mercier proclaimed that psychology was in fact a science and was no longer a branch of philosophy. Neoscholastic psychology would be the science of the soul. The plan was for experimental psychology to interdigitate with neoscholasticism, and that was the mission for the next seventy years. Of historical note is that William Wundt opened his first psychology laboratory that same year and within a few years William James opened another psychology laboratory at Harvard University. The goals of these and other labs were to operationalize psychology as a scientific endeavor.

The pope's hope was that a Catholic anthropology would emanate from this new focus on neoscholastic psychology. Unfortunately, defining psychology as the science of the soul was not well received by many non-Catholics. The emphasis on the soul as the basis for empirical research was the stumbling block. In fact, efforts to achieve this goal failed, even among Catholic psychologists. ACPA as an organization did not support the introduction of neoscholastic psychology in newly formed psychology programs at Catholic colleges and universities.

Because ACPA members and other humanistically oriented and spiritually oriented psychologists were sensitive to self-actualization and the spiritual domain, there was support for a broadened view of psychology. Accordingly, in the late 1950s through the 1970s, there was considerable support for humanistic psychology, existentialism, and, later, transpersonal psychology and positive psychology. Instead of using religious constructs like soul, these approaches emphasized constructs like self, person, and existence. This strategy seemed to work and as a result neoscholastic psychology slowly disappeared. About the same time, neoscholasticism ceased to be the official philosophy of Catholicism. These developments were greeted with hopefulness by some Catholics and wariness by others.

Catholic Anthropology

Many associate the term "anthropology" with the study of human persons from sociological, cultural, or even natural science perspectives. Others, including vocation directors and seminary formators, may think of anthropology in broader terms, including philosophical and theological perspectives. Philosophical anthropology refers to one's view of the human person derived from philosophical reasoning, whereas theological anthropology is derived from Christian revelation, particularly Scripture. Catholic anthropology is a combination of both philosophical and theological anthropology that addresses the emotional, mental, moral, relational, and spiritual health of the human person (Sperry, 2009b). It specifies the origins and purpose of human persons as well as the place of sin, suffering, personal effort, grace, and healing.

An individual's anthropology is important because it significantly influences one's thinking and actions. What vocation directors, seminary formators, spiritual directors, and consulting psychologists believe about human nature can and does influence how they conduct their personal and professional lives. For example, a seminary formator who is influenced by the Freudian view that human nature is basically bad, and that personal and spiritual transformation are merely illusions, can only expect to achieve some measure of adjustment to life circumstances. This sense of spiritual futility is not only inconsistent with a Catholic anthropology but will also influence the formator's homilies, teaching, counseling, and advisement of seminarians.

Catholic anthropology is, of course, an area of philosophical philosophy. There are some current efforts to articulate a Catholic anthropology in an updated neoscholastic framework (Brugger, 2009). Recently, there has also been a resurgence of interest in Catholic anthropology in the clinical training of psychologists (Brugger, 2008).

Clinical Psychology

Clinical psychology involves the assessment, diagnosis, treatment, and prevention of emotional and behavioral disorders. Clinical psychologists have largely served as consultants in the assessment of candidates for seminaries and religious orders, and to a lesser extent with psychological treatment of seminarians. Fortunately for seminaries and religious orders, clinical psychology's contribution can be much greater than assessment and treatment.

Historically, seminaries and religious orders profited from the publication of a two-part article by Dom Verner Moore, the Benedictine psychiatrist. This article, particularly the second part (Moore, 1936), reports on his 1935 study of hospitalized priests. The study is important because of its high response rate (about 90 percent) and its implication for the assessment of candidates to seminaries and religious life. Moore actually misinterpreted his data and concluded that high percentages of priests were psychotic, manic-depressive, or alcoholic. The publication of this article mobilized support for the psychological assessment of seminary candidates. In a reanalysis of Moore's data it was found that he confused proportions with incidence rates (Bier, 1970), which accounted for the inflated and false impression that major psychopathology was higher in priests than in the general population.

Moore's study set into motion a series of changes in the evaluation of priests and religious, not the least of which was a psychological study commissioned by the National Conference of Catholic Bishops. In the study conducted in the late 1960s and early 1970s, an alternative assessment protocol for candidates for seminaries and religious life was implemented. In contrast to the then current pathology-based assessment protocols that typically included the Minnesota Multiphasic Personality Inventory (MMPI) and the Rorschach Ink Blot test, this protocol involved growth-based assessments, and included the Personal Orientation Inventory, a measure of self-actualization (Kennedy and Heckler, 1972).

The early 2000s witnessed the rediscovery of virtue in psychology (Seligman et al., 2005). A number of new therapeutic approaches, including spiritually integrated psychotherapies, were developed as alternatives to conventional psychotherapy that focused primarily on symptoms and impairment

(Sperry, 2002; Sperry and Shafranske, 2005). Alternative therapies focus on virtues or values-in-action, as they are called by some researchers. Among these is "well-being therapy." Well-being therapy is an intervention compatible with a positive view of human nature that focuses on increasing virtue and well-being in seven domains of life, which include purpose in life, self-acceptance, and positive relations with others (Fava, 1999). This positive and focused approach with its emphasis on activating client development lends itself to use in counseling and psychotherapy, in personal coaching, and as an adjunct in spiritual direction (Sperry, 2010c). Presumably, it can have considerable value in priestly formation.

Research on God image, also called God representations, suggest these representations have considerable potential for both clinical and formation purposes. Beyond identifying God image as part of assessment of seminary candidates, such data can be quite useful in the process of seminary formation, including spiritual direction. For example, God image has been found to change over the course of conventional psychotherapy even when the therapy did not address spiritual matters. In one study God images changed from a harsh, negative view of God at the outset to images of God as loving and caring at the completion of treatment (Cheston et al., 2003). From the perspective of a Catholic anthropology this result is not unexpected.

These are just two examples of exciting developments that increase the potential contributions clinical psychology can and will make to priestly formation. As noted earlier, these contributions extend well beyond its traditional contribution of assessment of candidates. Seminaries can further benefit from such contributions to the extent to which they are open to them.

Social Psychology

Social psychology studies the influence of others on the individual, particularly in groups and social situations. Since the bludgeoning death of Kitty Genovese in 1965 that was witnessed by bystanders who watched but did nothing to help the victim, social psychology has focused largely on studying why individuals help and why they do not help others. Thus, it is not surprising that social psychologists have been fascinated by the Good Samaritan parable. Interestingly, this parable has significantly influenced everyday life in America. We have Good Samaritan laws. In medicine, specifically in oncology, there is considerable research on what are called Good Samaritan cells: that is, helper cells that activate when immunity is compromised and limit the proliferation of cancerous cells. In business, the "Good Samaritan effect" involves the intrinsic motivation of workers in corporations in North America, Europe, and Asia. All these suggest that helping others is a core value for some but not others (Tang et al., 2008).

With regard to seminarians, a famous social psychological study of the "Good Samaritan effect" was conducted in 1970 at Princeton Theological Seminary. In the study seminarians were invited to participate as research subjects. They were given a questionnaire to measure religiosity and then a task to give one of two talks: either on vocational careers of seminarians or on the Good Samaritan story (Darley and Batson, 1973). These three- to five-minute talks were to be given that same day under different time conditions, but en route to giving their talks, each seminarian encountered a "victim," a shabbily dressed man on the side of the alley who coughed, groaned, and slumped down when they passed by. The victim also had bruises on his face. The time conditions ranged from "hurry" ("you're almost late so get over there quickly") to "no hurry" ("your talk is in twenty minutes so you have time to prepare"). Overall, only 40 percent of seminarians helped the victim.

When the *New York Times* reported the findings of this study, a public outcry followed. Various explanations were offered for why so many seminarians—who presumably should have acted like the Good Samaritan—did not offer to help the victim. The "Is God Dead?" cover of the April, 8, 1968, issue of *Time* magazine shocked many. Some suggested the study results reflected that Princeton was an ultra-liberal seminary where many seminarians and faculty were godless so would not offer help to the victim! Others suggested that if the seminary rector had been observing the situation, all or most seminarians would have helped the victim.

Perhaps the most compelling explanation is that for many people, including the seminarians in the study, not helping reflects their core values. Subsequent research demonstrated that core values predicted the "Good Samaritan effect" and whether individuals would help or not help others in need (Tang et al., 2008). In short, like the priest and Levite in the parable, ministry personnel may not help because other core values are operative, for example, impressing superiors, being on time, career advancement, and so on. The insight and contribution of social psychology to priestly formation is that these core values can be measured, and perhaps should be in candidates for the priesthood and religious life. Interestingly, such core values are reflected in an individual's work orientation (Bellah et al., 1985), an area increasingly considered in the field of vocational psychology (below). It is noteworthy that the Lord's final words of the parable, "Go and do likewise" (Luke 10:37), are consistent with only one of the three work orientations.

Vocational Psychology

Vocational psychology studies factors that influence choice of an occupation, motivation for work, and work orientation. Work orientation is a leading area of research today in sociology and vocational psychology (Wrzesniewski et al., 1997). There are three orientations. In the job orientation, the focus is on making money and benefits so that workers can engage in activities consistent with core values of hobbies and entertainment. Their motto is "I work so I can play." In priestly ministry this orientation is not uncommon in those who are psychopaths and sexual predators (Sperry, 2005). In the career orientation the focus is on fostering career advancement. The motto of this orientation is "I work so I can get ahead." This orientation is not uncommon among those whose lives and ministry are characterized by clericalism (Conference of Major Superiors of Men, 1983). In the vocation orientation, the focus is on finding meaning in life and/or making a difference in the world. The core value is fulfillment in terms of wholeness and increased well-being. Here the motto is something like "My work is my play." Recently, a distinction has been made in the research between a vocation orientation and a calling orientation. The core values operative in the calling orientation have been identified as having a "transcendent summons" or "self-transcending reasons" for working, whereas the operative value in the vocation orientation is finding personal meaning in one's work (Dik, Duffy, and Eldridge, 2009). Because the operative values of the calling orientation are most compatible with priestly ministry, it may well have been that the Princeton seminarians who helped the victim internalized this orientation. It is also likely that if the seminary rector was observing the scenario, those with a career orientation would also have assisted the victim since the rector's positive evaluation of their helping behavior might be perceived as enhancing their career advancement. In any event, the assessment of core values and work orientations could be valuable in screening candidates, and since the calling orientation and its core values can be enhanced and reinforced, they could also be valuable considerations in seminary formation. In short, work orientation may be a significant contribution of vocational psychology.

Organizational Psychology

Organizational psychology studies the application of psychological theory and method to organizational issues, including the influence of the organization's structure, strategy, leadership, and culture. Culture always reflects the actual core values—in contrast to the stated values—of an organization or institution. The core values of clerical culture have been identified as privilege, entitlement, separateness, and status, and in the extreme of clericalism, these values are considered inconsistent with priestly ministry (Conference of Major Superiors of Men, 1983). The extent that priestly formation fosters these values will be reflected in the seminary's identity and the behavior of faculty administration and seminarians. While concern about clericalism has been expressed by church leaders (ibid.), this concern has not resulted in appreciable action. Arguably, the insights and change strategies of organizational psychology can contribute greatly to the process of priestly formation.

In contrast to the traditional clinical psychology model of individual dynamics, organizational psychology also offers a useful tripartite model of viewing behavior in terms of the influence of individual, situational and group, and organizational dynamics. The danger of ascribing to an individual dynamics model is that diocesan and seminary personnel can unwittingly accept the "fundamental attribution error." The fundamental attribution error is the belief that the best explanation for a seminarian's or priest's behavior or misconduct involves individual dynamics rather than situational and group, and organizational dynamics and influences. For example, church leaders commonly explain the sexual misconduct of priests as a result of fatal character flaws that were not detected during the admissions or formation process. This explanation reflects the individualistic perspective of traditional clinical psychology in which misconduct is viewed as a function of an individual's psychopathology. Another way of saying this is that a priest who engages in such behavior is a "bad apple."

This is a very limiting explanation that contrasts with the social psychology explanation wherein situational factors better explain a given behavior. In this perspective, called the "bad apples" explanation, a seminarian's or priest's behavior—such as sexual misconduct—is explained in terms of the influences of others with whom he lives or works, or knows who engage in such behavior. The third explanation is dubbed the "bad barrel" explanation wherein organizational or institutional dynamics can significantly, but often subtly, influence an individual's behaviors.

Essentially, it is the organization's culture, values, policies, and system of rewards and sanctions in combination with the individual dynamics of the seminarian or priest, as well as situational factors, that best account for sexual misconduct among priests or manifestations of clericalism (Sperry, 2003). Comparing the cultures, operative values, policies, and actions of officials of dioceses with higher incidence rates of sexual misconduct to dioceses with lower incidence rates can offer a compelling explanation for the misconduct. In the organizational psychology perspective, it is not individual, situational, or organizational dynamics that best explain behavior. Rather, it is a combination of all three that bears responsibility and explains behavior. In short, the insights and methods of organizational psychology regarding culture, organizational core values, and the tripartite model are very useful in explaining the behavior and actions of seminarians and priests, as well as the process of seminary formation.

Concluding Note

Despite the massive social, political, and economic changes of the past century, psychology has contributed much to seminary life. Still, some hold negative perceptions ranging from occasional wariness to serious skepticism and antipathy, that is, the belief that psychology is a godless science that has harmed the priesthood. This final section summarizes a number of concerns about psychology as well as its contributions.

Even though positive psychology has rediscovered virtue and is beginning to recognize the influence of how one's anthropology impacts one's actions, concerns remain. For example, in an effort to develop a spiritually sensitive psychology, what passes for spirituality can be little more than a "psychologization of spirituality" (Sperry, 2002), that is, a "reduction" of spirituality to psychology. Such a psychology is suspect in that it is likely to eliminate or underplay mystery, grace, and the person's likeness to God, and overemphasize spiritual narcissism, which is incompatible with the Catholic vision. Furthermore, certain philosophical premises are incompatible with a Catholic anthropology and are cause for concern. So is unwarranted optimism about psychology's promise to treat pedophilia and other sexual disorders. Likewise, the propensity toward the fundamental attribution error continues to be a concern, as is limited awareness of the impact of seminary culture on priestly formation. Table 3.1 summarizes these negative, as well as positive, views of psychology.

Table 3.1. Psychology's perceived positive and negative contributions to seminary formation

Perceived Positive Contributions	Perceived Negative Contributions
ACPA's and others' advocacy of psychological assessment: MMPI and projective techniques, e.g., Rorschach	Reductionistic and value-free psychology
Resurgence of interest in philosophical psychology of Catholic anthropology in clinical practice	Incompatibility of scientific naturalism and Freudian pansexuality with Catholic anthropology
ACPA's advocacy of psychological consultation in seminary formation	Psychologization of spirituality
Developments in social and vocational psychology, i.e., vocation and calling orientations	Death of virtue in psychology
	"Overselling" psychology's effectiveness in the treatment of sexual misconduct
Recovery of virtue in clinical psychology (positive psychology) for assessment and formation	"Overselling" of psychology's explanatory power/prediction of individual vs. institution influences,
Research in clinical psychology on image of God: assessment and formation	e.g., fundamental attribution error
Organizational psychology's insights of impact of seminary culture on seminarians	

Overall, psychology appears to have made—and presumably will continue to make— major contributions to the priesthood from seminary admission to seminary formation and beyond. Arguably, some of the suspicions and antipathies toward psychology were, and may continue to be, warranted. Nevertheless, to the extent that vocation directors, seminary formators, and consulting psychologists are able to conceive of psychology beyond the boundaries of traditional clinical psychology, they can appreciate the many and varied contributions of philosophical, social, vocational, and organizational psychology to seminary admissions and formation. Finally, this broadened view of psychology presumably will positively influence the inner life of seminarians and priests.

The Church and the Role of Psychology

Archbishop J. Michael Miller, CSB

Introduction

The purpose of this chapter is to review the history of the document Guidelines for the Use of Psychology in the Admission and Formation of Candidates for the Priesthood, published on October 30, 2008, by the Congregation of Catholic Education. My comments are those neither of a specialist in psychology nor of a longtime seminary formator. Rather, they stem from my experience as a diocesan bishop and as the former secretary of the Congregation for Catholic Education. During my tenure at the Vatican these Guidelines were in the final stages of their long period of preparation.

According to *Pastor Bonus*, the apostolic constitution that regulates the responsibilities of the Roman Curia, the Congregation for Catholic Education "gives practical expression to the concern of the Apostolic See for the training of those who are called to Holy Orders, and for the promotion and organization of Catholic education" (art. 112). Within the congregation this task is carried out by the Seminary Office, which, among other duties, oversees the publication of numerous documents that provide guidelines and directives for priestly formation.[1] Before looking at the Guidelines, it is helpful first to review its context: how the Roman Curia has viewed the role of psychology in priestly formation since Vatican II.

Vatican II and Response

For the first time ever, the council fathers recognized a role for psychology in the theological and pastoral formation of seminarians. They stated in *Gaudium et Spes*, "In pastoral care sufficient use should be made, not only of theological principles, but also of the findings of secular sciences, especially psychology and sociology: in this way the faithful will be brought to a purer and more mature living of the faith" (62).

The council fathers realized that theology could profit from other sciences so that a more profound knowledge of the human person would result; theology can be enriched by the contributions of the human sciences. According to the council fathers, in seminaries "the principles of christian education are to be religiously observed and appropriately supplemented by the latest findings of sound psychology and pedagogy. A well-planned formation program should therefore develop in the students a proper degree of human maturity" (*Optatam Totius*, 11).

Inspired by the council, in 1968 Father Pedro Arrupe, general of the Society of Jesus, proposed to the Congregation of Catholic Education that the Gregorian University set up a new Institute of Pastoral Psychology. Moreover, he envisioned this project as a concrete response to Pope Paul VI's encyclical on priestly celibacy, which affirmed that the human sciences, above all psychology, could make a contribution to "the difficulties and problems which make the observance of chastity very painful or quite impossible for some," since they "spring, not infrequently, from a type of priestly formation which, given the great changes of these last years, is no longer completely adequate for the formation of a personality worthy of a 'man of God'" (*Sacerdotalis Caelibatus*, 60). In those turbulent years this opening to the contribution psychology could make to formation was fostered by the sense of urgency felt because of the high numbers of those leaving the seminary and active ministry.

Those in Rome were very cognizant of two principal doctrinal and practical difficulties that the study and use of psychology presented in formation: first, the danger coming from the behavioristic tendencies widespread in the psychological sciences; second, the difficulty of finding professionals who can understand the particular needs of seminarians and know how to ensure that "a truly adequate formation should harmoniously coordinate grace and nature" (*Sacerdotalis Caelibatus*, 63), prudently integrating the findings of modern psychology with the church's theological and spiritual tradition.

The Gregorian's proposal was accepted by the Congregation for Catholic Education, approved by Paul VI, and established in 1971.

John Paul II and Benedict XVI:
Confidence and Diffidence

Pope John Paul II, with his great interest in Christian anthropology and the question of the human person, developed a comprehensive vision of priestly and religious formation. In his postsynodal apostolic exhortations, *Pastores Dabo Vobis* (PDV; 1992) and *Vita Consecrata* (1996), we find an approach to priestly and religious formation that is "dynamic, integrative, and holistic. . . . One of the important contributions made by Pope John Paul II has been to incorporate more systematically into the Church's anthropology of vocation and formation certain developmental perspectives drawn from the human sciences" (Costello, 2007). Indeed, throughout his pontificate, the pope encouraged the study of the human sciences, such as sociology and psychology, because he thought that "for a deeper understanding of man and the phenomena and lines of development of society, in relation to a pastoral ministry which is as 'incarnate' as possible, the so-called 'human sciences' can be of considerable use, sciences such as sociology, psychology" (PDV, 52). While incorporating into his Christian anthropology of vocation certain insights from the human sciences, he also insisted that it was necessary to go beyond a purely natural understanding. The human person can only be understood in light of Christ. On innumerable occasions he invoked the teaching of *Gaudium et Spes*: "In reality it is only in the mystery of the Word made flesh that the mystery of humanity truly becomes clear. For Adam, the first man, was a type of him who was to come, Christ the Lord. Christ the new Adam, in the very revelation of the mystery of the Father and of his love, fully reveals humanity to itself and brings to light its very high calling" (22).

On the one hand, then, a certain confidence is placed in the positive contributions of psychology and other human sciences. John Paul defended the conviction that "only a Christian anthropology, enriched by the contribution of indisputable scientific data, including that of modern psychology and psychiatry, can offer a complete and thus realistic vision of humans."[2] In a speech to the Roman Rota, the usual place of such remarks because of the use of psychology in annulment cases, the pope said, "Christian anthropology, enriched by the contribution of recent discoveries in psychology and psychiatry, considers the human person, under every aspect—terrestrial and eternal, natural and transcendent. In accordance with this integrated vision, humans, in their historical existence, appear internally wounded by sin, and at the same time redeemed by the sacrifice of Christ."[3]

At the same time, John Paul II warned against certain trends of contemporary psychology that, "going beyond their own specific competence, are carried into such territory and are introduced under the thrust of anthropological presuppositions which cannot be reconciled with Christian anthropology."[4]

In summary, Rome was still cautious, warning that every scientific discipline grasps only a partial dimension of the mystery of the human person. The Congregation for Catholic Education, in its Directives Concerning the Preparation of Seminary Educators (1993), aptly summarizes the view of John Paul II:

> The Church calls for an attitude of trust in these fields of scientific research and exhorts the maintaining of a climate of mutual comprehension and dialogue with her, but at the same time she marks its limits, inasmuch as "each particular science is able to grasp only a partial—yet true—aspect about man" (*Octogesima Adveniens*, 40). In fact, concrete dangers of generalization due to incomplete results, and the risk of ideological conditioning of such research exist, and cannot be ignored. (59)

The same wariness about the undue claims for the use of psychology is also evident in the teaching of Benedict XVI. During his visit to the Gregorian University in 2006, while praising the venerable tradition of cultivating the human sciences, he said, "For the very reason that these sciences concern the human being, they cannot set aside reference to God. In fact, man, both in his interiority and in his exteriority, cannot be fully understood unless he recognizes that he is open to transcendence. Deprived of his reference to God, man cannot respond to the fundamental questions that trouble and will always trouble his heart concerning the end of his life, hence, also its meaning."[5] There are few references—other than the very generic—to the discipline of psychology in Benedict's writings. This might lead one to conclude that he is little interested in its contributions. The Guidelines prepared by the Congregation for Catholic Education that he ordered to be published in 2008 tell, however, a somewhat different story.

The Development of the Current Guidelines

Study of the use of psychological expertise in the admission and formation of candidates for the priesthood began in earnest in the Roman Curia in 1975. The Congregation for Catholic Education first looked at this issue in light of a note prepared by the secretariat of state to which was attached a letter of Cardinal Villot. In this letter the cardinal underlined three points that the congregation needed to keep in mind in its deliberations on the role of psychology in formation.

First, the letter affirmed that no superior, either diocesan or religious, could have access to matters that touched upon a person's privacy without the prior, explicit, informed, and absolutely free consent of that individual. No use of psychological testing used either at the time of admission or during the course of formation could be legitimately used without such consent, which was not to be extorted in any way. Second, the psychologist must not reveal to third parties, whether religious or political (no doubt thinking of totalitarian regimes where such information could readily be used against a candidate), anything touching upon the privacy due the person, without the consent of the one being tested or treated. Third, the psychologist or expert should, for his part, respect the privacy of his client—the natural, professional, and committed secrecy proper to his role. With these cautions in mind, the congregation began to study in earnest the question of the use of psychology in formation. Nothing, however, was published as a result of this first investigation.

First Draft

In 1995 the need for the Congregation for Catholic Education to take up the question of the use of psychological testing before admitting candidates to the seminary was approved by the plenary assembly meeting in Rome. The bishops and cardinals asked that a draft document be drawn up for their next plenary session.

Typically a draft is prepared either in the congregation or, more usually, with initial input from a consultant who works closely with the officials within the dicastery.

Three years later, at the plenary of 1998, they received a first draft titled Psychological Screening and the Use of Psychology in the Admission and Formation of Candidates for the Priesthood and the Consecrated Life. In his discourse at the opening of the plenary assembly, John Paul II said,

> The great concern of the Seminaries Office is to see that candidates for the priesthood are given an integral formation, attentive to the human, spiritual, intellectual and pastoral dimensions. In this regard, there is a particularly important relationship between human and spiritual formation. It will be your task to set forth the criteria for using the behavioral sciences in the admission and formation of candidates for the priesthood. I consider

it useful to employ the contribution of these sciences for discerning and fostering growth in the human virtues, the capacity for interpersonal relationships, affective-sexual development and education in freedom and conscience. However, it must remain within the limits of their specific fields of expertise and not stifle the divine gift and spiritual inspiration of a vocation or diminish the place of discernment and vocational guidance which is the proper duty of seminary educators.[6]

For their part, the members of the plenary expressed certain reservations about the draft: they cautioned prudence about the nature of the test and about any generalized use of such testing, even though this practice had become commonplace in many dioceses and institutes of consecrated life. Furthermore, they asked for further precision regarding the appropriate time for administering any test and on its role in the overall process of vocational discernment. Despite these reservations, the members thought that this draft could serve as the basis for a future document, provided that the necessary changes were introduced.

Second Draft

At the conclusion of the plenary assembly, the text and the observations of the fathers were given to several experts of different psychological schools who were asked to help in the preparation of a second draft. Several other dicasteries were also invited to offer their observations, and those of the Congregation for the Doctrine of the Faith were given particular attention.

After receiving this input, the officials of the congregation prepared the second official draft; it was presented at the next plenary assembly in February 2002. At the beginning of this meeting, Pope John Paul II made the following remarks to the members of the assembly:

> You are going to examine some *Guidelines* for the use of psychological expertise in the admission and formation of candidates to the priesthood. This document is intended to be a useful tool for those involved in the work of priestly formation, who are called to discern the suitability and vocation of a candidate for his own good and that of the Church. Of course, the contribution of psychology has to be incorporated in a balanced way within the process of vocational discernment where it becomes part of the overall process of formation in a way that safeguards the great value and role of spiritual direction. An atmosphere of faith in which, alone, the generous response to the vocation received from God can mature, will lead to a correct understanding of the meaning and use

of psychology, that does not eliminate every difficulty and tension, but, encourages a broader awareness and freer exercise of personal freedom so that the candidate can take up an open and honest struggle; with the irreplaceable help of grace. It will therefore be right to pay attention to the formation of expert psychologists, who, with good scientific qualifications, will also have a sound understanding of the Christian vision of life and of the vocation to the priesthood, so as to provide effective support for the necessary integration of the human and supernatural dimensions.[7]

Clearly the pope agreed that a document should be published, though he again expressed some cautions.

Third Draft

The second draft, with the observations of the members of the plenary assembly, was next circulated to various congregations of the Curia, including that for the Doctrine of the Faith. Consultation was widespread. In light of these suggestions, a third draft was prepared for the 2005 plenary assembly. In his message to the fathers, John Paul II made only a passing reference to this document; not surprisingly, he put it in the context of celibacy, since the document on the admission of homosexual men to the seminary was under discussion. He wrote to the members,

> In light of current social and cultural changes, it can sometimes be useful for educators to avail themselves of the work of competent specialists to help seminarians acquire a deeper understanding of the requirements of the priesthood and to recognize celibacy as a gift of love for the Lord and for their brethren. At the time of the young men's admission to the seminary, their suitability for living a celibate life should be carefully assessed so that a moral certainty regarding their emotional and sexual maturity may be reached before they are ordained.[8]

As in editing any document, the decision about which suggestions made by the various Curia bodies and other consultors are to be accepted is crucial in revising the text. Those made at the plenary assembly and those from the Congregation for the Doctrine of the Faith undoubtedly have greater weight, though, in the last analysis, it is the responsibility of the superiors of the Congregation of Catholic Education to make such judgments: the prefect, the secretary, and the undersecretary.

The members of the 2005 plenary assembly did not recommend the publication of the third draft as it was submitted but asked for further modifications.

Fourth and Final Draft

In June 2006 the third draft, together with the fathers' observations and further ones from the relevant dicasteries consulted, was given to a consultor to edit the text. The fourth draft, shorter by nearly one-third than the previous version, was presented to the plenary assembly in January 2008. The members found the text to be satisfactory. They approved it with twenty-three *placet* votes, one *non placet* and five *placet iuxta modum*, and asked that it be submitted to the Holy Father for his approval before its publication. After inserting the final recommendations, the prefect, Cardinal Zenon Grocholewski, was received by Pope Benedict in an audience on June 13, 2008. The pope confirmed the submitted document, noting that one negative vote was insufficient to place a roadblock to its publication.[9]

Some Pertinent Concerns of the Instruction

In this section I would like to consider several of the questions that seem to have caused the most difficulty in preparing the various drafts of the Guidelines. First, however, it should be noted that this Roman document proposes to resolve neither theoretical disputes concerning the relationships between psychology, theology, and spirituality, nor questions about the merits of different schools of psychology. Rather, as Cardinal Grocholewski noted at the press conference that presented the Guidelines, they are limited to making "a practical contribution"[10] to the question at hand.

Real but Limited Role of Psychology in Vocational Discernment

A primary concern evident in the Guidelines is its insistence that there is a real but only limited role for using psychology in vocational discernment both at the stage of admission of candidates and in the course of their formation. The document is very clear in affirming, "Inasmuch as it is the fruit of a particular gift of God, the vocation to the priesthood and its discernment lie outside the strict competence of psychology. Nevertheless, in some cases, recourse to experts in the psychological sciences can be useful" (5). Chapter 3 of the document is purposely titled "Contribution of Psychology to Vocational Discernment and Formation" rather than, for example, "The Usefulness of Recourse to Experts in the Psychological Sciences," a title used in an earlier draft.

In the background two different, if not opposing, opinions can be discerned. On the one hand are those who stress the positive contributions that a proper use of psychology can bring to vocational discernment. They are aware, as the Guidelines affirm, that "errors in discerning vocations are not rare, and in all too many cases psychological defects, sometimes of a pathological kind, reveal themselves only after ordination to the priesthood. Detecting defects earlier would help avoid many tragic experiences" (5). On the other hand are those who are more aware of possible abuses in the use of psychology: where such experts in the discipline are given a role that—whether intentionally or not—obscures the spiritual formation of seminarians. For this reason the document affirms that "the priestly ministry, understood and lived as a conformation to Christ, Bridegroom and Good Shepherd, requires certain abilities as well as moral and theological concerns, which are supported by a human and psychic—and particularly affective—equilibrium" (2). While human formation is absolutely critical, the primacy of spiritual formation must be maintained: "The Church has the duty of furnishing candidates with an effective integration of the human dimension, in light of the spiritual dimension into which it flows and in which it finds its completion" (2).

Indeed, the role of psychology is to assist in, not substitute for, spiritual formation. The Congregation for the Doctrine of the Faith is particularly sensitive to situations where the use of experts in psychology has become obligatory and widespread for the admission of all priesthood candidates and in their subsequent formation. The Guidelines directly address the Congregation for the Doctrine of the Faith's concern that human formation could be equated with psychological well-being or that psychologists could replace spiritual directors and other formators: "The assistance offered by the psychological sciences must be integrated within the context of the candidate's entire formation. It must not obstruct, but rather ensure, in a particular way, that the irreplaceable value of spiritual accompaniment is guaranteed; for spiritual accompaniment has the duty of keeping the candidate facing the truth of the ordained ministry, according to the vision of the Church" (6).

And later, in its section on the "Specific Character of Spiritual Direction," the document adds, "It is a firm principle that spiritual direction cannot, in any way, be interchanged with or substituted by forms of analysis or of psychological assistance. Moreover, the spiritual life, by itself, favors a growth in the human virtues, if there are no barriers of a psychological nature" (14). Elsewhere the Guidelines unequivocally state the need for grace: "A certain Christian and vocational maturity can be reached, including with the help of psychology, illumined and completed by the contribution of the anthropology of the Christian vocation and, therefore, of grace. Nevertheless, one cannot overlook the fact that such maturity will never be completely free of difficulties and tensions, which require interior discipline, a spirit of sacrifice, acceptance of struggle and of the Cross, and the entrusting of oneself to the irreplaceable assistance of grace" (9).

Discernment and Formation are Ecclesial, Not Professional, Tasks

A second affirmation of the Congregation for Catholic Education that emerges with increasing clarity in the course of the various drafts is this: discernment and formation are above all an ecclesial matter. A vocation to the priesthood comes from God as his gift to the church, and so she has "the duty of discerning a vocation and the suitability of candidates for the priestly ministry" (1): "It belongs to the Church to choose persons whom she believes suitable for the pastoral ministry, and it is her right and duty to verify the presence of the qualities required in those whom she admits to the sacred ministry" (11). While carefully respecting every candidate's right to privacy and his good name or reputation, guaranteed by canon 220 and which the Guidelines vigorously protect, the church has the right and obligation to guarantee the suitability of her ministers.[11] In ensuring their suitability, the church may have "recourse to medical and psychological science." For this reason, "in cases of doubt concerning the candidate's suitability, admission to the seminary or house of formation will sometimes only be possible after a psychological evaluation of the candidate's personality" (11).

Bishop

Careful to avoid any impression that experts in psychology have a primary role in vocational discernment and formation, the Guidelines intentionally rank those responsible. Pride of place belongs to the bishop or major superior: "In fact, it belongs to the bishop or competent superior not only to examine the suitability of the candidate, but also to establish that he is suitable" (11). Then the congregation added a timely reminder: "A candidate for the priesthood cannot impose his own personal conditions, but must accept with humility and gratitude the norms and the conditions that the Church herself places, on the part of her responsibility" (11). The bishop's role confirms the essentially ecclesial nature of determining who can proceed to Holy Orders; he has the ultimate responsibility of recognizing and confirming the authenticity of the call (PDV, 65). The Guidelines cite three times canon 1052 in this regard. Before proceeding to a candidate's ordination, the bishop must have moral certitude about his suitability; that is, he must be satisfied that "*positive* arguments have proven the suitability of the candidate" (c. 1052.1).

Formators

The bishop's first assistants are the formators. Their concern is the good of the candidate who wants to be formed as a priest as well as the good of the ecclesial community that has a right to priests capable of carrying out their ministry. The formators' irreplaceable role in discernment is to help the bishop or competent superior reach a judgment about a candidate's suitability in every dimension, including the human dimension, which is "the foundation of all formation" (2). Their task is delicate, since they are expected "to understand profoundly the human person as well as the demands of his formation to the ordained ministry" (4). Hence the document insists that "every formator should have a good knowledge of the human person: his rhythms of growth; his potentials and weaknesses; and his way of living his relationship with God" (3). The bishop must see to it that they receive a suitable formation, including a psychological preparation, so that they can carry out their responsibilities.

A very heavy burden is laid on the shoulders of formators since, as far as possible, they should be able "to perceive the candidate's true motivations, to discern the barriers that stop him integrating human and Christian maturity, and to pick up on any psychopathic disturbances present in the candidate" (4). This is a tall order. Everyone would agree that such judgments should be reached about seminarians. Moreover, most formators are convinced that perhaps the use of experts, at least through an initial screening, might ordinarily be necessary. The help of such experts is needed because the congregation notes the limits of the formators when it affirms that "in consideration of their particularly sensitive nature, the use of specialist psychological or psychotherapeutic techniques must be avoided by the formators" (5). One wonders whether too much is expected from formators in diagnosing difficulties, frequently referred to as "psychological wounds" in the document, which are not readily discernible and could easily be missed.

Experts in Psychology

The Guidelines emphasize the need for a human formation that makes use of the insights of modern psychology, but they expect the formators to have a suitable knowledge in this area such that experts are not always necessary for successful discernment and formation. Indeed, and this is an important qualification, the document affirms that "*in some cases*, recourse to experts in the psychological sciences can be useful" (5). Ordinarily the formators, with the help of the spiritual director and confessor, deal with the difficulties inherent in the gradual development of the moral virtues, and help candidates overcome them "with the grace of God." Nevertheless, again "*in some cases* . . . the development of these moral qualities can be blocked by certain psychological wounds of the past that have not yet been resolved" and the help of experts can prove beneficial (cf. 5). Indeed, the document affirms that "it is useful for the rector and other formators to be able to count on the co-operation of experts in the psychological sciences . . . who [however] cannot be part of the formation team" (6).

Even if psychologists or similarly trained experts are not themselves formators, the congregation is very careful to insist that they, too, have the kind of preparation and sensibilities suitable for dealing with questions that touch upon the action of grace in the soul. The Guidelines point out that "it must be borne in mind that these experts, as well as being distinguished for their sound human and spiritual maturity, must be inspired by an anthropology that openly shares the Christian vision about the human person, sexuality, as well as vocation to the priesthood and to celibacy. In this way, their interventions may take into account the mystery of man in his personal dialogue with God, according to the vision of the Church" (6).

Si casus ferat

It is evident, therefore, that experts in the psychological sciences might be helpful, but only "in some cases" (*si casus ferat*). Everyone would acknowledge that experts be consulted for seminarians already in a formation program only if there is reason to believe that such a consultation is necessary. The fifth edition of the American bishops' Program of Priestly Formation, approved after the draft submitted to the plenary of the congregation in 2005, says as much. It acknowledges that "counseling is often a helpful tool in the candidate's human formation" and states that "the rector or his delegate should make provision for psychological and counseling services. . . . These services are made available to seminarians for their personal and emotional development as candidates for the priesthood" (105). Likewise, the Italian *ratio*, approved in the same year, states that "in the area of the seminarians' human formation the use of psychologists *can* be helpful."[12] Clearly both *rationes* fall within the limitation set by "in some cases," since there is no hint of psychological expertise being mandatory for seminarians.

The Guidelines, however, go one step further in affirming that such experts should not be used as a matter of course or prescribed, even in the *initial* discernment of those seeking admission to a program of formation in a seminary or institute of consecrated life:

"*Si casus ferat*"[21]—that is, in exceptional cases that present particular difficulties—recourse to experts in the psychological sciences, both before
admission to the seminary and during the path of formation, can help the
candidate overcome those psychological wounds, and interiorize, in an
ever more stable and profound way, the type of life shown by Jesus the
Good Shepherd, Head and Bridegroom of the Church. (5)

This restriction to using psychological expertise only "in exceptional cases
that present particular difficulties" applies, it seems, to candidates seeking
admission to the seminary. While acknowledging its usefulness, such use
is purposely circumscribed: "In the phase of initial discernment, the help
of experts in the psychological sciences can be necessary principally on
the specifically diagnostic level, whenever there is a suspicion that psychic
disturbances may be present" (8). In the footnote, the Guidelines cite the
Directory for the Pastoral Ministry of Bishops, published in 2004, which
supports this restrictive interpretation:

> The complex and difficult situation of young people in today's world
> requires that the Bishop be particularly attentive in assessing candidates
> at the time of their admission to seminary. In some difficult cases, when
> selecting candidates for admission to the seminary, it will be appropriate
> to ask them to undergo psychological testing, but only *si casus ferat*,
> because recourse to such means cannot be generalized and must be un-
> dertaken with the greatest prudence, so as not to violate the person's right
> to privacy. (88)

In the press conference given upon release of the Guidelines, Cardinal Grocholewski, commenting on this passage, stated, "In any case, it is clear that
the use of psychology must not be a practice which is either obligatory or
ordinary in the admission or formation of candidates for the priesthood."[13]
At the same press conference, Archbishop Jean-Louis Bruguès, secretary
of the congregation, acknowledged that the use of psychology "has become
obligatory in very many dioceses for candidates who wish to enter the seminary."[14] He did not, however, go beyond the straightforward statement of
fact, either affirming the practice or calling it into question.

Here a problem arises. In most countries and dioceses, at least in the
English-speaking world, it is common, in the stage of initial discernment
for candidates seeking admission to the seminary or a religious institute,
to use some kind of psychological testing and assessment. The Program of
Priestly Formation states that "a psychological assessment is an integral

part of the admission procedure" (52). The Italian *ratio* is more circumspect and speaks of the opportuneness of "offering" such testing and evaluation to all candidates.

Do the Italians have it right? Should we be considering a revision of what is a common practice in light of the congregation's Guidelines? The framers of the document appear to be aware of the widespread practice that makes psychological testing obligatory at the stage of initial discernment. Indeed, it seems to suggest the need for a change: "In faithfulness and coherence to the principles and directives of this document, different countries will have to regulate the recourse to experts in the psychological sciences in their respective *Rationes institutionis sacerdotalis*. The competent Ordinaries or major superiors will have to do the same in the individual seminaries" (7). Perhaps this conference will shed some light on this practice of obligatory recourse to experts in psychology in initial vocational discernment.

Conclusion

The preparation of holy and psychologically healthy men for the priesthood is among the church's noblest and most pressing responsibilities. May this writing enlighten all of us so we can carry out the work that the good Lord has entrusted to us so that he might bring it to completion!

Notes

1. Cf. The Teaching of Philosophy in Seminaries (1972), The Theological Formation of Priests (1976), Instruction on Liturgical Formation in Seminaries (1979), Guide to the Training of Future Priests concerning the Instruments of Social Communication (1986), Guidelines for the Study and Teaching of the Church's Social Doctrine in the Formation of Priests (1988), The Virgin Mary in Intellectual and Spiritual Formation (1989), Instruction on the Study of the Fathers of the Church in the Formation of Priests (1989), Directives on the Formation of Seminarians concerning Problems Related to Marriage and the Family (1995), and Instruction Concerning the Criteria for the Discernment of Vocations with Regard to Persons with Homosexual Tendencies in View of Their Admission to the Seminary and to Holy Orders (2005).

2. John Paul II, Address to the Roman Rota (10 February 1995), 3, *Acta Apostolicae Sedis* (AAS) 87 (1995): 1014.

3. John Paul II, Address to the Roman Rota (25 January 1988).

4. John Paul II, Address to the Roman Rota (5 February 1987), 2, AAS 79 (1987): 1454. This text is repeated by John Paul II, Address to the Roman Rota (10 February 1995), 3, AAS 87 (1995): 1014.

5. Benedict XVI, Address during Visit to the Pontifical Gregorian University (3 November 2006).

6. John Paul II, Address to the Plenary Assembly of the Congregation for Catholic Education (28 October 1998), 3.

7. John Paul II, Address to the Plenary Assembly of the Congregation for Catholic Education (4 February 2002), 2, AAS 94 (2002): 465.

8. John Paul II, Message to the Plenary Assembly of the Congregation for Catholic Education (1 February 2005), 2.

9. The material on the process is drawn largely from the intervention of Archbishop Jean-Louis Bruguès, secretary of the Congregation for Catholic Education, at the press conference announcing its publication, on October 30, 2008, http://www.vatican.va/roman_curia/congregations/ccatheduc/documents/rc_con_ccatheduc_doc_20081030_conf-orientamenti_it.html.

10. Zenon Cardinal Grocholewski, Press Conference for Presentation of the Guidelines for the Use of Psychology in the Admission and Formation of Candidates for the Priesthood (30 October 2008), ibid.

11. "No one is permitted to harm illegitimately the good reputation which a person possesses nor to injure the right of any person to protect his or her own privacy" (Code of Canon Law, cc. 1051–52).

12. Italian Episcopal Conference, *La formazione dei presbiteri nella Chiesa italiana: Orientamenti e norme per I seminari*, 3rd ed. (4 November 2006), n. 76; cfr. n. 93.

13. Grocholewski, Press Conference.

14. Bruguès, Press Conference.

5

Inner Life and Cultural Competence

Len Sperry

Several factors that influence the inner life of priests are described in this book. All of them are important; however, some are more foundational than others, such as self-control, affective maturity, and celibacy. To this list should be added cultural sensitivity and cultural competence. The temper of the times increasingly requires that priests exhibit cultural sensitivity and competence. Unlike most other factors influencing inner life, cultural sensitivity and competence are both individual and institutional traits. As noted in chapter 1 cultural sensitivity is a requisite feature of positive institutions—that is, communities and organizations that are healthy and high functioning. Institutions that exhibit cultural sensitivity typically foster an atmosphere of respect and tolerance and the expectation that cultural competence is expected of its members.

Cultural competence is a term that is increasingly being used in the church these days. Unfortunately, there is little consensus on what it means or what constitutes it. Many seem to intuitively understand it even though it is difficult to define. This chapter endeavors to define cultural competence and describe its components. Levels or degrees of cultural competence are introduced and then described and discussed. Finally, the three vignettes are then analyzed in terms of these components and levels of cultural competence. It begins by providing background and contextual information as well as some case vignettes.

Background, Context, and Case Vignettes

The American Catholic Church has always been a diverse church. At first, there were waves of Western Europeans immigrating here, followed by immigrants from Eastern Europe, Africa, and Asia. More recently, immigrants have increased from South America, Africa, the Caribbean, the Middle East, and elsewhere. A similar pattern occurred with immigrating priests. Initially, most were from Europe, particularly from Ireland, and more recently from all parts of the world. Until very recently, such diversity required some degree of cultural competence among at least some priests and ministry personnel in the American church. In the past, cultural competence was optional in that some priests would volunteer or be "volunteered" for ethnic parishes, while the majority were "safe" and relatively immune from the requirements of cultural competence. Today, however, diversity is requiring higher levels of cultural competence from a greater percentage of ministry personnel than ever before. It is hard to imagine that many, if any, priests will remain immune from this requisite in the near future. This is not to suggest that most priests and ministry personnel totally lack cultural competence. Not at all. In fact, most have some level of cultural competence, but these levels are insufficient in light of what is and will be needed.

The challenge of increasing the level of cultural competence in ministry personnel is immense. To deal with this challenge, both educational and organizational changes are needed. Changes in the education and formation of ministry personnel are inevitable. Changes will also be required in the organizational dynamics of diocesan and religious life, as well as parish life. The criterion by which such changes will be evaluated as successful is the extent to which ministry personnel can recognize cultural factors and respond appropriately and effectively to them.

Vignettes

Consider the following three pastoral situations. In each situation cultural factors are central and operative. Recognizing these factors and appropriately responding to them, or the failure thereof, significantly influences the outcome of each situation and reflects levels of cultural competence.

> *Juan Carlos is a twenty-two-year-old unmarried Mexican American male who is being interviewed for admission to a Midwestern diocesan seminary. He immigrated to the United States with his parents and younger sister when he was four years old. He is a recent college graduate who won a competitive scholarship to a Catholic university where he excelled as a literature major, a minor in religious studies, and was a student leader in campus ministry. It was there that he began to discern a priestly vocation. His letters of recommendation highlight his intelligence, posi-*

tive attitude, devoutness, and command of the English language. When asked about how he prays, Juan says that his favorite prayer forms are the rosary and litany to Our Lady of Guadalupe. He adds that he spent considerable time in the chapel of the Newman Center, where he would light a candle and feel consoled and connected. The vocation director was aggravated by the seeming absence of Jesus in the candidate's prayer life, but he was not convinced that there were sure to be problems with this candidate. Instead, he continued the mandatory interview by querying the candidate about reception of the sacraments.

Reverend Simon Oneko is a thirty-five-year-old Nigerian priest who is seeking initial faculties, the first step in incardination, in a southeastern diocese in which he is being recruited. The priest had trained and was ordained in Rome before returning to his native diocese. A diocesan policy requires a joint interview with both the vicar for priests and the bishop for anyone seeking such faculties. One of the standard questions asked of applicants is to give three examples of how they handled a difficult parish ministry problem or challenge in their old diocese. The second challenge the priest mentioned was preparing for a scheduled evening appointment with a female parishioner in that diocese. It so happened that a window had been left open, resulting in bugs swarming around the ceiling light. In an effort to remove the bugs he said, "Brothers, this is no time to be here, I pray that you leave me now so that I can attend to my parishioner." The vicar was aghast at the obvious reference to animism and ancestor worship but said nothing. However, the bishop said, "And what did you do then, Father?" The priest responded, "I told them if they didn't leave immediately, I would get out my can of Raid." In response, the vicar rolled his eyes. The bishop smiled and commented on the priest's command of English and bicultural experience. He then asked how the priest reconciled his native beliefs about ancestors and church teaching. Without hesitation, the priest went on to simply but convincingly describe the communion of saints as inclusive of his ancestors as manifest in his life. While the vicar was ambivalent about Father Oneko, the bishop decided to approve the request for faculties and agreed to his appointments as a chaplain at the Newman Center and as a weekend associate at a parish where a culturally sensitive pastor could mentor him.

The looming priest shortage was very real for Msgr. Jack McManus. At seventy-three, he was nearing mandatory retirement age at the same time his parish was facing the prospects of closure or merger. The bishop held out the prospect of assigning a priest who recently arrived from Argentina. He attended seminary in his native diocese, had limited command of English, and had no experience with US or Asian cultures. McManus's

*first thought was that there would be problems. His working-class parish
had been primarily white until fourteen years ago when Hmong refugees
from Thailand and Laos began settling within the parish boundaries.
The pastor had been quite successful in developing a welcoming and
growing community since then. During the Vietnam War he served as
a chaplain in Saigon, so he acquired knowledge of Hmong culture. He
began by educating his parish council about the gospel mandate regarding diversity, and established a Hmong Mass and a bilingual Mass in
addition to the English Sunday Mass. He incorporated Hmong leaders
on the council and interparish ministries. His efforts to "acculturate"
popular parish activities, like the monthly potluck to incorporate Hmong
cuisine and customs, were successful after some initial resistance. Now,
Hmong made up 60 percent of registered parishioners. Many, including
diocesan officials and pastors of adjoining parishes, attributed this to
McManus's unflappable personality and persistence. The question for
the bishop was, would this now largely Asian parish accept a Spanish-
speaking priest who would increasingly assume many pastoral duties
since their beloved pastor's health was declining? What would it take
for an effective "fit" to be achieved between this changing parish and
the priest under consideration?*

All three vignettes reflect obvious questions and concerns about the
suitability of an international seminary candidate or priest for seminary
admission or parish assignment. Questions of suitability or "fit" invariably
reflect the cultural competence of *all* parties involved. Typically, cultural
competence is considered a requisite for vocational directors, vicars, and
pastors and parishioners, but the cultural competence of the international
applicants and priests also needs to be considered. In short, it includes applicants and those interviewing them in the first two vignettes, as well as
the international priest and the pastor and parishioners in the third vignette.
Perhaps the designation "intercultural competence" more accurately reflects
this interaction and "fit."

Cultural Competence:
History, Definition, Components, and Levels

This section briefly describes and defines cultural competence and specifies its basic premises. It distinguishes four components of competence:
knowledge, awareness, sensitivity, and action. There are also various levels
of cultural competence. Four broad levels will be described. But first, some

background information is provided that briefly defines culture and summarizes early efforts to understand cultural competency.

Background

In its broadest sense, cultural competence is the capacity to interact effectively with other cultures. So what is culture? Culture can be defined as "the values, norms, and traditions that affect how individuals of a particular group perceive, think, interact, behave, and make judgments about their world" (Chamberlain, 2005, p. 197). Another way of saying this is that culture is a way of being embodied in a set of integrated values, beliefs, norms, and customs. Furthermore, providing effective ministry requires sufficient cultural competence and sensitivity for the differing values, beliefs, norms, and customs of ministry recipients.

While cultural competence has appeared on the ministry scene quite recently, this construct has been around for some time. The designation "multicultural competence" was first used by Pedersen (1988) nearly a decade before the broader designation cultural competence replaced it. However, those in health care and business have actively promoted cultural competence to increase positive outcomes and to reduce dire consequences (Betancourt, Green, and Carrillo, 2002; Johnson, Lenartowicz, and Apud, 2006). This includes the Catholic Health Association (Thies, 2010). The health professions promoted cultural competence because an incorrect diagnosis due to lack of cultural understanding can have fatal consequences. Similarly, cultural incompetence in a business transaction can result in the loss of a corporate client or a lawsuit for breach of contract. Not surprisingly, early definitions and models of cultural competence are to be found in the business and health care literature. New Jersey state legislators were so convinced of the need for culturally competent physicians that since 2007 they require physicians who practice medicine in that state to complete cultural competency training. Since then, other states have enacted similar provisions.

Pedersen's definition and model of multicultural competence emphasized three components: awareness, knowledge, and skills (1988). Other models added a fourth dimension, usually attitude or personal attributes. For the most part these definitions and models emphasized the repertoire of cultural knowledge, awareness, attitudes, and skills necessary to interact with others of different cultures, attitudes, or cultural sensitivities. Thus, cultural competence involves the possession of this repertoire. There is one obvious drawback to most of these definitions and models: they fail to include the individual's proficiency in responding and working with others while drawing on these cultural components (Johnson, Lenartowicz, and Apud, 2006). In other words, possessing these components does not mean that there will be positive outcomes.

Two other aspects of cultural competence have also been identified. The first is the recognition that individuals are embedded in organizations or institutions and so cultural competence emphasizes culturally informed organizational policies and practices. Thus, cultural competence is defined in terms of espoused values and demonstrated behaviors, attitudes, policies, and structures that enable an organization to work effectively cross-culturally. Second, other descriptions emphasize the developmental process of cultural competence. Accordingly, cultural competence evolves over an extended period, with individuals and organizations at various levels of awareness, knowledge, sensitivity, and skilled actions along a continuum.

With increasing recognition of the biblical and theological basis for cultural competence, as well as its practical necessity, the United States Conference of Catholic Bishops (USCCB) has established a Secretariat on Cultural Diversity in the Church. Allan Deck, SJ, its executive director, has become an articulate advocate for cultural competence in the church. At the Catholic Cultural Diversity Network Convocation in 2010 he said that because people of non-European descent constitute the majority of US Catholics, cultural competence is indispensable for the church. He insists that church ministers must understand cultural differences when they work in marriage preparation, faith formation in schools, the promotion of vocations, and the promotion of social justice and dignity (Odell, 2010). Earlier, at the 2009 meeting of National Federation of Priests' Councils, Deck described cultural competence as "learning opportunities that provide an adequate level of familiarity with the principles and dynamics of cultural interaction and relations so as to prepare priests, deacons, lay ministers and leaders of all ethnicities, races and cultural backgrounds to succeed in providing pastoral care for today's parishioners" (ibid.). Guidelines for developing cultural competence have been developed. Yet, it remains to be seen whether the USCCB will require that all priests complete cultural competence training, the kind of training that is now required of physicians and other professionals.

To date, the professional literature on cultural competence in ministry is in its infancy. This is unfortunate, since adequate definitions and models of cultural competency in ministry are essential to guide fruitful discussion of the challenge, as well as for the development of guidelines and training programs. Although there are a few training programs for preparing international priests for ministry in the United States, there is no research suggesting that these programs are effective. At this point, there is almost no research on cultural competency in Catholic ministry. One notable exception is the report of an important survey regarding international priests in the United States (Hoge and Okure, 2006). In short, there is a void in the literature and research in this area. It is hoped that this chapter will begin to address that void by proposing a model and structure for conceptualizing cultural competence in ministry.

Definition of Cultural Competence

Cultural competence is defined here as the capacity to effectively draw upon cultural knowledge, awareness, sensitivity, and skillful actions in order to relate appropriately and work or minister effectively with others from different cultural backgrounds. Possessing only the requisite knowledge, awareness, sensitivity, and skillful actions is insufficient; the individual must also apply them in often difficult and trying circumstances. A low level of cultural competence is evident when an individual demonstrates deficits in these requisite components, is unable to perceive the need to apply them, or is unable to do so. In contrast, a high level of cultural competence is evident when an individual knows, recognizes, respects, accepts, and welcomes, and takes effective and appropriate skillful action with regard to another's culture. In short, cultural competence requires both sufficiency of the requisite components and the proficiency to implement them.

Basic Premises of Cultural Competence in Ministry

The discussion of cultural competence in ministry that follows reflects four basic premises. They are the following:

1. Cultural competence is increasingly understood as a gospel mandate as well as a practical necessity. Consequently, it is becoming more commonly expected of ministry personnel, including seminarians and priests.
2. Cultural competence has various levels, and these levels range from "very low" to "very high."
3. Cultural competence has four components: culture knowledge, culture awareness, culture sensitivity, and culture action.
4. Effective ministry requires at least a "moderate" level of cultural competence, and the capacity to demonstrate all four of its components.

Until recently, these premises might have been considered unrealistic and even unnecessary for ministers. While it may have been sufficient to have possessed some level of cultural awareness, it was not required. Nor was effective ministry framed in terms of the capacity to demonstrate a moderate level of cultural competence in all four of its components. But the monumental changes sweeping across the Western world in the past decade have radically changed those expectations. Today, cultural competence is no longer considered desirable and optional; it is imperative and required. In other words, the necessary and sufficient conditions for effective ministry involve cultural competence. Fortunately, the church has recognized and is beginning to respond to this imperative.

Components of Cultural Competence

Four components of cultural competence have been identified (Sperry, 2010b; 2011b). These include cultural knowledge, cultural awareness, cultural sensitivity, and cultural action. Briefly, cultural knowledge is acquaintance with facts about ethnicity, social class, acculturation, religion, gender, and age (Sue and Sue, 2003). Cultural awareness builds on cultural knowledge plus the capacity to recognize a cultural problem or issue in a specific client situation. Cultural sensitivity is an extension of cultural awareness and involves the capacity to anticipate likely consequences of a particular cultural problem or issue and to respond empathically (Sperry, 2010b). Cultural action follows from cultural sensitivity (Goh, 2005). It is the capacity to translate cultural sensitivity into action that results in an effective outcome (Paniagua, 2005). In short, cultural action is the capacity to make appropriate decisions and respond skillfully with effective action in a given situation.

These four components are similar to the three dimensions of competency: knowledge, attitude, and skill, as described by the American Psychological Association and defined as this integration of cognitive, attitudinal, and behavioral dimensions (Kaslow, 2004). Unique to the understanding of competence proposed here, the four components overlap, inform, interact, and build upon one another.

Knowledge

The cultural knowledge component is cognitive, and refers to an acquaintance with a specific culture and facts and insights about that culture. There are two ways of achieving this knowledge. One is firsthand knowledge resulting from directly and personally spending time with, working alongside, visiting with, or talking to the other. The second way is indirect or secondhand knowledge resulting from reading about, talking about, or seeing a documentary about culture. It can involve the formal learning of a language at a distance rather than learning it by direct immersion in that culture.

Awareness

The cultural awareness component of cultural competence is largely cognitive. Cultural awareness is the recognition of impact of specific thoughts, attitudes, and feelings on culture; specifically, recognition that the other is or could be negatively impacted by these factors. It also includes recognition and anticipation of the likely consequences of that impact. Whereas cultural knowledge involves data or observations that are largely objective, cultural awareness always involves a subjective sense. Empathy involves two processes: awareness of another's needs and/or worldview, and a caring response that engenders the other's well-being and safety. Cultural awareness involves the first of these two processes.

Sensitivity

The cultural sensitivity component of cultural competence is its attitudinal dimension. Cultural sensitivity demonstrates an attitude of respect, welcoming, and acceptance. Genuine cultural sensitivity can be distinguished from "practiced" cultural sensitivity. Genuine cultural sensitivity requires an individual to become aware of the other's worldview and perspective, and then to respond in an empathic, caring, or helpful manner to the other based on understanding the other's perspective. In other words, cultural sensitivity involves the second of the two processes of empathy. Effective businesspeople are usually quite proficient at cultural awareness, although they may not demonstrate genuine cultural sensitivity. To do so might well mean that they would not sell or provide products or services that are not really needed or could be harmful to the other. Accordingly, they may engage in "practiced" cultural sensitivity where they appear to be caring and concerned for the other, but basically their primary concern is for their own financial well-being.

Action

The action component of cultural competence is its behavioral dimension. While cultural sensitivity is largely about intentions, cultural action is largely about decisions and actions that can impact the other. Individuals who demonstrate cultural actions respond with decisions and actions that foster the well-being of others.

For didactic purposes these four dimensions are often described separately, and are typically taught in a linear and sequential manner, that is, sensitivity building on cultural knowledge and awareness; the development of cultural competence is more accurately understood as a spiral in which development in one component fosters progress in the others.

Levels of Cultural Competence

It is possible to conceptualize cultural competence as a continuum (Sperry, 2011b; 2011c) ranging from destructive at one end to highly competent at the other end. For didactic purposes four levels of competence can be described, although any number of levels could be described, and differentiated. Figure 5.1 provides a visual illustration of the continuum of cultural competence and four designated levels.

Figure 5.1. Levels or degrees of cultural competence

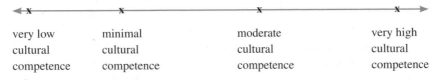

very low	minimal	moderate	very high
cultural	cultural	cultural	cultural
competence	competence	competence	competence

Level 1: Very Low Cultural Competence

This level reflects a lack or minimal acquaintance and recognition of cultural knowledge or awareness. Because there is a lack of cultural sensitivity, individuals do not take action or the decisions and actions taken are inappropriate or ineffective or both. Such actions can be harmful or destructive. Common at this level is cultural encapsulation, which is a way of relating to another from one's own worldview and perspective. Besides a failure to understand the worldview and cultural identity of another, it is the failure to incorporate whatever cultural knowledge one might have of the other into interactions with the other.

Level 2: Minimal Cultural Competence

There are two variants of this level. The first variant involves circumstances where limited cultural knowledge and awareness results in limited or misguided cultural sensitivity and subsequent cultural decisions or actions. The other may experience some degree of respect and/or acceptance, but not necessarily a sense of being welcomed as in higher levels. A second variant is not uncommon, particularly among individuals who are easily accepting, welcoming, or empathic toward others. Accordingly, they come across as culturally aware and culturally sensitive, although this awareness sensitivity may not be based on cultural knowledge but on the recognition of a sense of another's distress, shyness, discomfort, or uneasiness. This apparent cultural sensitivity is only partial because of an underappreciation of the consequences of the negative impact on the other. Because of such limited cultural knowledge and awareness, subsequent cultural decisions and actions are unlikely to be as appropriate, skillful, or effective as they otherwise could be. Some vestiges of cultural encapsulation may persist or there is inconsistency in responding to the other.

Level 3: Moderate Cultural Competence

This level reflects the availability of more cultural knowledge and aware-ness than in level 2. The experience of cultural sensitivity is qualitatively different than at level 2. The other is likely to experience some sense of respect, acceptance, and even welcoming, although this experience is not as consistent and unconditional as in level 4. Furthermore, cultural decisions and actions are more competent than at level 2. There are no obvious vestiges of cultural encapsulation, and the individual is likely to function at moderate or even high levels of professional or clinical competence.

Level 4: Very High Cultural Competence

This level reflects considerable cultural knowledge and awareness. Cul-tural sensitivity reflects this knowledge and awareness and is experienced by the other as respect and a sense of being welcomed and accepted. It is a sense of respect, acceptance, and welcoming that is ongoing. Unlike at level 3, this experience is consistent and unconditional. Cultural decisions and actions are appropriate and skillful. Conceivably, the actions are effective and the outcome may be positive, although this is not a requisite of this level of competence. These individuals are also likely to function at high levels of professional or clinical competence.

Analysis of the Three Vignettes

Pastoral Situation 1

Given that Juan is a first-generation Mexican American, he displays a rela-tively high level of acculturation as evidenced by his command of the English language, degree in English literature, and involvement in university activities, particularly leadership in campus ministry. The vocational director demon-strated relatively little knowledge or cultural sensitivity of Juan's religious heritage. A culturally sensitive question would be, "How do you relate your devotion to the Blessed Mother with what you know from your university study of Christology and ecclesiology?" Such a question would allow the candidate to demonstrate either some integration of the two, no integration, or confusion. However, by failing to pursue such questioning, the vocational director summarily concluded that Juan's spirituality would be problematic if admitted to priestly studies. Overall, it appears that the vocational director exhibits limited cultural knowledge and awareness, and an absence of cultural sensitivity and action. Accordingly, he appears to be at level 1 of cultural competence.

Pastoral Situation 2

Overall, it appears that the vicar for priests exhibited some cultural knowledge and awareness. However, rolling his eyes at Father Oneko's response to the bishop's question suggests low sensitivity. That his initial evaluation was not very encouraging suggests a low level of cultural action. Accordingly, he appears to be at or just below level 2 of cultural competence. In contrast, the bishop demonstrated a higher level of cultural knowledge, awareness, and sensitivity. This was reflected in his complimenting Father Oneko on his English, his bicultural experience, and his response to the bishop's follow-up theological question. His cultural action was reflected in the chaplaincy and part-time parish appointments and, particularly, the request that the pastor, a culturally sensitive friend of the bishop, mentor the newly arrived priest. Overall his level of cultural competence was at level 3, or even slightly beyond.

Pastoral Situation 3

Msgr. McManus comes across as a pastor with high cultural knowledge, awareness, and sensitivity. Perhaps this reflects his experience as a chaplain in southeast Asia, but it could have resulted from concerted effort to personally and earnestly relate to his Hmong parishioners. Particularly noteworthy is the extent the pastor's cultural actions in transforming the parish to being a welcoming community for Hmong immigrants. Overall, the pastor's level of cultural competence is at or around level 4. Possibly, the pastor's previous cultural transformation efforts would generalize to the parish welcoming someone like the Argentinean priest. But this is conjecture. Furthermore, there is insufficient information provided to identify a level of cultural competence for the bishop.

Concluding Comment

Cultural competence is increasingly important in ministry decisions today. This chapter defined cultural competence in terms of its requisite components, proficiency applying them, and its levels. Cultural competence was defined as the capacity to effectively draw upon cultural knowledge, awareness, sensitivity, and skillful actions in order to relate appropriately and work successfully with others from different cultural backgrounds. Unlike other definitions and models of cultural competence, this one requires both sufficiency of the requisite components and the proficiency to implement them.

It bears repeating that a basic premise of this chapter is that at least a moderate level of cultural competence is necessary for effective ministry. An analysis of the three opening cases illustrated these components and levels of cultural competence. It should be clear that this analysis emphasized only the cultural competence of the decision makers—vocational director in the first vignette, vicar for priests and bishop in the second vignette, and pastor and bishop in the third vignette. It did not directly address the competence of the seminary candidate or priests in the vignettes. Nevertheless, the overall conclusion of this chapter is that developing cultural competence leads to an increase in the capacity to understand, respect, relate to, and effectively interact with those in other cultures.

It should also be noted that cultural competence is not just an individual requisite; it is also an organizational or institutional requisite. Unfortunately, a discussion of this organizational aspect of cultural competence is beyond the scope of this chapter. Suffice it to say that cultural competence in a church organization, such as a parish, diocese, or ministry situation, is a set of congruent behaviors, attitudes, and policies that come together to enable ministry personnel to minister or work effectively in cross-cultural situations. Finally, a broadened understanding of intercultural competence, mentioned earlier, is exceedingly important in ministry, as is the capacity for it. A more exhaustive discussion of it would need to emphasize the components and levels of cultural competence of all parties involved and their interaction and "fit."

As noted at the outset, the professional literature on cultural competency in ministry in the Catholic Church is in its infancy. This limited literature is problematic and needs to be urgently addressed with competent scholarship and research. It is hoped that this chapter has added both substance and direction to this literature by providing a heuristic model for conceptualizing. Presumably, this and other models can be empirically operationalized so that, in time, cultural competence in Catholic ministry can be measured and evaluated, and as a result of this evaluation, ministry formation and training programs can be improved.

6

The Journey Within
and Intercultural Competencies

Gerard J. McGlone, SJ, and Fernando A. Ortiz

Historical Underpinnings

Recent opportunities and challenges facing the church in the United States demand a sophisticated interiority and an integrated understanding of culture and difference (Hoge and Okure, 2006). The landscape and features of the church in North America are changing, and changing rapidly (CARA, 2010). Few descriptions of most interactions between religion and culture begin with the indigenous peoples who were colonized by the cultural conquests of France, Spain, Portugal, and England. "American" history most often begins with the founding of Plymouth Rock —"America" most often begins its history with the white, Anglo-Saxon or English, Protestant views of religion and the "manifest destiny" inherent in the "American" founding (Bolton, 1921). It often does this while taking little account of the Catholic and Spanish experience, which preceded this settlement on the North American continent by almost a century. Both of these histories also tend not to mention the indigenous religious traditions of the "first peoples" in both North and South America. These historical accounts form the contextual backdrop of a long, tumultuous, and often troubling, if not shameful, historical context and understanding. The tales of our past are most often the histories written by the "winners" with little regard to the peoples and cultures of the "losers." The historical religious and cultural dramas in North America certainly seem to reflect this tendency. The first necessary interiority might be an intellectual one. Bias, racism, colonialism, and prejudice often shape our historical understanding; they can also shape our current realities and perspective. Few writers describe this reality from a properly critical and spiritual perspective.

Understanding Intercultural Competency

The gospel imperative given to the apostles thousands of years ago echoes forth through time and place: "Then Jesus approached and said to them, 'All power in heaven and on earth has been given to me. Go, therefore, and make disciples of all nations, baptizing them in the name of the Father, and of the Son, and of the holy Spirit, teaching them to observe all that I have commanded you. And behold, I am with you always, until the end of the age' " (Matt 28:18-20). Practically speaking, more sophisticated inner awareness, sensitivity, appreciation, and knowledge might be essential to develop such a competency. *Intercultural* competency by definition means that each feature of the situational interactional experience demands appreciation and respect, as an example, the candidates' culture and the culture within which the candidate is being formed or sent. Sperry (2011b) outlines the dimensionality of these competencies quite clearly. The gospel imperative of Jesus Christ is at the root of any competency within this faith tradition: the commandment to love others as you love yourself and most especially the commandment to love and serve those less fortunate than you (Matt 22:26-34; John 10; Luke 10; Matthew 11). The seminary, religious institute or community, parish, assessing psychologist, or diocese must first become aware of their own views and their beliefs about culture itself (fig. 6.1).

Figure 6.1. Interaction of self-culture beliefs

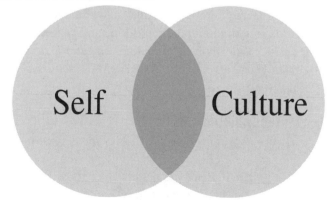

"Foreigner," "immigrant," "international," "foreign-born" seminarians or priests might connote several meanings to any one of us. These men typically refer to themselves as "missionaries." Indeed, they are. The essential question is whether the communities, dioceses, seminaries, and parishes view themselves as mission territory. This is a rather interesting difference of perspective as one considers the more standard and more dominant white, Anglo, Eurocentric, or Americentric worldview that permeates most seminaries, dioceses, religious communities, houses of formation, programming, and perspectives. As Fr. Allan Deck states, "from a pastoral point of view, the growing diversity of the clergy requires more *intercultural competence* among all clergy, religious men and women, and lay pastoral agents . . . decades ago the church sought to provide a fairly homogeneous environment for the many Catholic cultural groups, each with its own clergy." Now, in contrast, "bishops are hard-pressed to find priests from among all the diverse groups" that seem to be emerging in the United States. The full reality is that "parishes are becoming more and more multicultural or 'shared' by several groups. . . . Clergy, religious and lay ministers from abroad are often finding themselves in positions of leadership in the local parish. They are called upon to serve the whole community, not just those of their particular culture" (Deck, 2009, emphasis added).

In addition to this fact, Deck (2009) points out how rarely anyone takes into account the multigenerational realities within the "immigrant" classes. A sizable number of Hispanics have been in the United States for several generations. These could have been from anywhere in both Latin America and the Caribbean. If this is the case with the Hispanics, it is likewise analogous that many more from many different countries and cultures have immigrated to the United States. The places from which these missionaries seem to be coming include Mexico, Colombia, Africa (mostly Nigeria and Ghana), and Southeast Asia (India, Philippines, and Vietnam). The US Conference of Catholic Bishops has developed "guidelines on cultural competency for implementation at every level of the church's life, including, of course, parishes" (Deck, 2009).

Challenges and Opportunities

There clearly are enormous possibilities for the church in the United States, if we embrace these efforts in these multiple arenas of competency. It can and ought to change us for the better. The church has always been a place where anyone can find a home and where the "stranger" is always welcomed, the hungry are fed, and the homeless find shelter. In the spirit of the social teaching since Pope Leo XIII, the long and amazing history of social service, social activism, and social justice ministries should allow us to welcome and become more welcoming as a country and as an ecclesial community of faith. This is our tradition and one hopes that we retain that aspect of our tradition. We can and will become a more diverse country and a more diverse church. Most research clearly indicates that the majority of communities and the majority of "missionaries" or "internationals" are doing well in the seminaries, religious communities, and parishes to which they are sent and enrolled.

Within this arena of possibility is also a dark side; it will challenge us to become less prejudicial, less racist, less closed as a society and as a faith community. Can our systems and perspectives adapt? Writers and researchers point out three consistent areas of concern:

1. Problems with language and accent reduction
2. Orientation programming
3. Appropriate and consistent support

These areas need consistent and persistent care, attention, and sensitivity if we are to succeed in these challenging times. Equally important, there are some legitimate concerns in the arenas of child safety, harassment of lay-women within pastoral settings, and sexual misconduct/abuse of women.

As the USCCB states in the Charter audit report (2010), "The CARA 2002 priest poll identified 11% of priests as foreign born; 19% of the recently ordained priests were foreign born. The statistics from the ordination class of 2009 show us that 25% of the class is foreign born, the largest numbers coming from Mexico, Vietnam, Poland and the Philippines with the mean age at entry to the US being 23. The percentage of ordinands who are foreign born increased from 22 percent in 1999 to 38 percent in 2003, but has declined since that point and is now at 24 percent in 2009. These statistics and trends show just how large the gift of foreign born priests is. However, along with this gift come some challenges."

The Charter audit report continues, "this is a matter for the *Charter for the Protection of Children and Young People* for two reasons. First, *Charter* compliance audit findings in 2007 showed that 50 percent, or six out of 12 credible allegations concerning current minors, involved foreign priests. This finding came to light when the Secretariat of Child and Youth Protection studied the status of the 12 priests credibly accused of sexually abusing young people who were minors in the 2007 audit year. No one expected to find that six of the 12 came from outside the United States, and that most of them had returned to their native country" (ibid.). The second reason, compliance and the necessity within dioceses to monitor and report about the safe environment trainings, was also mentioned as an important and consistent issue with these men. These issues and this data do not seem to be changing nor do they seem to be improving, and they warrant new and consistent attention and care.

Current Data

An increasing number of candidates to the US priesthood with immigrant or international backgrounds or from US ethnic minority groups[1] are being psychologically evaluated as part of their application process (Batsis, 1993; Niebuhr, 2000). The latest data from the Center for Applied Research in the Apostolate (CARA) at Georgetown University reports that almost 27 percent of all seminary and religious institute candidates are from foreign countries and that 80 percent of those are studying for dioceses or religious orders here in the United States (CARA, 2011a). Their assessment usually involves the administration of widely used psychological measures that have been constructed, normed, standardized, and published in the United States (Hennessy, 1994). More specifically, these measurement instruments include intelligence, personality, vocational, behavioral, and symptom inventories, which are mostly used with English-speaking populations by examiners trained in doctoral level institutions accredited by the American Psychological Association. However, as this chapter hopes to point out, assessment practice with these ethnic minority populations in the United States generally requires cultural competence and sensitivity (Dana, 1995a, 1995b, 1996, 1998). Several researchers have identified serious shortcomings in the multicultural utilization of the most widely used assessment instruments (Allen and Dana, 2004; Dana, 1995b). This includes biases in measurement (Lu, Lim, and Mezzich, 1994; Malgady, 1996; Oldham and Riba, 1995; Sue, 1996), inaccurate and invalid interpretations of psychological findings attributed to ethnic minorities (Ramirez et al., 1996; Rollack and Terrel, 1996; Sandoval et al., 1998; Sundberg and Gonzales, 1981), and method and item biases (van de Vijver and Leung, 2001). The consideration of cultural factors in psychological assessment has become an imperative (Jones and Thorne, 1987; Miller-Jones, 1989; Westermeyer, 1987). In order to minimize or eliminate some of these limitations associated with the assessment process of ethnic minority candidates, we offer the following reflection and practical applications.

Psychological Assessment: Catholic Perspectives

The psychological assessment of candidates to the priesthood should be accurate, thorough, and, most important, ethically informed, culturally sensitive, and theologically sound. These are among some of the *sine qua non* recently outlined in church documents addressing priestly formation. In the document Guidelines for the Use of Psychology in the Admission and Formation of Candidates for the Priesthood, Pope Benedict XVI highlighted the methodological accuracy of psychological assessment that is obtained through multiple sources of data in an ethically responsible context of free consent, that is, "to arrive at a *correct evaluation* of the candidate's personality, the expert can have recourse to both interviews and tests. These must always be carried out with the previous, explicit, informed and free consent of the candidate" (5, emphasis added). Moreover, psychological experts conducting these psychological assessments "must be inspired by an anthropology that openly shares the Christian vision about the human person" (ibid., 6). A holistic and multidimensional approach is of paramount importance, given that "today's candidates represent a considerable diversity—not only of differing personal gifts and levels of maturity but also significant cultural differences—that must be taken into account. All those involved in the evaluation of applicants for priestly formation must appreciate cultural, generational, educational, and familial differences and be able to recognize which are gifts, which are liabilities, and which are simply indications of a need for fuller growth" (Program of Priestly Formation [PPF], 38). Thus, the recommendation is that all those involved in the assessment and evaluation of candidates should make sure that "due care should be observed in correctly interpreting the results of psychological testing in light of the cultural background of applicants" (ibid., 52).

A Conceptual Framework for Culturally Sensitive Assessment: Suggestions for Psychological Evaluators and Seminary Formators

Consistent with the outlined Catholic perspectives, we propose a conceptual model that integrates specific assessment competencies and practices and that strictly defines a cultural assessment competency as comprising (a) self-awareness, (b) knowledge, and (c) skills within the context of a (d) Catholic anthropology. Given that psychological assessment always occurs within a cultural context (Ridley, Li, and Hill, 1998) and that, unfortunately, cultural factors are often ignored or overlooked in psychological evaluations (Dana, 1995a), evaluators and formators should be cognizant of the following dimensions during the entire assessment process:

1. Self-Awareness
   1.1 Be aware and sensitive of your own cultural background and worldview when relating to culturally different candidates.
   1.2 Monitor how your own experiences, attitudes, values, and biases may influence the assessment process.
   1.3 Be comfortable with differences that exist between yourself and candidates in terms of cultural values.
   1.4 Explore issues of acculturation, language, racial/ethnic identity development during the assessment process.
2. Knowledge
   2.1 Recognize the limits of your knowledge of cultural concepts and worldviews.
   2.2 Acquire specific knowledge of personal worldviews in your own culture and in other cultures.
   2.3 Establish consultative relationships with cultural experts and cultural consultants (e.g., interpreters).
3. Skills
   3.1 Learn about culture-specific or indigenous psychological experiences, and use them to understand the candidate's frame of reference.
   3.2 Incorporate into the assessment practice and evaluation of candidates the use of culturally meaningful expressions to establish rapport.
   3.3 Consult and get feedback on the practice of ethically responsible and culturally sensitive assessment practice.
4. Catholic Anthropology
   4.1 Use multidimensional conceptualization of psychological issues that considers a holistic approach to the human person during assessment, with close consideration of Catholic anthropology of multiple dimensions of the human person (body, mind, spirit) across multiple dimensions of existence (natural, spiritual, supernatural, etc.).
   4.2 Appreciate the overlap and interrelation between internal subjective experience reflective of culture (cognitions, emotions, beliefs, perceptions, values, attitudes, orientations, epistemolo-

gies, consciousness levels, expectations, and personhood) and external correlates of culture (roles and cultural practices).

Vignette

This brief vignette exemplifies the complexity of psychological assessment with culturally diverse candidates and the following are some practical suggestions we have gleaned from the scientific literature.

José, a nineteen-year-old Mexican male, arrived in the United States two years ago. Since his arrival he has been very active in his predominantly Spanish-speaking home parish in Los Angeles, California. He graduated from high school in his native country and recently has completed the intensive English as a Second Language (ESL) program to acquire more fluency in English. He has a strong interest in discerning his vocation to the priesthood and has already started the screening process with the vocation director. During the interview process, he stated that he misses his hometown in Mexico. He maintains a strong sense of loyalty to his family and participates in Mexican cultural practices. As part of the customary screening process, the vocation director refers José to a licensed psychologist for a fully integrated psychological evaluation. José reported that he has never seen a therapist before or previously talked to a psychologist.

1. Pre-Assessment
   1.1 Be aware of José's familiarity with psychological resources and his cultural attitudes toward psychology. In some Latino cultures, for example, the profession of psychology may be negatively stigmatized and considered culturally undesirable.
   1.2 Facilitate José's participation in the assessment process by informing him of reasons for evaluation and expectations. Explaining the purpose, goals, and process of assessment to culturally different candidates may ease misunderstandings.
   1.3 Recognize that culturally related defenses to assessment may be normative for some culturally diverse candidates.
   1.4 Identify a qualified evaluator (preferably bilingual) who has received training, and has supervised evaluation experiences with Hispanic/Latino and Catholic examinees.
2. Assessment
   2.1 Establish culturally sensitive rapport with José (e.g., assess level of bilingual skills and culturally related test-taking attitudes).

2.2 Evaluate level of acculturation and racial/ethnic identity development.

2.3 Use standardized instruments in culturally appropriate ways. Commonly cited problems in using commonly used instruments are bias in item content, differences in test-taking skills, lack of appropriate norms for various cultures, misinterpretation of test data, and problems in test translation. Evaluator may need to consult specialized literature and manuals on more specific guidelines (e.g., see Fernandez, Boccaccini, and Noland, 2007, for the professionally responsible test selection for Spanish-speaking clients).

2.4 Use culture-specific instruments that have been constructed, normed, and validated with Mexican populations. In this case, the use of the Acculturation Rating Scale for Mexican Americans (ARSMA, Cuéllar, Arnold, and Maldonado, 1995), or the use of the Hispanic Stress Inventory (Cervantes, Padilla, and Salgado de Snyder, 1991), both of which were specifically developed with Mexican and Mexican American populations, would augment the assessment process.

2.5 Use interpreters/translators who, at a minimum, (a) share José's racial/ethnic background, and (b) are trained on the use of Spanish for psychological assessment.

3. Post-Assessment

3.1 The referring source (i.e., vocation director) and evaluator should have a collaborative professional relationship. In this case, the vocation director may inquire about culturally appropriate protocol used to evaluate José and what specific steps were taken to address cultural factors in his assessment.

3.2 Discuss with José major findings of the psychological assessment and provide him with feedback based on evaluation results in a culturally sensitive manner.

Conclusion

We would like to offer some caveats regarding the suggestions made in this chapter. First, psychological assessment is a very individualized task and there is diversity in how psychologists conduct evaluations. Second, not every suggestion herein presented can be used with every culturally diverse candidate, given the heterogeneity and diversity of candidates to the priesthood. We have carefully reviewed the existing psychological literature and extracted what we consider helpful suggestions. Ultimately, it is the expertise of the evaluator and his or her clinical judgments following best practices and ethical guidelines on assessment that will yield ethically informed, culturally sensitive, and theologically sound psychological evaluations.

Notes

1. Comparing the 2000 to the 2011 study conducted for the USCCB by CARA, it was found that 93 percent of priests are white non-Hispanic, 3 percent are Hispanic/Latino, 1 percent is African/African American/black, 2 percent are Asian or Pacific Islander, and less than 1 percent is Native American or other. From the same study, the top sending countries for international priests (in descending order by number of identified international priests) were Ireland, India, Philippines, Poland, Vietnam, Mexico, Colombia, and Nigeria.

The Inner World of Today's Celibate

Gerard J. McGlone, SJ

"Love is seen in deeds, not words."
—*Saint Ignatius Loyola, 1540*

In the wake of the church's sexual abuse crisis, few issues are more pertinent than healthy celibacy and sexuality for Roman Catholic clergy and religious. The church considers such healthy celibacy and sexuality one aspect of "affective maturity" (AM). AM also pertains to many different capacities that need maturing—including healthy and ecclesiastically appropriate interpersonal relationships, pastoral leadership, dealing with authority and being an authority figure, to mention just a few. These are not my focus in this chapter, though some aspects mentioned already will be pertinent. Nothing is more critical than a healthy way of loving that speaks more than any words one could utter or policies and charters that can be promulgated. Interestingly, a recent picture in a local Philadelphia newspaper shows a Buddhist monk completely wired while his head was covered with implants to measure his "mindfulness" while meditating (*Philadelphia Inquirer*, July 25, 2011). This image causes mixed emotions—excitement that science is finally measuring the effects of spirituality upon our well-being and health yet also sadness that we look only to the East for such models. Regrettably, the current societal model or image of "spiritual and sexual health" is not the image of a Roman Catholic priest.

Too often, one reads the stories of disordered sexuality among the clergy and inept, if not utterly incompetent, pastoral leadership in response to such criminal and scandalous behavior. In order to better understand what needs to be done, some basic definitions, information, data, and models of affective maturity, sexuality, and celibacy must be explored. Two case illustrations will be used to help distinguish high versus low sexual affective maturity. Additionally, some new contextualizations need to be detailed and the dynamics of a healthier model of celibacy might then emerge. It is in this deep and profoundly sacred experience of sexuality that this crisis most clearly challenges and induces fear. Healthy sexuality and unhealthy sexuality most often develop and are understood in a deeply private and personal interior world. It is essential to understand the current context in order to better place this fuller and needed discussion of healthy affective maturity and healthy sexuality.

The Current Context

Clergy across the country have described what they have experienced in the wake of the sexual abuse scandal. They report shattered images of ministry and priesthood, lost hopes and dreams about who they saw themselves to be and what they had hoped their leadership to be in the face of such horrible betrayals and tragedies. Time after time, they lament most especially the broken trust between themselves and their bishops, between themselves and the leadership in Rome, and the shattered trust among and between themselves as priests and those they serve in their apostolic works. Sexual violence is challenging society and the church most especially at a core and primal level: what the church calls *affective maturity*. This term will be discussed more fully later, but suffice it to say here that this aspect of the clergy's development was often not part of their religious or seminary training. The sexual abuse scandal, then, draws critical attention to two interrelated issues: the underdeveloped affective maturity of the perpetrators and the need for addressing affective maturity in the initial assessment and ongoing formation of the religious and clergy.

At a recent gathering of priests, one cleric stated, "At my ordination, I placed my hands into the very hands of my archbishop and pledged my entire self, my obedience to him and through him to Christ. I believed in those bonds, that promise, and now . . . this current crisis puts all of that into question." In diocese after diocese, in religious order after religious order, in parish after parish, the question is the same: Where is the accountability for the bishops—the church leadership—that we have had as priests in the Dallas Charter written by these very same bishops? Where is their charter for their betrayal, lack of accountability, and lack of leadership?

As a result of this broken trust, most clergy experience a deep and abiding sense of fear and abandonment. Their sense of faith, trust, and fidelity is in serious jeopardy. This fear is often based on the question, Who is next; will it be me? The very ground upon which they used to walk is not safe. There were credible reports in Philadelphia after the latest Grand Jury Report was released in February 2011 that when a priest was crossing a Catholic school playground, one of his own students, an eleven-year-old, screamed, "Pedophile!" The pastoral landscape has changed just a bit since the actor Bing Crosby portrayed an available, happy, and engaged priest in *The Bells of Saint Mary's*! Imagine for a second, the images of self, priesthood, church, relationships, sexuality, and celibacy that now have been put into question by that one child's scream across the playground.

These new images create fears and questions that are most often managed in the interior life of the cleric or religious. There is little question that the sexual abuse crisis certainly raises questions and concerns about the ability and capacity of any cleric or religious to live a celibate life. It was in and through a mature interiority and spirituality—the life of emotions—that their celibate desires first arose and currently exist for most men in pastoral ministry. If this interiority is healthy and integrated, this crisis is a challenge and most often experienced as an opportunity for further grace and growth; on the other hand, if this interiority is not integrated and unhealthy, this crisis is most often managed as a shame-based assault and a very deep neurotic threat.

This interiority is challenged by the current times, and it is not what many would choose for themselves, for their parishioners or students, anyone whom they serve. It challenges us at every level of our being and our existence as celibate males and as Catholics. Ron Rolheiser (2002) in his article "On Carrying the Sexual Abuse Crisis Biblically" writes about how one might see this crisis not as something to be *gotten through* but more as an opportunity and grace that we are given to stand *within* as with Mary and the Beloved disciple and *be at the foot of the cross, be in this moment*. If one stands in that same courage as Mary, one is asked to face the multitude of feelings that might be experienced and what one needs to do with them. We could run away from them and the crucified Jesus as many did; Peter certainly can be a model of what we can do with those difficult emotions. It is not, however, what affective maturity and its management requires of us as men and women, as leaders and as a community. Violence, and indeed sexual violence, is not something for which we have been trained and from which we can expect to recover easily. It will take patience, new capacities, and time. For Rolheiser, Mary's action is not a passive or even a weak stance, but it is one of enormous strength, vision, and courage. Perhaps this same call is the call for each of us, priest and parishioner, believer and unbeliever, and for the church itself. The foot of the cross is not an easy place to be precisely because the cross subverts the ordinary understanding of human identity even as it simultaneously reveals the divine essence of human identity. The cross challenges who we are and what we are, while it is also about a passionate love and our ways of loving in their deepest and most striking forms. Perhaps it is forcing or eliciting both an individual and organizational affective maturity not seen or imagined before. Perhaps it is an act of love that must be seen as St. Ignatius taught in the sixteenth century. Ignatius of Loyola taught the tools of discernment that allow us to see our desires and passions as the very place within which God can communicate and most often dwells. While this love and action are a standing within the moment that few are prepared to do, want to do, or are maturely capable of doing, this just may be the model of celibacy, sexuality, and affective maturity given to us from the Gospel itself.

Affective Maturity

The understanding of affective maturity may seem obvious to some at first glance but it is far from simple or easily defined. The term affective maturity is used constantly in the church documents about the assessment and admission of candidates to seminary and religious life, formation in seminaries, and ongoing formation for the ordained and fully professed. Simply understood psychologically, it is the ability to know what one feels, express those feelings, and manage them appropriately through the psychological phases and/or stages from adolescence into adulthood. However, that is not what the church documents have conceptualized nor is it the full ecclesial understanding. It is a more complex and nuanced demand, expectation, and capacity. As can be seen in figure 7.1, affective maturity must first be contextualized within the "four pillar matrix," the four pillars essential in the formation process (the intellectual, human, spiritual, and pastoral, shown in fig. 7.1) that Pope John Paul II described in his now famous exhortation *Pastores Dabo Vobis* (PDV, translated "I Will Give You Shepherds," 1992). It is in a sense a maturity (developmental growth process) of affects (emotions) that can and must be seen intellectually, humanly, spiritually, and pastorally. This full concept deserves a much fuller and longer treatment in another book or several chapters, but suffice it to say for this chapter, we will only look at affective maturity across each of these pillars, and only in regard to healthy sexuality and celibacy.

Figure 7.1. Four-pillar matrix

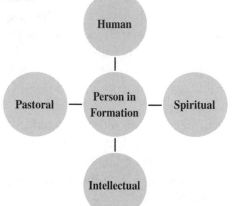

In this extraordinary document, the late pope highlighted the essential root cause of any vocation and our call to be a celibate priest or a religious: the life and breath of Jesus Christ, as reflected in the Trinity and manifested through his church. It is at one and the same time a powerful vision of the human person, God, Christ, and the church. Any discussion of this aspect of what and who a priest or religious might be comes in and through this extraordinary vision portrayed in PDV. A vocation and call is first and foremost the work and action of God. The church discerns with the person the nature and scope of that call: "The center and foundation of all formation is Jesus Christ" (PDV; and Program of Priestly Formation, fifth edition [PPF], 2006). It also is clearly a process that is always dynamic and therefore in development, that is, changing, as the person grows, ages, and hopefully matures into adulthood (PDV, 30). In summary, formation must be and is "ongoing and dynamic." It dies and/or finishes when the person dies.

In the PPF, "the seminary [and religious life] and its programs foster the formation of future priests [and religious] by attending specifically to their human, spiritual, intellectual, and pastoral formation—the four pillars of priestly formation developed in *Pastores dabo vobis*. These pillars of formation and their finality give specificity to formation in seminaries as well as a sense of the integrated wholeness of the different dimensions of formation" (70). A person of balanced affective maturity might look like the integrated vision of the overlapping spheres in figure 7.2. The core of affective maturity is seen in this chart as the primary circle. Here is the capacity that manages the emotions on an everyday basis, which of necessity leads to a maturity in dealing with authority feelings, while dealing with the everyday sources of stress and conflict that could be manifested internally or externally. This emotional/affective capacity might foster the ability to become a healthy model of authority in the pastorally appropriate exercise of power, which finally comes into full circle in the overarching maturity within the development of the integration of this emotional life with thoughts and values in the person. It is this center of the priest's identity that is being most challenged today. Feelings or affects are managed in every aspect of the person and within each of the four "pillars" of John Paul II's vision—human, intellectual, pastoral, spiritual. The PPF describes these attributes as existing, being measured, and developing within the full framework of the formational or seminary life of the seminarian or religious. But, it is known in and through relationships— mentorship, supervision and intimacy of celibate friendships, and fraternity of community or the presbyterate. It continues developing after ordination in the pastoral and active life of the priesthood and is most especially found in the sustained, supported fraternity of the "brotherhood" of brothers (see PDV, 17; PPF, 18). It is this need to know and feel the support of fellow celibates that needs and warrants the most attention today. This "brotherhood" is essential especially because of the diminishment of the number of men in religious life and the priesthood coupled with the theological divisiveness that often causes more dissension, isolation, and loneliness.

Figure 7.2. A vision of affective maturity

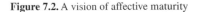

Integrating affects with
thoughts and values

Managing power as a
healthy authority figure

Dealing well with
stress and conflict

Dealing well with
authority

Growing in
awareness and
managing emotions
well on a daily basis

The PPF states that "*'sexuality* affects all aspects of the human person in the unity of his body and soul. It especially concerns affectivity, the capacity to love and to procreate, and in a more general way the attitude for forming bonds of communion with others.' For the seminary applicant, thresholds pertaining to sexuality serve as the foundation for living a life-long commitment to healthy, chaste celibacy. As we have recently seen so dramatically in the church, when such foundations are lacking in priests, the consequent suffering and scandals are devastating" (41). The goal of human formation in the seminary or religious training is the fullest development of this person. "In general, human formation happens in a three-fold process of self-knowledge, self-acceptance, and self-gift—and all of this in faith" (PPF, 80). Affective maturity seen in this framework allows the person of faith to be known, accepted, and seen as gift.

Affective maturity in sexuality can be further seen in a summary of three different dimensions or areas of expertise in the candidate or religious (fig. 7.3). As such, these dimensions might best be seen and understood as continuums within which a person changes, adapts, learns, and develops at the same time. According to the PPF, the priest or religious needs to master a certain basic knowledge and intellectual skill set about the physiological and psychological dimensions of sexuality, the various meanings associated with this knowledge, and the incumbent skills to live these factors out in ordinary life within a society that may not value these skills or lifestyle. In other words, all four "pillars" need to be nurtured and developed in this one aspect of living "affective maturity" within these three areas of competency.

A man must be schooled additionally in the virtues of chaste loving, with ascetical and theological knowledge of what is required in this marital love between himself and the church, while learning to love healthfully and chastely the particular men and women within whom God gifts him in this present time and place. He is essentially a "man of communion." As with Aristotle's virtues, these skills need practice over time to develop. This development occurs through the proper use of the sacraments of Eucharist and confession, various forms and types of prayer, regular and ongoing use of spiritual direction, devotions, and an ascetical discipline of living celibacy itself. These are not innate skills but learned behaviors, skills, and disciplines within this broad contextual framework and understanding. The goal is being a healthy and happy integrated celibate. This ability to develop affective maturity does not happen in a vacuum; it arises from the early modeling or experiences of childhood, the family, schooling, and the culture. It is filled with mistakes and sins, joys and hopes. It is also most especially filled with

Figure 7.3. Dimensions of affective maturity

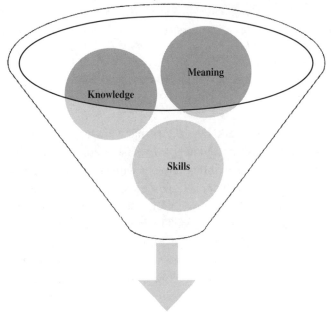

Integrated Celibate

the capacity to reflect upon oneself and one's problems. It is an ability to seek and receive feedback and criticism. It is most especially seen in the ability to be able to seek and to ask for help if one is in need of it.

Case Illustration: Low Affective Maturity

This case is fictional but based on real cases.

Father Fred is a twenty-nine-year-old priest who always had trouble in seminary, was often isolated from his peers, and developed few long-standing friendships. The staff thought about delaying his ordination, but his bishop decided to ordain him because the diocese needed him. He reports coming from a fairly close but small family with no real extended family ties. He goes home regularly but rarely socializes with any class-mates. He did not have many friends in high school and was considered odd for his religiosity, being bullied occasionally for being the "nerd," and dated infrequently. He recently stated to a spiritual director that he does not think that he is straight or gay but celibate. He is consistent and regular in saying the office and attending to his sacramental and devotional life of prayer. He seems awkward socially in his first pastoral assignment and seems a bit lost in the parish. He is quite bright and did well in his academics but did not seem to integrate his vast and expansive theological knowledge into ordinary pastoral or everyday situations. His homilies are often long and people find them irrelevant to their daily living. People are complaining to the staff and the pastor. He refuses to get help and does not try to get help from his pastor and the staff; he thinks that they do not like him and it's their problem, not his.

Case Discussion

This case illustrates several key factors that were noted above; he has not developed peer relationships and hence he is isolated. His lack of affective maturity shows itself in his inability to work with staff and the parishioners. His prayer life seems superficial and he seems emotionally-affectively immature, distant from his God, himself, and others. His sexuality is underdeveloped in key areas and most especially in his inarticulate sexual identity. This is a high risk factor for possible emotional and interpersonal sexual acting out in the future. His lack of sexual integration and affective sexual maturity stands as a red flag. In each of the spheres of capacities of affective maturity and in each of the dimensions, this man is underdeveloped or immature.

Case Illustration: High Affective Maturity

Father Felix is a thirty-four-year-old priest. He has been ordained for about six years. He is quite shy by nature and bookwormish. He seems to have a couple of good friends with whom he talks and socializes regularly. He was an average to good student and was involved in various activities in the schools that he has attended. He was not the most popular guy at the seminary but he seemed to get along with everyone. He would work in various activities and was appreciated by many. The faculty confronted him on several issues related to his interpersonal engagement and study habits and he seemed to benefit from these interventions. He comes from a divorced family but has stable and consistent contact with both parents who have remarried. They seem to have good relationships with the ex-spouses. He has several stepbrothers and stepsisters and gets along with most of them well but has some siblings with whom he is distant. He is regular in his prayer life and sees a spiritual director often. He states to the director that he struggles with his erotic fantasies but he is certain of his sexual identity and sometimes masturbates. He is developing a more active prayer life and states that he has found a priest's prayer group helpful because they discuss their prayer life with one another monthly. He says that this keeps him "honest." He is active and engaged with the parishioners and finds them life-giving. He is quite a good homilist and people appreciate his presence in the parish community. He seems comfortable with men and women. They say he is quite shy but likable once you get to know him.

Case Discussion

Father Felix seems to be open emotionally or affectively; he seems to be growing or maturing in this capacity by the fact that he has been open to confrontation and feedback in his formation. He seems to be adaptable, though shy, and able to engage in both pastoral and personal relationships without too much difficulty. He talks honestly and openly with his director in a mature way in regard to his struggles with being celibate. He seems to ask for feedback by bringing these topics up in direction. He is not complete in his sexual knowledge or development and is not withholding of his need to grow. He is open to both men and women and does not seem exclusive in this manner of pastoral care and engagement. He seems to possess an affective maturity in his capacity to stay intimate with his family, friends, and parishioners. He seems to have been able to walk through fairly difficult conflicts or relationships (divorce and stepfamilies) in his family and at the seminary and seems to have grown from these experiences. He seems open to growth.

Early Models of Sexuality

In the various theories of healthy sexual development, typically, a young female or male will go through the usual urges and first experiences of sexuality in the silence and sacredness of her or his body. There seems little question that the fields of biology and genetics will help us further understand and explore the vast beauty and complexity of healthy sexuality. The purpose of this chapter is not to review that research. Suffice it to say that the framework and the template for how one becomes sexual and what becomes a healthy expression of one's sexuality is clearly indicated in the biological and genetic makeup that each of us is given in conception and at birth; any affective maturity builds upon this nature. More recent research in sexology has suggested the early experience has an enormous effect on the development of the child and the healthy and unhealthy aspects of who he or she will become as a sexual creature (Kann, Telijohann, and Wooley, 2007). As a child, the young boy or girl is exposed to familial, societal, and cultural aspects and views of sexuality the minute that he or she is able to see, hear, and touch.

The tender touch of a mother or father teaches the child about his or her value in the world, his or her body as valued and precious. Freud was famous for saying that the first sense of self is a "body self." The ability to have someone respond to the cries and concerns of the child often creates a sense of hope, security, or trust and that this new world is safe, dependable, and can be trusted. The ability to enjoy pleasure and endure pain becomes part and parcel of the young child's small yet growing repertoire and capacity. Cultural and familial senses and views of gender will be taught very soon just in the colors and expressions of the child's room and dress chosen for him or her and reinforced by actions and beliefs of family and relatives. The genetic and biological markers of sex will become expressed in their nascent and primitive forms. Central to this new creature's sexual world will be learning *how to feel, what is appropriate and what is not,* the new life and the new way of emotions, of affects. This is excitement; this is joy; this is pleasure; this feels good, and this does not. Feeling is everything for the child. As Freud would say, the child at this point is pure and utter urge, impulse or "id."

The young person continues to develop and goes through various stages of what we refer to as "normal" human and sexual development as has been described elsewhere (Erikson, 1950; PPF). The focus for this chapter is on the knowledge and sexual experiences that a normative development might look like in male clergy in the United States. Typically, a young man will see and model what he sees the parental figures, siblings, and/or caregivers doing in the full range of what healthy touching, kissing, and caressing might be like and how that might be expressed. One can see this same innocence in the play of children with one another, or one also might see the unhealthy versions in that play. A child can't help but express what he or she has known and seen in the daily and nightly rituals. A healthy child might touch tenderly and play innocently. An abused child may act out that abuse with other children or with himself or herself. Children learn quickly what is socially appropriate and what is not socially appropriate for young girls and boys to do. The capacities that were given biologically and through the genes find expression in the social interactions and value-laden world of the situation within which the child either thrives or is challenged to make sensible.

Clergy describe their early "sexual education" or their learning about sex in a similar manner as most males in the United States. Affective maturity is stunted or often hampered when this is not done well. It is exceedingly rare for males to hear about sexual information, education, or matters from their parents. Catholic clergy's first knowledge about sexual matters being similar to most men's experience and knowledge in the United States is both normative and troublesome. "Schoolyard or alley sexual education" is most often the place where the facts, or lack of facts, knowledge, or lack of knowledge, fantasies, tall tales, and myths about sex are learned and very hotly debated by the more extroverted and "mature." Priest after priest, religious after religious, often describe the same experiences of how they were taught about "the birds and the bees" and all other matters sexual. They were not taught as the church encourages parents to be the first teachers of all matters sexual in canon law (Code of Canon Law, 1996; see PDV; PPF). This does not impugn the ideal set forth in the Code of Canon Law but it places our current discussion within a necessary framework that becomes critical to understanding the how and where (the mechanisms and places) a young man matures in his own knowledge about sexuality, himself, and his sexual affectivity or emotions in the church today. Sexual education is most often done in secret within a learning environment less than ideal or sacred. The young man may learn rightly or wrongly not to ask about these matters and most especially may not learn to feel anything in a healthy manner. A first and early model about sexual maturity is most often a model that teaches quite well about misinformation, secrecy, and silence. It rarely teaches about knowledge, sacredness, and health. It rarely teaches that an affect or feeling can be managed effectively and appropriately. The ability to manage and become affectively mature was very limited or nonexistent.

Additionally, clergy describe their early, primary, or first sexual experiences in a similarly secretive, solitary, sometimes isolative and myth-laden atmosphere (McGlone, 2001). They often state that they might have had some engagement, act, experience, or fantasy within their early formation in sexuality, which could include sexual experimentation of some kind with same sex or opposite sex individuals. It might also have been pleasant, exciting, and erotically playful and/or awkward, scary, painful, and/or odd. But, most often when they describe early sexual experiences, they report little conversation, understanding, and healthy integration about those experiences and little ability to feel secure about what actually happened or did not happen. The second aspect to this still developing and myth-laden model reveals how now one's sexual experiences are reinforced most often in more secrecy, silence, and awkwardness. As a result, sexuality for some clerics and religious might become shame-based and fear-driven; for others, it can become healthy and integrated; for many others, it might be on a continuum between these two extremes.

Early Models of Celibacy

As one can see, this early typical and first model of sexual development for the cleric today seems both troubling and challenging. It does
suggest that the early model of sexuality and the early model of celibacy are
strikingly similar. This model does not suggest that everyone experiences
sexuality in this one manner or way. It merely is an attempt to suggest that
most males and most clerics describe these two aspects of their development in strikingly similar ways. It is also much more useful to understand
sexuality as developing along a continuum. If we were to have a 3-D version
or schemata of this in front of us, the biological, genetic, familial, societal,
interpersonal, intrapsychic, situational, and environmental influences upon
sexuality interface and interact at many and varied levels, often at the same
time, almost like a modern art piece suspended like a hologram in mid-air
(fig. 7.4). These schemata and dimensions develop and grow as the individual matures and ages. The tasks that one must complete in the natural
maturation process are difficult enough. If we now consider this added
dimension of sexual maturity in celibate identity, one wonders how or if
anyone can be "healthy" in today's hypersexualized, visually overloaded,
and impulsively oriented society. It is even more striking that the secretive
and private nature of this learning model kept and keeps most seminarians
and clerics in the dark, both spiritually and psychologically. Formation and
seminary life today confront the candidate to religious life and/or seminary
with several challenges that might not have been understood nor fully analyzed in the past. This sexual person within his model in all of its knowledge
and mystery, its wounds and scrapes, its joys and hopes, its fantasies and
dreams, its health and lack of health, its integration and confusion already
in place, then, is confronted with a new and even more challenging world
of celibate life and living. This model now must fit within another unknown
and even more challenging model: celibacy.

Celibacy is a gift; it is also a learned discipline. One would think, like
the soldiers who were trained in a "boot camp" manner of initiation to be
good marines or great pilots in the air force, that most houses of formation and seminaries would teach the young man *how* to be celibate. Such a
"celibate boot camp" might teach the young man/seminarian/religious the
very basics about living and thriving in a celibate world. It might teach him
how to manage well his God-given sexual feelings—his erotic fantasies
and attractions, his urges and what to do with his sexual frustrations, his
masturbatory struggles, and his sexual hurts and joys. However, most cler-

Figure 7.4. Sexual development

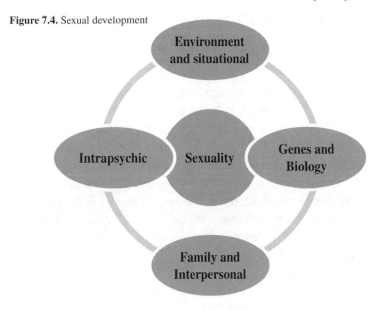

ics and religious report the direct opposite happened in their formation and seminary training.

Cleric after cleric, religious after religious, reports the same fundamental manner of learning how to be celibate. Clergy describe their education in celibacy as "it sort of just happened." It was not to be touched, literally and figuratively (Loftus, 1999). Most clerics and religious consistently reported about the early expectations and experiences in seminary and religious formation houses. They were often "schooled" *not* to talk about, *not* to deal with, anything like sexuality because if you did, you were seen as deficient, weird, or sexually obsessed. Simply put, it was a taboo within a taboo. Spiritual direction or friendships were the "places" wherein one began possibly to speak about the struggles or questions. In seminary after seminary and in religious order after religious order, education about sexuality was fairly nonexistent. The former "street, alley, or schoolyard knowledge" about sexuality and sex often sufficed till one was in a morality class in theology or in a confessional "practicum." For many religious and clergy, healthy celibacy never got discussed. It was something you learned about in private or secretive discussions; friendships were seen as necessary yet no one was ever taught how to have celibate, healthy, and intimate friendships that were life-giving and necessary for being "a man of communion" (PPF). To the contrary, friendships in this context were often seen as suspicious places to avoid, lest you be accused of being "gay" or "too needy." In Latin the expression was *nonquam duo, semper tres*, translated into English, "never in twos, always in threes." Healthy ways of relating and friendships were not to be trusted.

Many just left the seminary or religious life because they could not see (did not learn) themselves living this "way" or lifestyle anymore. For many, the early model of celibacy pretty much mirrored the same one they brought with them into the seminary or religious order. It was secretive, private, superficially knowledgeable, and full of myths about themselves and others. This early celibate model failed most often in its ability to manage the most fundamental and important affect, that is the basis of one's ability to be celibate: If one cannot see, know, and love one's own sexual feelings and identity as appropriate, gifted, and sacred, how could there possibly be celibacy, and a healthy celibacy at that? It was also expressed most consistently in an "immature affectivity" and an adolescent-like response style to seminary and/or religious life. It was this same adolescent-like immaturity that was theorized to be at the heart of the sexually offending behavior of the priests (McGlone, 2001). Perhaps we are seeing this same phenomenon today.

Figure 7.5. Comparison of early lay and celibate sexuality

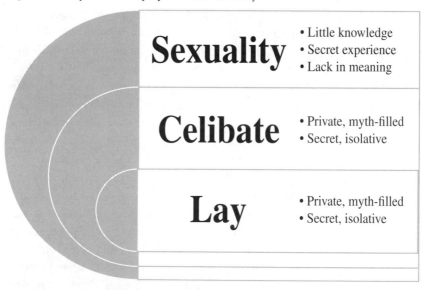

Eugene Kennedy's 1977 research, which concluded that priests and religious were "underdeveloped," is one of the few studies that exist on the sexual and psychological development of priests and religious. Of note, and

often missed in the preface of that study, Kennedy mentions that priests and religious described in that study were quite *similar* to males in the general population of the United States. Essentially, these men looked like most men in the United States—they all were underdeveloped.

The general population of Roman Catholic clergy is similar to the general male population in the United States in several key ways. Surprisingly, they are within the norms on the sexual knowledge portion of the Multiphasic Sex Inventory. In other words, they have about the same basic sexual knowledge, which is not that good, as the general population of men in the United States; though of particular note, a little under the norm, Roman Catholic clergy (98–99 percent) show themselves to be *without any* admitted sexual deviancy in the realm of sexual fantasies (McGlone, 2001). This is clearly different from the norm of most males. Their fantasies were not deviant psychologically; they were always of opposite or same sex partners. They did not indicate a *paraphilic* or a sexual disorder. The latest John Jay report (Terry, 2010) issued recently at the USCCB also supports this observation. The nuanced and sophisticated nature of this study clearly indicates that some of the more recent efforts at prevention through education seem to be working and having a great deal of positive and measurable effects in the church.

Additionally, it is essential to assess and explore psychological mechanisms and realities with which these men engage this question. Longitudinal and developmental studies are necessary, and Loftus (1999) has suggested several appropriate designs for doing this type of research, psychologically. After extensive analyses on the Rorschach test data in several groups of clergy, there is little doubt that this test provides us with helpful and important information (McGlone, 2001). Normal celibates look far less dependent than sex offenders; they appear far more resourceful psychologically. Normal celibates tend not to be narcissistic but there is a subgroup (approx. 12 percent) that does seem to be a little more *avoidant* in dealing with people and reality than the normal population of males in the United States. In general, however, the results here in this study indicate no noteworthy psychological illness or disorder. They do not, as a group, seem to be "psychologically underdeveloped" at all. This becomes essential to measure especially since clergy and religious tend to present well on most tests and objective assessment measures. Most important, the Rorschach and its utility seem quite clear in this research.

Furthermore, on several key assessment variables within this Rorschach test, they do look different from the clerical offenders. This information can be quite useful for screeners of candidates for seminary and for future assessment of clergy who might be experiencing psychological difficulties in their ministry (McGlone and Viglione, 2003). Perhaps more than anything, this supports recent research about seminary education and training about sexuality, and that teaching sexuality must include and concentrate on relational and intimacy issues that are ongoing and developmental, and not on the accurate provision of purely anatomical and biological data/knowledge about sexuality. Relational and interpersonal capacities, resources, and issues that naturally arise from this discussion are essential to creating a new model. Who has this person been involved with, to whom do they relate, and what is the nature and quality of intimacy in those relationships? As was already indicated, the priests in the research show a history of having had both chaste and sexual relationships that they attempt to understand and integrate (Sipe, 1999; McGlone, 2001). This, therefore, points to a question regarding sexual development that both future researchers and clinicians in the field might benefit from looking at; that is, *the how* of Roman Catholic clergy's attempt to integrate their sexuality and intimacy needs within church doctrines.

Models of Celibate Life

There might be certain emerging *models of celibacy* that exist and seem to be more present. These models are not meant to be exhaustive but are descriptive from data in the interviews that were done in the study (McGlone, 2001). There exist in the history of the church many saintly men and women who have attempted to live a celibate, holy, and integrated sexual life. They are often stories of virgins, sinners, and saints. We see in the lives of Augustine and Monica, Francis and Clare, Dominic, Benedict and Scholastica, Ignatius of Loyola, and many others various struggles and graces in the attempt to live a chaste and celibate life. Perhaps these figures and lives of the saints are the stories or models of today also and perhaps they are challenging us in a similar way. Many of these stories are filled with previous or preconversion experiences of fairly clear and overtly promiscuous sexual activity. It was only after much work, prayer, and the grace of God that many were able to live a celibate life. For many clerics and religious, celibacy and living a chaste life might be something that one enters into after failing to do so repeatedly or as one priest said, "I learned to become celibate, after I failed miserably and learned to love and live differently."

A *first* model and ideal of celibacy exists for some who clearly come to celibacy without effort or second thought, a truly graced group for whom celibacy is an "effortless gift," as one priest described it. They have not had sexual genital experiences and they are virgins. They were called and have not struggled with this call. These individuals model for us a virginal, holistic, and innocent-like approach to living the celibate life. They have described a happy family life where sexuality was seen as a gift and a vocation to the priesthood or religious life as a model of one of many vocational choices that any member might be called into following. These men seem to be untouched by the societal images and assaults upon the ego.

A *second* model seems to have emerged in those who lived a fairly active sexual life prior to being called or having experienced a conversion; the members of this group have not struggled with the call to be celibate and live within that original grace. This group seems to have experienced a clear vocation but these clerics struggle often with their commitment and admit to "falling from grace." They fall into masturbatory activity and/or experiences of genital sexual activity but return to their call and love of the discipline. They are able to confess their sins and feel forgiven of them and return to the effort to be holistically integrated and dynamic celibates.

A *third* model arises among those who seem to have the desire to live celibately but do not have the skills and the vocation to do so. They want to live the rule of celibacy but fail often at it and see themselves as being called to struggle with this in spite of the failings. They may often reject the church's teaching. These priests and brothers want the discipline/rule changed to facilitate a married clergy or a relational clergy with full sexual activity.

What becomes interesting and important in a qualitative analysis is how clerics justify, rationalize, and/or integrate their sexual activity in a theological and/or psychological manner. Most clergy who report being sexually active both in the present and in the past have opted not to accept the church's doctrine on celibacy and chastity. They are in direct conflict with church rule and discipline, while still exercising ministry within the church. In their interviews, the overwhelming majority said in effect, "I choose not to accept this particular form of church doctrine, and I still love exercising my ministry, and the church is not going to determine that for me." Whether straight or gay, the priest clearly has struggled with this aspect of his sexual development and sexual history.

Sexual activity seems to happen among both the heterosexual (29 percent) and homosexual (24 percent) priests. Contrary to myth, and to what seems to be popular in the media about the gay priest, he is not the predominantly, nor the only, sexually active priest. Additionally, 28 percent report having no past or present sexual activity, and 40 percent report only having past sexual activity; hence, 68 percent are currently celibate. Some (5 percent) report being sexually active in the present and others (28 percent) report being sexually active in both the present and past. Further statistical analysis also found no significant psychological deficits/disorders between the nonactive and the sexually active groups of priests. Sexual abuse was reported to have occurred in about 19 percent of these participants. This fits with most studies of males in the United States.

This seems to both confirm and challenge the oft-quoted *Kansas City Star* article of April 1999, which suggests that there is a higher than normal proportion of gays, AIDS-related deaths, and HIV infection in the Roman Catholic clergy, and that these homosexuals are indeed promiscuously sexually active. This study confirms a higher than normal percentage of gays (31 percent in the RC priesthood) but challenges their rate of HIV infection (1 percent). This clearly contradicts the *Kansas City Star* article in a significant manner.

A rather striking piece of demographic data that would be of interest to psychologists and those in formation houses or seminaries is that 59 percent of the priests and religious identified themselves as having received some form of psychological treatment or counseling (McGlone, 2001). Additionally, 41 percent indicated that they had not received any psychological treatment or counseling. Among those who sought treatment, 1 percent identified themselves as having psychological treatment that included inpatient care, while 78 percent of these said that they sought outpatient treatment only. The remaining 21 percent did not distinguish the type of treatment. The primary reasons for inpatient and outpatient psychological help were issues related to depression, sexual orientation, sexual identity issues, and issues surrounding alcoholism.

This compares to the data by Falkenhain and others (1999), who reported that only 1.7–2.5 percent of clerical sex offenders ever sought psychological help prior to inpatient assessment and treatment for their sexual offenses. This seems to be quite a salient difference. It should also be kept in mind, however, that these were two different samples or groups of priests. However, it does point to a "psychological mindedness" that might be present in the normal celibates that is not present in the sexually offending clerics.

As previous research suggests, observing violent behavior in the family often leads to a child imitating that violent drama. In the control group of priests, as a child or adolescent, 16 percent remember their parents fighting physically and 84 percent deny *any* physical fighting of their parents; 13 percent report being involved in fighting between their parents, 5 percent report sometimes being involved in verbal fighting between their parents, and

82 percent report that they were not involved in any fighting between their parents. Over 56 percent reported that there was never any severe verbal or physical fighting in their family.

In this same control group, 48 percent identified a history of alcoholism in the family and 52 percent denied any history of alcoholism or drug abuse in their family. This seems to match the available data on clerical offenders that, according to Connors (1994), was about 45 percent. However, Loftus and Camargo (1992) reported no substance abuse in the clerical sex offender population as a whole and in their families of origin. Perhaps differences exist in this data as a result of selection bias because the data from Connors (1994) comes from a treatment center that had a history of treating clergy for alcoholism.

A Healthier Model

These three phenomena discussed above—the current sexual abuse context, the early sexual modeling prior to entering seminary or religious life, and the celibate models—seem to coalesce into a fairly challenging and difficult set of factors within which any celibate can manage and choose to live a more healthy celibate lifestyle. A healthier model seems to be emerging that must include better sexual education and knowledge; training in intimacy and interpersonal skills; education on managing boundaries, stress, conflict and anger management skills; and, most important, spiritual discipline and skills in the mystical tradition of the church. The following elements seem to be key factors in this new model:

1. It must first and foremost teach the basics of an attentive awareness and sensitivity to each of these realities in an ongoing, dynamic, and developmental fashion.
2. A new affective maturity creates a need for more sexual knowledge and awareness as well as the skills to access these in the capacity for a more healthy intimacy that is both celibate and free.
3. This intimacy skills development should be an essential, though heretofore missing, link in seminary and religious formation. Interpersonal skills training, stress and anger management skills, and effective conflict resolution skills are a must.
4. The skills necessary to manage this complicated and new pastoral landscape seem to be fairly obvious and yet quite nuanced and challenging.

More effective management of pastoral boundaries and education about them is necessary.

5. Ongoing education, knowledge, and awareness of this changed landscape are a must for those the celibate serves and for his own pastoral needs. This could address the rising and persistent fears experienced by clergy and religious.

6. It seems obvious that this new *interiority* that might be necessary to handle the complicated and ever-changing realities of the sexual abuse crisis is a new and important spiritual, human, pastoral, and intellectual development in maturity.

7. It is a new *mysticism* that is necessary, calling the celibate into a new way of understanding, knowing, and being present to that from which we want to flee. This new mysticism of these *holy longings*, as Rolheiser (2002) has suggested, seems not only necessary but also warranted. This is a spiritual and psychological discipline that is in our tradition in the art and practice of meditation.

8. An integrated, healthy, and Catholic anthropological view and understanding of himself, his brother priests, and those he serves (Sperry, 2010b) is necessary to assess and manage.

9. Creating and becoming a "brotherhood of brothers" is as necessary as a new interiority for this new model to be both manageable and transformative.

One single approach will not be helpful and sufficient nor appropriate to the challenge at hand. The values and character necessary in what Rolheiser puts forth in the current pastoral moment is strikingly similar to the values and priestly character necessary and expressed by John Paul II in his encyclical *Pastores Dabo Vobis*. It is this *affective maturity* that he saw as being both multidimensional and dynamic in its developmental view of the human being. If the cleric or religious neglects one "pillar" or one aspect of who he is, he is doomed to fail. If he also does not have the patience to endure this as a dynamic or unfolding process, he is likewise doomed to fail and make it more complicated than it already is.

One could try to pray through this time and become too piously disengaged; one could read more and be doomed to rationalize/intellectualize it away; one could be pastorally more active to all those in need and become more easily burnt out; one could try to do all that is humanly possible and suffer a long-standing and persistent depression. Or, one could try to embrace it at every level and allow the richness of this new mysticism/interiority to emerge slowly and stand within it in a courageous and Marian perseverance. It would demand a spiritual conversion or, even more aptly, a new affective maturity that would allow each celibate to see, feel, and know his weakness and sin and the weakness and sin of the church more clearly.

The vision that John Paul II put forth in PDV seems right on point in this regard; this document points to a dynamic human growth process within a relational ontology, built upon a relational and trinitarian view of God and a relational and dynamic view of priestly fraternity and intimacy. Creating a "brotherhood of brothers" is deeply rooted in the ability to function and thrive in the current ecclesial and pastoral situation facing religious and priests in their ongoing formation. It is a profoundly relational theology and it is psychologically quite sound, if only the presbyterates and religious communities were able to actualize this theory. Concerning affective maturity, awareness and management of these sexual and celibate realities, one cannot leave it to the silence and assumptions of society and culture, nor to seminary and religious life. Again, this kind of love must be seen in a new concrete action; perhaps the action, this new way of loving, is as simple and direct as a new way of being priest to ourselves and to each other, and thus becoming a new brotherhood. Additionally, we priest the people of God every day we serve in and before the crucified one, the Body of Christ—and maybe we, like Mary, may be able to stand in strength, dignity, and grace at the foot of the cross. This might be the very grace of a more *healthy inner life for today's celibate.*

Assessing the Journey Within

Len Sperry

Priesthood is a journey. The stages of that journey extend from birth and family upbringing, seminary, active ministry, and then to retirement and/or death. Irrespective of the twists and turns the journey takes, it reflects the unique inner life of each priest on that journey. Consulting psychologists and psychiatrists are tasked with the responsibility of assessing that journey at various stages, most commonly at the seminary admission stage.

For some time I have been concerned about the adequacy of the psychological assessment of candidates for seminary admission. This concern follows from my experience with evaluating seminary candidates as well as priests accused of various forms of misconduct, including sexual misconduct. Usually, there was a report of psychological assessment in the files of the priests that I evaluated. Typically, these reports included results on a Minnesota Multiphasic Personality Inventory (MMPI), Rorschach, and a Weschler Adult Intelligence Scale (WAIS). It was somewhat disappointing that the reports contained few, if any, clues suggesting that misconduct might occur. It could be argued that assessments of candidates with such clues were, in fact, screened out of priestly formation. Yet, the reality is that a significant percentage (28 percent) was admitted despite a negative psychological assessment report (Batsis, 1993). It could also be argued that the assessment protocols of those who went on to become priests and then engaged in misconduct were incomplete and so could not be sufficiently predictive.

Assuming that the typical assessment protocol is incomplete, what additional components or factors would increase predictability? To begin to answer this question requires that a typical assessment protocol be specified.

Unfortunately, this is problematic since consensus on what constitutes a standard assessment protocol has yet to be achieved. This problem is long-standing, beginning in the late 1930s when the psychological screening of candidates began in response to Moore's famous study involving "pre-psychotic" priests (Moore, 1936). Surprisingly, not even the sexual misconduct crisis of the past two decades has led to a standardized protocol or a national applicant database (Plante and Boccaccini, 1998). It was not until the fifth edition of the Program of Priestly Formation, published in 2006, that psychological testing became normative in the seminary admission process. Fortunately, an important step forward was the recent report on the national survey of testing and screening practices of seminary candidates. The report, "Psychological Assessment: The Testing and Screening of Candidates for Admission to the Priesthood in the U.S. Catholic Church: A Survey Study Conducted by the NCEA Seminary Department"—hereafter referred to as the report or NCEA survey—provides the first documentation of the current practices of psychological assessment in the United States.[1] The report identified what appears to be "a standard, core set of measures [WAIS, MMPI-2, the Rorschach Inkblot Test using the Exner system]" (NCEA, 2010, p. 52) and the clinical interview. The report indicates that the psychologists assessing seminary candidates also utilized other measures to assess additional considerations. But what are these additional considerations and what is the basis for conducting such additional assessments?

This article attempts to address these questions. First, it briefly reviews the Vatican document making psychological testing normative. Then, it compares national survey data on current assessment practices with that document and concludes that the conventional model of psychological assessment of seminary candidates has both theoretical and technical shortcomings. Finally, it proposes additional assessment factors that presumably provide a fuller, more comprehensive psychological assessment model.

Rationale for Psychological Assessment

To date, what constitutes the psychological assessment of seminary candidates has been largely the decision of individual seminaries and psychologists. In other words, there is no consensus on a systemic and theological basis or rationale on which specific factors are to be assessed. As noted previously, the Program of Priestly Formation (PPF) made psychological testing for seminary candidates normative, but specified no directives about the factors to be assessed, nor was a specific test battery designated.

Instead, seminaries were charged with specifying what constituted "sufficient growth" necessary for seminary admission.

Nevertheless, the PPF did outline several markers or attributes of maturity that it expected viable candidates would have achieved prior to seminary admission. "Candidates for admission . . . should have attained, at least in some measure, growth in those areas represented by the four pillars or in the integrated dimensions of formation identified in *Pastores dabo vobis* [PDV]: human, spiritual, intellectual, and pastoral" (37). The document then specifies what it considers to be "sufficiency"—presumably an indicator of minimal competency—for each of the four pillars. It indicates that sufficient *human formation* involves the absence of serious pathology and the proven capacity to function competently in ordinary situations without requiring extensive psychotherapy or remedial work. It also involves psychosexual maturity, empathy, and the capacity for personal and relational growth and for conversion. Finally, it involves a "deep desire to be a man for others in the likeness of Christ," which presumably reflects the candidate's capacity to live celibate chastity (ibid.). Sufficient *spiritual formation* involves daily prayers, belonging to a parish, regular participation in the Eucharist and penance, and a draw to deepen his spiritual life and share it with others. Sufficient *pastoral formation* involves understanding the church's mission and the willingness to promote it as well as the priest's contributing to it. It also involves sensitivity to the needs of others and the desire to respond to them, and the willingness to initiate actions and assume leadership of individuals and communities. Sufficient *intellectual formation* involves a proven capacity for critical thinking, understanding abstract and practical questions, and sufficient understanding to communicate effectively orally and in writing (ibid.). In other words, the PPF does provide a systematic and theological rationale for the assessment of seminary applicants.

Conventional Assessment Model

This rationale is not only reasonable, but because the stated markers of sufficiency are specific enough to serve as behavioral markers, these markers can be assessed. In fact, the NCEA survey appears to have adapted these markers, generated a list of "assessment components" (e.g., psychosexual development, capacity for empathy, capacity for critical thinking, capacity for leadership, etc.), and incorporated them as survey items.

The results of this survey are enlightening. Psychologists report that they are very likely (ratings of "very likely" with percentages of 70 percent or more on components) to assess eight of the eighteen assessment components.

These include "psychosocial development," "affective maturity," "history of substance abuse," "interpersonal skills," "sexual orientation or inclination," "sexual experience," "capacity for empathy," and "capacity to live celibate chastity." Less emphasized are "dealing with authority," "capacity for growth and conversion," "capacity for critical thinking," and "cross-cultural adaptability." Although the report indicates that "pastoral leadership formation, decision-making skills, and the manner of dealing with authority are areas that seminaries typically address during the formation process" (p. 11), it appears that the assessment components related to pastoral formation were, in fact, assessed by some psychologists. Table 8.1 lists all eighteen assessment components categorized in terms of the four pillars of formation. What is noteworthy about these survey results is that most of the assessment components identified as human formation were assessed in contrast to the other three areas of formation, wherein only "capacity to live celibate chastity" was very likely to be assessed. The results of this national study operationalize what will be called the conventional assessment model in this chapter.

Table 8.1. NCEA survey assessment components related to the four pillars of formation

Human Formation	Spiritual Formation	Intellectual Formation	Pastoral Formation
psychosocial development*	capacity to live celibate chastity* †	capacity for critical thinking	capacity for leadership
affective maturity*	capacity for growth and conversion	ability to grasp practical questions	manner of dealing with authority
history of substance abuse*		ability to grasp abstract questions	decision-making skills
interpersonal skills*		cross-cultural adaptability	
sexual orientation or inclination*			
sexual experience*			
capacity for empathy*			
ability to communicate effectively			

* Denotes components that were very likely to be assessed by surveyed psychologists.
† Some may also consider this to be a component of the human formation pillar.

In the psychological literature the term "sufficiency" denotes a "minimal level of competency" (Sperry, 2010a). The PPF implies that the process of priestly formation should result in higher levels of sufficiency and increased maturity, which have been called "proficiency."[2] Nevertheless, because the primary concern of this article is on the assessment of seminary candidates, it focuses on the assessment of sufficiencies. A logical question is, does the typical or conventional psychological assessment of seminary candidates actually measure or assess these sufficiencies? Assuming that the NCEA survey represents conventional assessment practice, the answer to this question is found by comparing conventional practice against the sufficiencies specified in the PPF. Table 8.2 provides a visual depiction of this comparison.

Table 8.2. Comparison of the PPF markers to conventional assessment focus and methods

PPF Pillars	PPF Markers of Sufficiency	Assessment Factors	Assessment Methods
Human	a. absence of serious pathology	1. Psychopathology (a)	1. MMPI-2; Rorschach, others
	b. function competently without extensive therapy or remediation	2. Coping Capacity (b)	2. Interview & tests
	c. psychosexual maturity	3. Sexuality (c)	3. Interview & tests
	d. capacity for empathy e. capacity for personal & relational growth f. capacity for conversion g. capacity to live celibate chastity	4. Relational Capacity (d & e)	4. Interview & tests
Spiritual	a. daily prayer b. active parish membership c. regular Eucharist and penance d. desire to deepen spiritual life & share it		* *
Intellectual	a. critical thinking b. understand abstract and practical questions c. effective oral & written communication	5. Intelligence (a & b)	5. WAIS, WASI or others

Pastoral	a. understand & promote church's mission b. sensitivity and responsiveness to others' needs (including culture) c. willing to initiate actions & assume individual & communal leadership		**

** Information from interview by formator or vocation director or document review such as transcripts and the pastor's recommendation letter

What should be obvious from table 8.2 is that conventional psychological assessment only assesses some of these markers. An obvious omission of the human formation dimension is the capacity for personal and relational growth, a critical element of affective maturity. It also appears that markers of the pastoral formation dimension are less likely to be formally a part of the conventional psychological assessment, although, as indicated, such information is likely to be elicited by the vocational director or seminary personnel.

Comprehensive Assessment Model

Attention now turns to the question, are there other key factors that may be useful indicators of effectiveness and satisfaction in priestly ministry besides those already being assessed? A basic premise of this chapter is that the conventional approach to psychological assessment of seminary candidates has some value but also has some shortcomings. A second premise is that psychologically based information on factors such as the spiritual and pastoral pillars is an essential and necessary addition to the assessment data collected by vocational directors and seminary personnel. What is proposed here is a "comprehensive assessment" that bolsters the conventional psychological assessment foci or areas of psychopathology, coping capacity, intelligence, sexuality, and relational capacity with eight additional foci. These are self-control, affective maturity, acculturation and cultural adaptability, God image, anthropology, theology of ministry, leadership and work orientation, and "fit" with seminary culture. Each is described in this section and identified in table 8.3.

Table 8.3. The four pillars and conventional and comprehensive psychological assessment

Four Pillars	Conventional Psychological Assessment Factors	Comprehensive Psychological Assessment Factors
Human	Psychopathology Sexuality Coping Capacity Relational Capacity	Psychopathology Sexuality Coping Capacity *Affective Maturity* *Self-Control*
Spiritual		*God Image* *Anthropology (Implicit)*
Intellectual	Intelligence	Intelligence
Pastoral		*Leadership & Work Orientation* *Acculturation & Cultural Adaptability* *"Fit" with Seminary Culture* *Theology of Ministry (Implicit)*

Italicized items are the proposed added factors or components of a comprehensive assessment.

Self-Control

The inner life of priests reflects either virtues or vices, or some combination of the two. From a psychological perspective, virtues are more commonly referred to as "strengths" and, psychologically speaking, a priest's inner life would be conceptualized in terms of strengths. The exception is the developing field of positive psychology, which unabashedly researches virtues as a synonym for strengths. Positive psychology focuses on those virtues that enable individuals and communities and institutions to thrive. The goal of positive psychology is to foster positive individuals and positive institutions. Positive individuals are understood as embodying virtues that include the capacity for love and work, courage, compassion, resilience, creativity, curiosity, integrity, self-knowledge, moderation, wisdom, and self-control, as well as the expression of positive emotions and affective maturity. Positive institutions are recognized by justice, responsibility, civility, nurturance, leadership, mutual support and teamwork, tolerance, and cultural sensitivity.

From a psychological perspective, self-control is considered the central or master virtue. It is argued that morality is a set of rules that enables individuals to live together harmoniously and that virtue involves internalizing those rules. Insofar as virtue depends on overcoming selfishness and antisocial impulses for the sake of what is best for the community, self-control can be considered as the master virtue and moral muscle (Baumeister and Exline, 1999). While self-control is specified as a dimension of self-management, one of the four core abilities of emotional intelligence, recent research suggests that all other domains are influenced by self-control. Research also indicates that higher levels of cognitive intelligence is linked to higher levels of self-control. Furthermore, intelligence and self-control are the two traits that best predict "positive outcomes" in life, which includes inner life. It is also linked to relationship difficulties and dissolution (Baumeister, Vohs, and Tice, 2007).

So what exactly is self-control? Self-control is the capacity for modifying one's responses to conform with ideals, values, morals, and social expectations, and to achieve long-term goals. In the past self-control was known as willpower.

High self-control is associated with better physical health, lower rates of obesity, and emotional stability. Accordingly, those with high self-control are less likely to experience anxiety and depressive symptoms or psychiatric conditions. In addition, they can form and maintain secure, satisfying attachment to others, and are better at empathizing and taking on another's frame of reference. In contrast, low self-control has been linked to behavioral and impulse-control problems, such as overeating, alcohol and drug abuse, smoking, criminal acts, violence, overspending, and sexually impulsive behavior. It is also linked to emotional problems, underachievement, lack of persistence, various failures at task performance, and relationship difficulties and dissolution (Baumeister, Vohs, and Tice, 2007).

Affective Maturity

In the NCEA survey, 89 percent of psychologists reported that they were very likely to assess affective maturity. However, since there is no consensus among psychologists about the definition of affective maturity or its assessment, it is unclear what psychologists were assessing. There is also no obvious consensus in the definition of affective maturity in Vatican documents addressing seminaries (McGlone, Ortiz, and Viglione, 2009). For example, in PDV affective maturity is defined as the capacity to "relate correctly to both men and women." It involves "a responsible love that touches the person in his physical, psychic and spiritual dimensions." Affective maturity assumes that a seminarian can bring to all human relationships a serene friendship and a deep brotherliness, with the capacity to renounce anything that is a threat to it. It requires self-mastery and the capacity to be a "sincere gift of self" to all (43–44). The PPF defines a person of affective maturity as "someone whose life of feelings is in balance and integrated into thought and values; in other words, a man of feelings who is not driven by them but freely lives his life enriched by them." It then specifies four ways in which affective maturity is manifested: the "ability to live well with authority," the "ability to take direction from another," the capacity to effectively exercise authority among peers, and the "ability to deal productively with conflict and stress" (76). Even though PPF specifies affective maturity as part of human formation, the capacity to deal with stress and conflict is clearly related to the human formation dimension, while the other three seem to relate more closely with the pastoral formation dimension as described in number 37.

In contrast to these theological definitions, the psychological literature emphasizes the link between affective maturity and intimacy. For example, Kevin McClone (2009) suggests that the effective priest is expected to "relate in more honest and conscious ways with oneself, with others and with God. These various relational dimensions are interconnected and influence each other's growth" (p. 6). Intimacy and affective maturity are central to such relationality and include relating to God. Intimacy is described as being in touch with one's real self and it presumes the capacities for self-awareness, self-intimacy, and self-disclosure. More specifically, affective maturity is the capacity to "effectively identify, understand and express my real feelings with the diversity of persons that make up the contemporary church while having a growing capacity to listen, understand, and empathize with their experiences" (ibid.). In short, affective maturity is an indicator of an individual's capacity for intimacy, and seems to be central to both human formation as well as pastoral and spiritual formation.

Some view affective maturity and sexual maturity as overlapping realities. Both involve the capacity for intimacy, specifically to develop and maintain friendships and relationships of significance. For celibates—seminarians and priests—it involves at least three dimensions: the capacity for self-knowledge and awareness, the willingness to risk being loved and loving as celibates, and an integrated sexuality and comfort with this identity (G. J. McGlone, personal communication, October 26, 2010).

Although there may be some conceptual confusion about affective maturity, depending on how it is defined, it may actually overlap some of the formation areas. Accordingly, it could be concluded that affective maturity is actually a central component of at least three pillars of formation: human, spiritual, and pastoral. But what about the remaining pillar? Is there any relationship between affective maturity and the intellectual pillar? Are not a priest's affective life and his intellectual development closely interrelated?

Should not seminarians have a passion for learning and ongoing formation that keeps their minds and hearts continually challenged and open to growth? Theological and psychological literature supports this link. For example, affective maturity and the intellectual pillar appear to be closely related in PDV (71–72), wherein John Paul II implies such a link and provides a model for it.

The psychological literature also suggests a strong link between the two, particularly in the literature on cognitive and emotional development. For instance, seminarians are expected, at a minimum, to utilize formal-operational thinking (FOT). FOT is the capacity to think abstractly and use inductive and deductive reasoning to make decisions and solve problems based on logic. A higher level of intellectual development is called post-formal thinking (PFT). PFT is more complex than FOT and involves making decisions based on situational constraints and circumstances, and *integrating emotion* with logic. It relies on subjective experience and intuition as well as logic, and is useful in dealing with ambiguity, contradiction, and compromise. Four stages of PFT have been identified (Commons and Richards, 2003).

The distinction between FOT and PFT is important and can be observed in seminary candidates. It is not uncommon for candidates with a limited capacity for PFT to experience more difficulty with emotionally charged situations than candidates with a greater capacity for it. Discussions involving emotional issues often reveal differing responses that reflect the capacity for PFT: those with little PFT tend to believe that there are clear right and wrong ways in dealing with complex situations, while those with much more PFT are likely to be open to nuance. Accordingly, it would seem essential to assess a candidate's capacity for FOT and PFT.

Related to general intelligence, emotional intelligence (EI) overlaps with both PFT and affective maturity. As such, it is a necessary component of effective, compassionate, and intelligent behavior. EI is the ability to understand and regulate emotions. It involves four competencies: self-awareness, self-management, social awareness, and relationship management in which a person can develop others, exert influence, communicate effectively, and function effectively as a leader (Mayer, Salovey, and Caruso, 2008).[3] In short, PFT and EI overlap with affective maturity. Accordingly, a case can be made that affective maturity is a necessary factor in all four pillars: human, spiritual, pastoral, and intellectual.

God Image

Research on God image, also called God representations, suggests these representations have considerable potential for both candidate assessment and formation. God image refers to ways in which an individual views or represents God. The image can vary from positive, for example, loving and caring, to negative, for example, stern and wrathful. Explanations for how God images develop vary. The most common explanation or theory is that a child's image of God is linked to the child's perception of his or her parents. There is convincing evidence that individuals project characteristics of their fathers onto their images of God, which suggests a link between God image and one's biological father (Hood et al., 1996). Other research suggests that a child's attachment style influences his or her experience of God later in life (Tisdale et al., 1997). It also appears that God image reflects an individual's theological anthropology (Sperry, 2009b).

Other factors such as transformational experiences and psychotherapy have been shown to modify God image. For example, researchers report that an adult client's God image changes as a result of successful psychotherapy even when the therapy did not address spiritual matters. God images changed from a harsh, negative view of God at the outset to images of God as loving and caring at the completion of treatment (Cheston et al., 2003).

Assessing the candidate's God image adds value to the psychological assessment process. Furthermore, because God image reflects an individual's relationship with his father, his attachment style with his mother or caretaker, and his theological anthropology, assessing the God image provides indirect verification of the candidate's attachment style, relationship with his father, and his theological anthropology. If a candidate reports having a "good and happy childhood" but later in the interview portrays a negative image of God, further inquiry is indicated to clarify this apparent discrepancy.

God image can be assessed in the clinical interview or by formal measures. The interviewer can simply ask the candidate how he imagines God when he prays, when he is sick, or when he feels he has failed. The most common psychological measure is the God Image Scale, or its shorter version, the God Image Inventory (Lawrence, 1997). Beyond identifying God image as part of assessment of seminary candidates, knowledge of a seminarian's God image can be quite useful in seminary formation, including spiritual direction.

Acculturation and Cultural Adaptability

The number of international applicants to US seminaries continues to rise. The diversity of American society means that an increasing number of candidates were born here of recent immigrants. Acculturation is the process by which individuals adapt to a new culture and reflects the level or degree to which they integrate new cultural patterns into their original cultural patterns. Individuals with lower levels of acculturation can find seminary extraordinarily challenging.

At the same time, highly acculturated candidates, often of European ancestry, will inevitably find themselves—assuming they are accepted and complete seminary training—assigned to culturally diverse parishes. They will be expected to be culturally adaptive. The same expectation will be held for international priests, since they may be assigned to parishes with cultures that are different than theirs. In short, future priests will be increasingly expected to demonstrate cultural sensitivity and competence. For that reason, formal assessment of acculturation and cultural adaptability should become a necessary factor in the psychological assessment of seminary candidates.

There are several ways of assessing acculturation. A short and clinically useful method is the Brief Acculturation Scale. This scale measures three levels of acculturation (low, medium, high) based on the client's language (native vs. English), generation (first to fifth), and social activities (preferences for friends—native vs. mainline). The scale and its scoring system for three levels of acculturation is available in Paniagua (2005, pp. 11–12). In addition, the Cross-Cultural Adaptability Inventory (Kelley, 1995) is a device useful in assessing an individual's cross-cultural adaptability. It measures psychological factors critical to success in cross-cultural situations.

Leadership and Work Orientation

Capacity for leadership is one of the indicators of sufficiency for pastoral formation expected of seminary candidates (PPF, 37). So is the capacity for understanding and promoting the church's mission, which reflects the candidate's capacity for leadership as well as his work orientation. Both leadership and work orientation are discussed in this section.

Leadership

Leadership refers to a process of influence whereby an individual in the role of leader influences others to pursue and achieve the intended goals of an organization, such as a parish. Today, while leadership is being distinguished from management, both deal with five functions of influence: planning, organizing, staffing, directing, and controlling. While those in management are expected to operationalize the planning, organizing, staffing, and controlling functions, those in leadership roles are primarily involved with the directing function (Sperry, 2003). In a parish setting, a priest, particularly the pastor, is expected to be proficient at all five functions. Highly effective priest-pastors are masters of directing and are able to create a vision that tells parishioners where the parish is going and how it will get there, and then galvanize their commitment to the vision by being ethical, open, empowering, and inspiring. Less effective priest-pastors have less mastery of this function. Fortunately, it is possible to become a better leader-manager. Unfortunately, assessing a candidate's capacity for leadership is not often a part of the psychological assessment except for organizational psychologists. But, it can be. There are inventories such as the Leadership Practices Inventory (Kouzes and Posner, 2007). It is an assessment tool for measuring leadership competencies. It was developed by two luminaries in leadership research, Jim Kouzes and Barry Posner, and has demonstrated its value as a useful measure of leadership potential.

Work Orientation

Four work orientations have been described: job, career, vocation, and calling (Wrzesniewski et al., 1997; Dik, Duffy, and Eldridge, 2009). In the job orientation, the focus is on making money and benefits so that workers can engage in activities consistent with core values of hobbies and entertainment. In priestly ministry this orientation is not uncommon in those who are psychopaths and sexual predators (Sperry, 2005). In the career orientation the focus is on fostering career advancement. This orientation is not uncommon among those whose lives and ministry is characterized by clericalism (Conference of Major Superiors of Men, 1983). In the vocation orientation, the focus is on finding meaning in life and/or making a difference in the world. The core value is fulfillment in terms of wholeness and increased well-being. Recently, a distinction has been made in the research between a vocation orientation and a calling orientation. The core values operative in the calling orientation have been identified as having a "transcended summons" or "self transcending reasons" for working, whereas the operative value in the vocation orientation is finding personal meaning in one's work (Dik, Duffy, and Eldridge, 2009). The operative values of the calling orientation is most compatible with priestly ministry. Accordingly, the assessment of candidates' core values in clinical interviews, particularly as candidates express themselves in work orientations, could be valuable in screening candidates. Since the calling orientation and its core values can be enhanced and reinforced, they could also be valuable considerations in seminary formation.

"Fit" with Seminary Culture

Every seminary is an organization with its own unique mission, structures, policies, system of rewards and sanctions, and culture. It is a truism in organizational psychology that culture always reflects the actual core values—in contrast to the stated values—of an organization. A seminary's culture can range from healthy to disability-prone (Sperry, 2003). Healthier seminary cultures are less likely to reflect values associated with "clerical culture" and "clericalism" than less healthy and disability-prone seminaries. Clerical culture reflects values associated with privilege, entitlement, separateness, and status. The extreme is clericalism, the pathological version of the clerical culture that is considered inconsistent with priestly ministry (Conference of Major Superiors of Men, 1983).

A seminary's identity as well as its actions, including the attitudes and behaviors of faculty administration and seminarians, are subtly and not so subtly influenced by clerical culture values. A candidate's individual dynamics interact with the organizational dynamics of a seminary. That interaction or "fit" can foster either growth or regression and psychopathology in the candidate. In other words, seminary candidates with a "good fit" between their healthy core values and the seminary's healthy core values are more likely to experience health, well-being, and increased sufficiency in terms of the four pillars than if there is a "poor fit."

Because the emotional and financial stakes are so high, assessing fit is a necessary and vital component for psychologists evaluating managers and executives who are applicants for corporate positions. Similarly, assessing fit should also be a necessary component in the psychological evaluation of seminary candidates. Assessing such fit will require that psychologists assess a candidate's core values and become sufficiently familiar with the cultural values of the seminaries and religious orders in a geographical area. Occasionally, it happens that the psychologist finds a particular candidate is judged not to be a good fit with the seminary to which he is seeking admission, but is assessed to be a better fit with another one.

Anthropology and Theology of Ministry (Implicit)

Implicit theory refers to the common sense but unarticulated explanations individuals use to make sense of their world (Bruner and Taguiri, 1954). In contrast, explicit theories tend to be technically informed and articulated explanations. While implicit theories may be life-giving and useful, they can also be harmful and ineffective particularly when they are shortsighted, injurious, or biased. A reality of life is that the lives of many individuals are based on implicit theories. More specifically, seminary candidates hold many implicit theories including their anthropology and theology of ministry. Arguably, these implicit theories can and should be assessed. Presumably, effective priestly formation assists seminarians in examining and articulating their various theories and explanations. Both anthropology and theology of ministry are described in this section.

Anthropology

Everyone has a theory or explanation of what it means to be human, the meaning of life, and the view of human nature. Technically, this theory, which may be implicit or explicit, is called an anthropology, and it profoundly influences one's attitudes, decisions, and actions (Brugger, 2009). While psychologists may associate the term "anthropology" with the study of human persons from sociological, cultural, or even natural science perspectives, vocation directors and seminary formators are likely to think of anthropology from the philosophical and theological perspectives. A Catholic's anthropology may or may not be compatible with the Catholic vision. Candidates may have been taught that Catholics believe that all individuals are made in the image of God and that human nature is good but influenced by original sin, but are redeemed and restored by Jesus Christ, and can respond to grace and achieve fullness of life.

An individual's anthropology *always* reflects one's basic personality dynamics and core values, that is, basic convictions or views about self and the world that are significantly influenced by early life experiences and confirmed and reinforced by one's ongoing experiences. Therefore, an individual's anthropology may not be consistent with the individual's formal learning and Catholic beliefs. Understanding a candidate's anthropology is vitally important because it significantly influences his thinking and actions. Accordingly, a candidate's view of human nature can and does influence how he conducts his personal as well as professional life. For example, a candidate who operates from a Calvinistic view that human nature is corrupted and that change is nearly impossible may have very limited expectations about personal and spiritual growth. Needless to say, such spiritual futility is inconsistent with a Catholic anthropology.

Since a candidate's operative anthropology can be identified, presumably this information can be useful in making admission decisions and guiding priestly formation. Because an individual's view of human nature is a reasonably accurate marker of his anthropology, it can be assessed in a number of ways. Carefully listening to the candidate's narrative may reveal his basic convictions or views about self and the world. In addition, individuals' views of human nature will be reflected in their attachment styles and God images.

Theology of Ministry

A candidate's theology of ministry is typically implicit. Because it can greatly influence the approach one takes to ministry, it is important that it be made explicit. Just as anthropology reflects one's core convictions about self, the world, and human nature, so does theology of ministry. Basically, theologies of ministry can be thought of as a continuum with two very distinct theologies of ministry at each end of the continuum.

At one end of the continuum is the more effortful view. Here, ministry is understood as a personal responsibility in which the minister focuses talent and energy on serving others. Often, but not always, upholding established policy and authority, maintaining control, and preserving the status quo are involved. In this view, the health and well-being of the minister is a secondary consideration to accomplishing the mission. The focus is on action and results, and the "doing" pole of existence. There is a sense of compulsiveness with this theology of ministry, and often the candidate (or minister) has perfectionist tendencies. Accordingly, he may believe that he should have full knowledge about the ministry, be highly competent, and be available to those served at all times. He may also find delegation difficult, believing that if it is to be done right you have to do it yourself (Sperry, 2003). Not surprisingly, loneliness is not uncommon among these individuals. Furthermore, those who operate from this theology of ministry are at risk of experiencing burnout and compassion fatigue.

At the other end of the continuum is the more effortless view. Here, ministers assume that their ministry is in God's hands and that things will work out. "Being" with others is favored over planning and focused efforts at implementing the mission or plan. Shared leadership is valued and this is not problematic as long as parishioners are ready for mutual collaboration and the minister exerts appropriate leadership. Those who operate from this theology of ministry are not likely to experience burnout and compassion fatigue. Instead, they may be viewed by others as lazy, not sufficiently involved, failing to provide necessary leadership, or emphasizing faith over works.

The implicit theology of ministry of a suitable candidate is likely midway between these two extremes: an individual who is focused, effective, and can practice a ministry of presence. In this view, a balanced lifestyle and mutual concern become the terms upon which the kingdom comes about. Doing springs from the "being" pole of existence, as action is more likely to flow from contemplation than compulsiveness. Achieving such balance may require considerable experience, so it is not often seen in candidates.

In his classic book *Theology of Ministry*, Thomas F. O'Meara (1999) indicates that a variant of the effortful theology of ministry and its resulting model of priest-parishioner relationships was normative throughout Christian history. It was commonplace in America with its emphasis on "doing rather than being." The laity's expected role in this theology of ministry translated to the "pray, pay, and obey" model that characterized most priests' expectations for the subordinate role of parishioners in priest-parishioner relations (O'Meara, 1999, p. 8). This theology of ministry was widespread in America. Fortunately, *Lumen Gentium* has somewhat modified this theology of ministry and the model of priest-parishioner that results from it.

Unfortunately, like anthropology, theology of ministry is influenced by an individual's early life experiences and personality dynamics. As such, it does not change simply because the individual decides to change it. Thus, individuals with compulsive and perfectionistic dynamics are likely to operate out of the effortful theology of ministry and, unless a transformational experience occurs, they may be on a pathway to model hard work but not necessarily the love of God. They may also be predisposed to some degree of burnout or compassion fatigue. Since priests' theology of ministry can significantly impact both themselves and others, assessment of the implicit theology of ministry of seminary candidates seems advisable. Since there do not appear to be formal measures of theology of ministry, a review of the candidate's life history and personality dynamics and the clinical interview may be helpful in making this assessment.

The Next Steps

This proposed comprehensive assessment model is the beginning of a process. Feedback, input, and an empirical evaluation of it are indicated and necessary. Feedback and input from psychologists, seminary personnel, and vocational directors is essential so that these factors can be refined or replaced by factors or components that are more accurate and potent indicators of sufficiency of the four pillars. So also are efforts at empirical evaluation. It would also be useful to review how similar efforts could increase the viability of the assessment process. One notable example is a recently published assessment tool for evaluating seminarians. The tool evaluates seminarian performance with regard to four pillars of formation, nine basic ministerial duties and related tasks (e.g., provides pastoral care, leads parish administration, practices a ministry of presence with parish groups), and four performance levels (Ippolito, Latcovich, and Malyn-Smith,

2008). Another is an assessment model for formation that incorporates the four pillars (Ortiz and McGlone, 2010). Finally, it is not inconceivable that proficiency in performing such a comprehensive psychological assessment may necessitate specialized training and experience for psychologists, and perhaps even certification.

Concluding Note

In short, there is a failure to assess a number of key factors. This failure reflects both theoretical and technical shortcomings of the conventional model of psychological assessment of seminary candidates. The main theoretical shortcoming of the conventional model is the absence of a sufficient systematic and theological rationale informing the conventional model. Fortunately, the PPF provides such a rationale for establishing a comprehensive model of psychological assessment that remedies the theoretical shortcoming. The conventional model represents the typical practice of most psychologists and the NCEA survey has been useful in specifying this model. Mapping the survey results against the "sufficiencies" of the PPF depicts the shortcomings of this model.

The main technical shortcoming of the conventional model is that psychological assessment primarily evaluates components of the human and intellectual pillars of formation, and virtually ignores the spiritual and pastoral pillars. The NCEA survey seems to support this observation. Survey results demonstrate that the actual practice of psychological assessment is largely limited to the human and intellectual pillars of formation. It also appears that aspects of affective maturity, specifically intimacy and relatedness with self, with others, and with God, are not adequately assessed. My conclusion was that while affective maturity is largely within the domain of the human pillar, it is also a key factor in the intellectual, spiritual, and pastoral pillars.

Furthermore, the proposed comprehensive model of psychological assessment is consistent with the PPF—which provides a systematic and theological rationale—and adds eight factors to the conventional model. As such it remedies a major technical shortcoming of the conventional model. My presumption is that a comprehensive model of psychological assessment should provide psychologically informed input on all four pillars, not just the human and intellectual pillars. This input supplements—but does not replace—information from vocational directors, seminary personnel, and others on the spiritual and pastoral pillars. The next steps in this process are to refine and empirically validate the factors and components. Hopefully, the end result of the process will be a comprehensive model that provides more valuable, psychologically based information to better inform decisions about a candidate's suitability for priestly ministry.

Notes

1. Survey data on seminary rectors and vocational directors is not reported here.

2. Three levels of proficiency, "approaching proficiency," "proficiency," and "above proficiency," are used to rate seminarian performance (Ippolito, Latcovich, and Malyn-Smith, 2008).

3. It would appear that EI overlaps with at least three pillars: human, pastoral, and intellectual.

9

The Psyche and the Soul:
Personality and Spirituality

Len Sperry

Among the personality dynamics most influential for the inner life of priests is narcissism. Narcissism is alive and well in all spheres of American life, particularly in the priesthood. It is particularly fascinating that Americans have a largely positive view of it. Many picture narcissists as engaging, charming, and successful individuals despite some degree of self-absorption. Such individuals are often popular entertainers, sports figures, politicians, corporate leaders, and priests. This favorable and benign view of what psychologists call the "healthy narcissist" stands in marked contrast to the experience of those who work or live with an unhealthy or "pathological narcissist."

In my professional experience with priests, it seems that both healthy and pathological narcissism is increasing—an observation that parallels the increasing prevalence of narcissism in the general population. The impact of such narcissism can be positive or devastating to Catholic institutions and ministry recipients, whether they are parishioners, students, patients, employees, or other ministry personnel. But, it would be shortsighted to attribute narcissism only as an individual concern, when it is also an institutional or organizational concern. The reality is that both personality dynamics and organizational dynamics are operative in the rise of narcissism in ministry. This chapter describes both the personality and organizational dynamics of narcissism. It describes and illustrates four types of narcissism, followed by the manifestations of pathological narcissism in ministry. Then, it discusses the organizational dynamics of clerical culture and clericalism. Finally, it briefly considers some spiritual and ministry implications of narcissism for the inner life of priests. First, some background and context is provided.

Some Background and Context

While narcissism has been present since the nation's beginning, it has become increasingly common in the past few decades. Since the "me-ism" of the 1970s was analyzed in the 1979 best seller *The Culture of Narcissism*, dealing with narcissism has preoccupied psychiatrists and other clinicians as well as employers and formation personnel. In that book, historian Christopher Lasch argued that Americans were becoming increasingly self-preoccupied and narcissistic to the extent that pathological narcissism became normalized and socially acceptable in American culture. Lasch's impressionistic appraisal has since been empirically supported by various research studies. For example, national survey data from the National Opinion Research Center indicates that a major shift in values took place in America in the late 1960s. Before that shift, Americans valued duty, hard work and a high work ethic, and delayed gratification. After the shift, these values began to be replaced by pleasure, a reduced work ethic, and immediate gratification. The authors of *The Narcissism Epidemic: Living in the Age of Entitlement* recount several research studies and chronicle social trends that fueled what they call "the relentless rise of narcissism in our culture." Chief among these trends were the "self-esteem movement" and the movement away from "community-oriented thinking" and toward self-actualization and entitlement. Perhaps the most defining trend was the shift that occurred in parenting: from limit-setting toward letting children have their way and get whatever they want. The authors conclude that this changed attitude toward parenting has significantly "fueled the narcissism epidemic" (Twenge and Campbell, 2010).

While narcissism has been present since the nation's beginning, it has become increasingly common in the past few decades.

Types of Narcissism

While many ministry personnel and most psychologists who consult to dioceses and religious orders recognize two types of narcissists, there are actually four types of narcissism. These four are described in some detail in this section. While these types are noted in priests, religious, and seminarians, examples of seminarians illustrate these types.

Healthy Narcissists

Healthy narcissism can be described as the capacity to love oneself and to maturely love others. It requires the ability to distinguish reality from fantasy, and the capacity to demonstrate empathy and genuineness to others. Healthy narcissists possess an adequate sense of self-esteem, which enables them to both function effectively in the world as well as share in the emotional life of others. For Freud, good mental health reflects the capacities to both work well and love well.

Freud contended that healthy narcissism is an essential part of normal development. He argued that adequate parental love and caring results in meeting the self-needs of that child. Just as important, the parent's attitude toward the child is understood as a revival and reproduction of their own narcissism. He believed that children experience omnipotence of thought and that parents stimulate and reinforce that feeling because in their child they see the things that they have never fully achieved themselves. Accordingly, parents tend to overvalue the qualities of their child. However, when parents act in an extreme opposite manner and the child is rejected or inconsistently reinforced, the self-needs of the child are not met, and pathological narcissism is likely to result.

Case Example

> Jack Frankel is a second-year seminarian at a diocesan seminary. He is a top student and athlete with many friends, and commands the respect of his peers, seminary faculty, and administration. He impresses others with his charm, self-confidence, leadership ability, communication and interpersonal skills, and sense of humor. He has been heard joking with his friends that he has not met a mirror that he doesn't like! He recognizes that he is gifted and admired by many. Yet, despite his occasional braggadocio, he is a sincere individual whose priority is personal and spiritual development. He is realistic about his potential and believes he can and will become an effective preacher and pastor. Nevertheless, at the present time his primary concern is "learning as much and growing as much as I can before ordination."

James F. Masterson (1993) has described compelling portraits of two types of pathological narcissism, which he calls the exhibitionist narcissist and the closet narcissist. Unlike the healthy narcissist, he describes the developmental trajectory of both pathological types as the failure to adequately develop an age- and phase-appropriate sense of self. The primary reason for this failure is assumed to be a defect in the attachment style with the primary caregiver—usually the mother—and the inability of the caregiver to provide adequate and consistent psychological nurturance.

Overt Narcissists

Overt narcissists, also called exhibitionistic or classic narcissists, believe they are better than others, continually seek attention, lack emotionally warm and caring relationships, seek status, power, and possessions, and tend to be overly concerned with their physical appearance. Overt narcissism is the only type described in the *Diagnostic and Statistical Manual of Mental Disorders, Fourth Edition, Text Revision* (DSM-IV-TR) description and diagnostic criteria. The DSM-IV-TR is accepted as the official diagnostic classification by the medical, psychological, and counseling professions as well as the government, insurance carriers, and health maintenance organizations that reimburse professionals for mental health services provided.

Overt narcissism differs from other types of narcissism in several important ways. The overt narcissist is described as having an inflated, grandiose sense of self with little or no conscious awareness of the emptiness within or the emotional needs of others. While they may boast and exaggerate their importance to others, inside they typically experience a sense of insecurity and worthlessness. This experience of inner emptiness requires the recurrent infusion of external confirmation of their importance and value. As a result, they constantly seek and demand confirmation of their worth and specialness. When they succeed in receiving such confirmation in the form of status, admiration, wealth, and success, they feel an internal elation.

Arnold M. Cooper (1998) notes that they commonly behave in an overtly grandiose manner and treat others—particularly those perceived as lower in status—with contempt. Not surprisingly, they typically lack empathy for others. When others fail to provide such evidence, they often feel depressed, shamed, and envious of those who succeed in attaining what they lack. Their lack of pleasure in work or love is painful to witness. Furthermore, when they feel rejected, thwarted, or frustrated, they are likely to act out their insecurities in outbursts of anger—called narcissistic rage, verbal abuse, and obnoxious behaviors.

These individuals spend considerable energy evaluating themselves against others, and will defend their wounded self-esteem through a combination of idealizing and devaluing others. When they idealize another, they feel more special or important by virtue of their association with that person. When they devalue someone, they feel superior. Not surprisingly, their colleagues and significant others tend to feel unreasonably idealized, unreasonably devalued, or simply disregarded by them.

Case Example

> *Jerry Winters is a second-year seminarian who is an energetic, confident, and engaging individual who enjoys the limelight. Because of his ability*

and good looks, he has become a student leader in the seminary and was selected as a regular cantor and an occasional homilist at seminary liturgies, both remarkable distinctions since fourth-year students are usually assigned these roles. He greatly enjoys his reputation as the "alpha male" among his seminary peers and envisions his priestly career as a "rising star in the church." He insists he will be a compelling presider, highly organized, detail oriented, and a beloved and highly effective diocesan official or pastor. On occasion, particularly when he is "on a roll," he boasts of "being appointed a bishop in the not too distant future." When challenged about how this might come about, his disdainful response is "How can they keep this from me? Look around, guys. I've got everything it takes and more!"

Covert Narcissists

By contrast, the covert narcissist, also called the shy or closet narcissist, is highly attentive to the needs of others. In fact, they come across as humble and unassuming individuals who avoid being the center of attention. Still, they are exquisitely sensitive to criticism and slights from others and are likely to respond with harsh self-criticism. Like the overt narcissist, the covert narcissist has grandiose fantasies, feels a sense of entitlement, and is exploitive, but is characterized by worry, ineffective functioning, and unfulfilled expectations. When they are overly stressed, they are likely to become defensive, hostile, or self-reproachful. Because of intrapsychic dynamics, their grandiose fantasies are seldom, if ever, expressed in overt behavior since they are believed to be beyond their conscious attainment. Instead these individuals are conflicted and guilty over their exhibitionistic, competitive, and aggressive desires, which lead them to suppress or repress any awareness of the existence of these qualities. Basically, their severe inner conscience finds these fantasies unacceptable and demands that they suppress them and experience guilt. As a result, they can attribute all goodness and power to themselves but relegate all weakness and badness to others.

Like others who know them, covert narcissists tend to perceive themselves as shy, unassertive, and incapable of achieving their dreams. The first hint of their underlying grandiosity appears when they realize that adolescent daydreams of being heroic and acclaimed have persisted into adult life. Such fantasies and lack of achievement leads to increased guilt, continued attacks from their conscience for not meeting self-set standards, and feelings of worthlessness. Their inability to sustain ambitions or to pursue even attainable goals with full dedication results in significant self-pity, feelings of hurt, and depression. If they seek psychotherapy, it is typically because of depression and a sense of inner deadness since nothing in life matches the thrill of triumphant achievement that they imagine is due them.

Despite believing that they deserve to be recognized for their specialness, they are plagued by self-doubts and so do not seek the affirmation of others for what they believe they are due. Moreover, they are unlikely to seek out appropriate friends or close intimate relationships because they fear exposure as frauds. As a result, they surround themselves with others who are conspicuously inferior to themselves, and so when these individuals offer them praise, they discount this admiration as phony and insincere. Instead they ruminate about how little their true worth is appreciated and how others get the recognition for their achievements, and they procrastinate about accomplishing achievable tasks because they fear they will fail. As a consequence, their overt demeanor is decidedly retiring, modest, and shy. Unlike overt narcissists who demand special attention from others in recognition of their superiority, covert narcissists are more likely to fawn over others whose accomplishments they envy while secretly harboring strong feelings of resentment and contempt.

Though they experience guilt and shame for their ambitions or accomplishments, they may still relentlessly pursue them without genuine regard for others, since the feelings of others are viewed as less important than theirs. While they tend to hide their strivings and accomplishments for fear of engendering envy in others, they know envy well. They suffer intensely from it, even as they fiercely disavow it. Because they seldom show arrogance and aggression, they are seldom perceived by others as "narcissistic," even though they manifest less obvious traits and the underlying sense of vulnerability common to all narcissists. Their attentiveness should not be taken for empathy, for it is as difficult for them to connect emotionally to others as it is for the classic narcissist.

Case Example

> *Jeffrey Bender is in the same year of studies as Jack and Jerry. He admires and is quite solicitous toward Jerry but is secretly angry at and envious of him. He sees his future in the priesthood as a career trajectory aimed at a top leadership position in the diplomatic corps for the Vatican Department of State or even at the chancery. Yet, he keeps these career aspirations to himself. Those around him would hardly suspect these strivings since Jeff has done little to cultivate relationships with key diocesan officials and establish a reputation as a "company man" like Jerry and other seminarians who are hierarchy-bound. Instead, he comes across to others as a congenial, likeable, and unassuming seminarian who is loyal and can*

be counted upon to extend a helping hand. While he receives average grades, his instructors suspect that he is underachieving. He has been known to berate himself and become self-reproachful when criticized— even mildly—by his peers or the faculty. Lately, his spiritual director has become increasingly concerned at Jeff's worried, guilt-ridden, and depressed manner, and puzzled because there is no obvious cause, such as a loss or failure.

Malignant Narcissists

A more pathological version of the classic narcissist is the malignant narcissist. This type is only briefly noted here since it is presumed to be un- common in ministry. Besides overt narcissistic features, malignant narcissists also exhibit sadistic, paranoid, and antisocial or psychopathic features. Like the overt narcissist, they appear as self-sufficient and successful, yet their inner experience is that of being fragile, vulnerable to shame, and hypersensi- tive to criticism. Failure to succeed in their grandiose endeavors is likely to result in prominent mood swings with feelings of emptiness, irritability, rage, suspiciousness, and sadistic aggression. Suspiciousness and sadistic aggres- sion tend to distinguish these individuals from overt narcissists. Furthermore, when these individuals are not involved in narcissistic pursuits, they tend to be cold, unempathic, exploitative, and indifferent toward others.

Malignant narcissists typically present with features of the paranoid per- sonality disorder and the antisocial personality disorder. This means that psychologists evaluating such candidates for the priesthood or religious life may find that these candidates may meet or come close to meeting the criteria for these other personality disorders. As a result, the candidate is likely to be screened out. In my thirty plus years as a psychiatric consultant to dioceses and religious orders, I have encountered only a few malignant narcissists in active ministry. Since they are so rare in ministry, no case example is provided.

Assessing Narcissism

Clinical psychologists who evaluate candidates for admission to diocesan seminaries and religious orders find that a narcissistic pattern is relatively common among such applicants. Generally, the healthy narcissistic pattern is a better fit with ministry than the pathological types or patterns of narcis- sism. Unfortunately, because clinical practice in America is significantly influenced by the diagnostic criteria of the *Diagnostic and Statistical Manual of Mental Disorders* (DSM)—which we have already noted reflects the overt type of narcissism—this DSM version of the narcissistic personality disorder is the only one that exists in the minds of many clinicians. That means that the covert pattern of the narcissistic personality is unlikely to be identified and diagnosed. The result is that many covert narcissists are not offered and do not receive the kind of psychotherapeutic help that could reduce their suffering and increase their ministerial effectiveness and well-being.

The *Psychodynamic Diagnostic Manual* (PDM) was recently developed as a complement to the DSM. PDM describes both healthy and disordered personalities and symptom patterns. In addition, it provides profiles of mental functioning that include patterns of relating, comprehending, and expressing feelings. Unlike the DSM—which focuses exclusively on external behavior and seeks to answer the question, What is likely to be observed for a specific mental health disorder?—the PDM focuses primarily on internal experience, and seeks to answer the question, What is it like to experience a specific mental health disorder?

Diagnostically, the DSM-IV-TR specifies nine behavioral criteria (i.e., grandiose sense of self-importance, sense of entitlement, belief in being special, etc.), of which five are needed to make the diagnosis of narcissistic personality disorder. In contrast, the PDM indicates that the pathogenic belief about self for the narcissistic personality disorder is "I need to be perfect to feel okay." The characteristic pathogenic belief about others is "Others enjoy riches, beauty, power, and fame; the more I have of those, the better I will feel."

Unlike the DSM, the PDM can be of considerable clinical value and utility to clinical psychologists and others evaluating candidates for the priesthood, religious life, and other ministries. In addition to clearly and succinctly describing the intrapsychic dynamics of the narcissistic personality disorder and providing treatment considerations, it recognizes both the overt and the covert types of narcissistic personality disorders.

It is essential that the narrow DSM view of the narcissistic personality disorder be extended or broadened. Elsa Ronningstam (2011) has offered a revised set of diagnostic criteria for DSM that address the limitations of the description and criteria of the disorder. She has broadened the definition of grandiosity and has reformulated the characteristics and criteria of grandiosity as it differs among the overt, covert, and malignant types. She also adds the criteria of vulnerability as central to understanding this disorder. Presumably, such reformulated criteria will increase its validity of the disorder and reflect the lifelong pattern of dysfunctionality that defines a personality disorder. Interestingly, these suggested criteria seem to not only better reflect clinical practice but also are consistent with the PDM description of narcissistic personality disorder. Such a revision of the DSM description and criteria would result in all three types of pathological narcissism being assessed and not just the overt type.

The Manifestation of Pathological Narcissism in Ministry

Ministry provides a ready-made forum to reinforce and reconfirm the narcissist's grandiose self. For the overt and covert narcissists, the theological formulation of vocation as a "call" from God, a sign of "being set apart," confirms their belief in their inherent specialness and superiority over others. For those with public ministries, such as presiders and homilists, liturgies and other religious services are viewed as a forum to exhibit that special call. Even though most would publicly deny it, they may secretly harbor the belief that the real purpose of a religious service is "worship" of themselves! Accordingly, liturgies are primarily a performance where the worshiping congregation "mirrors"—that is, admires and praises—the minister.

God-Image and Beliefs

Because of their self-absorption and self-deceiving tendencies, pathologically narcissistic ministers must creatively distort the precept to love God and neighbor to fit their pathological perspective. For them, God and everyone else exist for one purpose: to love and take care of them. Their basic spiritual deficits are a lack of awareness of grace and an incapacity for gratitude. Not surprisingly, they imagine God as an all-giving father, and they perceive faith as magical entreaty. Consequently, they believe God will do exactly as they ask in their prayers, with no regard to the kind of claim God has on them.

Prayer

For narcissists, particularly pathological narcissists, there is only one kind of prayer: the prayer of petition or demand. Prayer as praise, self-examination, forgiveness, or thanksgiving has little meaning for them. Some narcissistic ministers may have intense mystical leanings that pull them in the direction of mystical experience, including the occult. This is understandable in light of their sense of specialness and grandiosity. However, they are more likely to experience an exaggerated state of self-exaltation than a true mystical state. When prayers are not answered as they expect, they become narcissistically wounded and feel deeply rejected. As a result, they may reject God, becoming atheists for an instant or forever, because God has let them down.

Relations with Those to Whom They Minister

The pathological narcissistic minister is typically insensitive to the suffering and needs of others. While they may offer to help others in need and engage in acts of charity, they will do it only if their charitable deeds are noticed by others. If their efforts do not bring attention to them, they are unlikely to make a donation, extend a helping hand, lend a listening ear, or continue these actions when the attention and praise of others stop. Still, these ministers have learned the art of manipulation and will, on occasion, act opportunistically. While they may come across as lacking in warmth and consideration, their sense of inner direction allows them to inspire others and create a common cause, transcending petty self-interests. Nevertheless, exploitativeness and coercion are features of the overt and malignant narcissism. These features are not uncommon in sexual misconduct involving ministers with narcissistic personality disorders, particularly with the malignant pattern.

Intimacy, Sexuality, and Celibacy

Individuals with pathological narcissism are often incapable of giving and receiving emotional intimacy because of their low self-esteem and maladaptation about relationships. As a result they have considerable difficulty or an inability to integrate sex and intimacy. Still, they may be preoccupied with sex and sexual activity and view themselves as being accomplished lovers. They are likely to exhibit a casual attitude toward sex and possess an inflated sense of their sexual skills. Nevertheless, they are dependent on significant others yet tend to blame them for sexual dissatisfaction.

Males with pathological narcissism tend to prize their bodies. "They may praise themselves monotonously for the size of their organs, proficiency, longevity, and special skills in eliciting orgasm. They do not even ask questions. It is not, 'Look at me, am I not the most wondrous of men?' but rather 'Be privileged to behold me, I am the miracle.'" (Offit, 1977, p. 69).

According to Reid Meloy (1986), sexuality for narcissistic ministers is basically autoerotic. This autoerotic preference is usually consciously denied but will be seen in a pattern of transient and multiple sex partners. Paradoxically, the narcissist's search for the perfect body to mirror the narcissist's sexual desire, as well as the desire to be young and attractive forever, may be accompanied by impotence. Without a physiological cause, the inability to achieve an erection may result from the narcissist's fear of dependency.

Meloy points out that celibacy may support their autoerotic preference, because they are allowed the freedom of sexual fantasy that has no limits or the imperfections, awkwardness, messiness, or inconvenience of actual contact with another person. Sexual images can be perfectly gratifying. Furthermore, he contends that by requiring celibacy, church authorities may be unwittingly sanctioning the narcissistic minister's preference for fantasy and masturbation.

With regard to masturbation, it might be assumed that narcissists frequently engage in self-stimulation with flair, such as in front of three-way or ceiling mirrors. But some regard masturbation as an embarrassment and social and sexual failure. They reason, why should I do it myself when I can get someone else to do it for me? Accordingly, Offit observes that they will seek out others using whatever charm, cunning, and exploitativeness necessary to achieve both the satisfaction they demand and the control and admiration to which they believe they are entitled.

Narcissism and Clericalism

It would be remiss not to mention clerical culture and clericalism when discussing narcissism in ministry. The reason is that a priest's identity, attitudes, and behaviors are influenced by culture and, particularly, the clerical culture in which they function. Clerical culture reflects values associated with privilege, entitlement, separateness, and status—values consistent with narcissism. Clericalism is the extreme, and some would say pathological, version of clerical culture, and is considered inconsistent with healthy priestly ministry (Conference of Major Superiors of Men, 1983).

A priest's individual dynamics continually interact with the organizational dynamics of a diocese or religious community. That interaction—called "fit"— can foster either growth and development or regression and psychopathology in the priest. In other words, priests with a "good fit" between their healthy personality dynamics and core values and a diocese's or religious community's healthy culture and core values are more likely to experience psychological and spiritual health and well-being. Similarly, a diocese or religious community that reflects the values of clericalism is more likely to reinforce existing pathological narcissism in a priest. A "poor fit" exists when a priest's personality dynamics and values are the opposite of a diocese's or religious community's culture and core values. Sometimes a discrepancy or "poor fit" can actually foster neutral or positive growth. This can occur over the course of several years when a priest's pathological narcissism begins to diminish as he functions in a diocese or community with healthy organizational dynamics.

Because "fit" can significantly influence an individual's well-being and job satisfaction positively or negatively, it is not surprising that individuals seek to increase their level of "fit." For example, when professionals move from a job or position to what they believe will be a more "compatible" position, it is usually to increase the "fit" between their own personality and values and the organizational dynamics and culture of the new position. Savvy psychologists who assess candidates for the priesthood may actually recommend a candidate for seminary Y over seminary Z based on their evaluation of a "fit" between the candidate's personality dynamics and organizational dynamics of the seminary. Finally, some would argue that the individual dynamics of pathological narcissism is, in and of itself, a poor "fit" with the priesthood, and a candidate's relative contraindication for ordination to priestly ministry.

Concluding Comments

Narcissism continues to influence American culture, and for the most part this influence has been negative. The diagnosis of narcissistic personality disorder came into being just as narcissism and immediate gratification overtook duty and delayed gratification as cultural values in America. Unfortunately, there are significant problems with current DSM diagnostic criteria for the narcissistic personality disorder. Presumably, in the future the DSM description of the disorder will expand to include all three types of pathological narcissism and diagnostic criteria will be revised accordingly. If it does not, perhaps psychologists consulting with seminaries and religious orders will utilize the PDM instead.

As to ministry, few would question that pathological narcissism is incompatible with effective ministry. Accordingly, those charged with screening candidates for the priesthood, religious life, and other church ministries would do well to assess candidates for pathological narcissism in all its guises, including overt, covert, and malignant narcissism.

Finally, it should also be noted that while healthy narcissistic ministers can be ambitious, manipulative, and sensitive to criticism, they typically possess sufficient self-confidence, adaptability, and humor to be effective in ministerial settings and interpersonal challenges. Unlike pathological narcissists who create havoc in their ministries, healthy narcissists seldom create such havoc and have the capacity to grow personally and spiritually and become effective ministers.

10

Reclaiming Our Catholic Anthropology

Len Sperry

Every priest has a theory or framework for understanding what it means to be a human person, how sin and brokenness occur, and how healing, restoration, and redemption result. For some, this theory is *implicit*, meaning that it has not been consciously and logically articulated. While it may be life-giving and useful, it can also prove to be harmful and ineffective. For others, this theory is philosophically (and perhaps even theologically) *explicit*, informed, internally consistent, and life-giving (Sperry, 2009a). Technically, such a theory of human personhood, life's meaning, and a basic view of human nature is called an anthropology, and it profoundly influences one's attitudes, decisions, and actions (Brugger, 2009). Furthermore, an anthropology compatible with the Catholic vision is a Catholic anthropology. Whether explicit or implicit, this anthropology guides the priest's inner life.

While this anthropology may or may not be compatible with the Catholic vision, it *always* reflects one's basic personality dynamics and core values. As such it is influenced by one's early life experiences and perceptions, although it may not be consistent with one's formal learning or Catholic beliefs. Presumably Catholics, including priests, have been taught the Catholic vision of human nature, brokenness, and restoration. Central to this vision is the belief that all individuals are made in the image of God (Gen 1:26-27; *Catechism of the Catholic Church*, 396) and can respond to grace. Thus human nature is viewed as good, although tainted by original sin. However, there can be a disconnect between knowing this and acting in light of it because negative early life experiences, including trauma and deprivation, can distort or override an individual's formal learning and religious beliefs. Because of its pervasive influence, consulting psychologists, vocation directors, and seminary formators would do well to recognize the importance of a candidate's anthropology in the process of seminary formation. As such, its identification should be incorporated in the assessment process.

This chapter begins by defining various meanings of the term anthropology and then describes three common anthropologies, illustrating one of these in a seminary context. Next it describes the implications and applications of this construct in assessment. Emphasized are three markers of a candidate's anthropology and how it can be assessed.

Meaning and Varieties of Anthropology

Psychologists are likely to associate the term "anthropology" with the study of human persons from sociological (applied anthropology), cultural (cultural anthropology), or even biological perspectives (medical anthropology or forensic anthropology). Others, including vocation directors and seminary formators, are just as likely to think of anthropology in broader terms, including philosophical and theological perspectives. Philosophical anthropology refers to conceptions of the human person derived from philosophical reasoning, while theological anthropology is derived principally from Christian revelation, particularly Scripture. Catholic anthropology is a combination of both philosophical and theological anthropology that addresses the emotional, mental, moral, relational, and spiritual health of the human person (Sperry, 2009b). It specifies the origins and purpose of human persons as well as the place of sin, suffering, personal effort, grace, and healing.

One's anthropology is important because it significantly influences one's thinking and actions. There are at least three dominant anthropology models, based on Catholic assumptions, on cultural Calvinism, or on scientific naturalism.

The *Catholic model* is a hopeful one that assumes that humans are made in God's image and likeness. Therefore, human nature is considered to be good but tainted by original sin. Although sin and suffering are realities, so is personal effort aided by grace and healing. There is redemption and life has a transcendent purpose, which is to increase the kingdom of God in the world. Moreover, healing, spiritual growth, and living life to the full are not only possible but also considered normative (Brugger, 2009).

In contrast, the *cultural Calvinism model* views human nature as bad and that individuals are controlled by internal and external conflicts with little hope for ultimate fulfillment. It is similar to Freud's view of human nature, a mechanistic view of life in which repressed sexual desire accounts for one's problems and there is little expectation for growth. In fact, the most that is possible is some degree of adjustment to life circumstances. Christians who hold that human nature is basically depraved and that only the good—and not the bad—will merit eternal reward, might bristle at the notion that they espouse a Freudian-like worldview without the element of sexual repression. Nevertheless, such beliefs are more consistent with cultural Calvinism, as described by Cardinal Francis George, OMI (2010), than with a Catholic anthropology.

Table 10.1. Comparison of scientific naturalism, cultural Calvinism, and Catholic anthropologies

Scientific Naturalism	Cultural Calvinism	Catholic Anthropology
Life is a material phenomenon, where mind is the expression of matter; God and afterlife are false projections of the mind. Human nature is neutral.	Life is a material phenomenon, and human nature is essentially bad. Or, there may be Calvinist or cultural Calvinist views on the depravity of human nature and the division between those who are good and bad.	Humans are created in God's image and likeness; therefore, human nature is good but has been tainted by (original) sin.
Humans are only the products of evolution. Freedom and free choice are also false projections of the mind. Individualism is emphasized over the communal.	Human behavior and feelings are the results of biological (id) impulses and other unconscious processes and conflicts. Individualism is emphasized over the communal.	The human person can be influenced by past experiences and concupiscence but has free will, and can respond to grace, which builds on nature. Relationships with others and God are important. There should be a balance between the communal and the individual.
Human life has no transcendent purpose. The only reasonable purpose in life is to maximize pleasure and minimize pain.	Human life has no transcendent purpose. But through insight and effort it is possible to achieve some degree of personal adjustment in life while indulging in pleasure.	The human person is redeemed and has a transcendent purpose, which is to increase the kingdom of God in the world; healing and living life to the full are possible and normative.

Similarly, the *scientific naturalism model* views all reality as a function of matter. Although human nature is viewed as neutral—and sometimes as bad—there is no provision for choice or free will. Neither is there a transcendent purpose to life other than maximizing pleasure and minimizing pain. Unfortunately, this third model underlies most undergraduate and graduate education in the Western world, particularly in the sciences. E. Christian Brugger (2008) is probably accurate in his observation that most psychologists, irrespective of their religious affiliation or training program, "accept" the scientific naturalistic or Freudian models, albeit unwittingly.

A brief comment is in order about a less common model of anthropology that is reflected in certain forms of existentialism. While some of the existential schools, and even Carl Rogers's client-centered therapy, view human nature as good, such approaches have no place for original sin and redemption. Table 10.1 further elaborates the three most common anthropological models.

Implications of Anthropology for Priestly Ministry

As noted earlier, what vocation directors, seminary formators, spiritual directors, and consulting psychologists believe about human nature can and does influence how they conduct their personal and professional lives. A reasonable question is, do faculty and formators with Freudian and scientific naturalism anthropologies—whether held implicitly or explicitly—have a place in Catholic seminaries? In my opinion, the answer is no.

The reason is that a priest's operative view of human nature is reflected in how he preaches, functions as a confessor, provides spiritual guidance, and develops—or fails to develop—emotionally and spiritually. For example, a priest influenced by the Freudian anthropology will operate from beliefs that human nature is hopelessly flawed, evil, or bad, that individuals cannot be trusted, and that the only change possible is mere adjustment to life circumstances. Such a sense of spiritual futility is not only inconsistent with the Catholic vision but it can also adversely affect the personal and spiritual well-being of the seminarians under the influence of that faculty member or formator.

Illustration of Fr. Sisyphus

Reverend Jason Sisyphus[1] has been on the seminary formation team for the past year and a half. He provides spiritual direction to five seminarians in first- and second-year theology. While he seems congenial and has a dry sense of humor, the rector was somewhat taken aback by a homily in which Fr. Sisyphus described how he deals with lifelong issues of impatience and criticalness, and a recent incident of road rage. His solution to the road rage was to refrain from driving in heavier traffic, at least until it interfered with his priestly responsibilities. His overall message was life is tough, human nature does not change, and the best one can do is continue to work against one's shortcomings and vices. This is similar to his advice to his directees: avoid difficult circumstances and accept that life is difficult, so just "grin and bear it." His anthropology is one of spiritual futility that is more consistent with a Freudian, rather than a Catholic, anthropology. Furthermore, the rector's concern about Fr. Sisyphus's influence on a future generation of priests is more than justified.

This illustration points out the importance of identifying the operative anthropology of formators as well as seminarians and seminary candidates. Identifying an individual's anthropology provides a baseline for making admission decisions as well as for endeavoring to modify or change anthropologies that are inconsistent with the Catholic vision.

Assessing Anthropology

An individual's anthropology is a set of core convictions about self and the world that are significantly influenced by early life experiences and have been confirmed and reinforced by one's ongoing experiences. Furthermore, that anthropology parallels one's psychology, that is, psychological core convictions. Accordingly, that anthropology does not easily change. Lectures and academic advisement tend to have little or no influence in changing it when compared to transformation resulting from psychotherapy, spiritual direction and growth, or other life-changing experiences.

Since an individual's operative anthropology can be identified, presumably this information can be useful in making admission decisions and guiding priestly formation. Because individuals' view of human nature is a reasonably accurate marker of their anthropology, it can be assessed in a number of ways. This section reviews three ways of identifying an individual's view of human nature with the assessment of attachment styles, family functioning, and God images.

Attachment Style

Attachment is an emotional bond to another person. John Bowlby hypothesized that the earliest bonds formed by children with their caregivers—usually mothers—greatly impacted other relationships throughout life. The basic premise of attachment theory is that mothers who are available and responsive to their infants' needs establish a sense of security. His colleague, Mary Ainsworth, identified three major styles of attachment in infants and children: secure attachment, ambivalent-insecure attachment, and avoidant-insecure attachment (Ainsworth and Bowlby, 1965). Later, other researchers (Main and Solomon, 1990) added a fourth attachment style, disorganized-insecure attachment. Research has supported Ainsworth's conclusions and found that these early attachment styles can predict behaviors in adulthood. Four attachment styles are identified in adults: secure, anxious-preoccupied, dismissive avoidant, and fearful avoidant. The secure attachment style in adults corresponds to the secure attachment style in children. The anxious-preoccupied attachment style in adults corresponds to the anxious/ambivalent attachment style in children. However, the dismissive avoidant and the fearful avoidant attachment styles, which are distinct in adults, correspond to a single avoidant attachment style in children.

An individual's expectations and belief systems, called working models, that develop in early years tend to persist throughout life. These beliefs guide our perceptions of ourselves and the world, including others. Models or views of self and the world range from positive to negative. Negative models of the world reflect negative views of human nature, that is, human nature is bad. These models of self and the world interact and are reflected in specific attachment styles. As might be expected, individuals with insecure attachments tend to have negative views of self, negative views of human nature, or both. Accordingly, adults with dismissive and fearful styles tend to view human nature as bad.

How are attachment styles to be assessed in adults? There are a number of commonly used assessment measures of attachment styles (Crowell and Treboux, 1995). These include three interview schedules: Adult Attachment Interview, Attachment Interviews, and Current Relationship Interview; and three questionnaire and rating scales: Adult Attachment Styles, Relationship Questionnaire, and Reciprocal Attachment Questionnaire. In addition, the Attachment to God Inventory (Beck and McDonald, 2004) measures one's relationship with God in terms of an attachment bond. It is a twenty-eight-item self-rating scale with good psychometric properties.

Family Functioning

Family functioning can effectively be understood and measured with the Global Assessment of Relationship Functioning (GARF) scale that was patterned after the Global Assessment of Functioning (GAF) scale, which measures individual mental health on a continuum from superior mental functioning to serious mental illness. GARF was designed to measure relational health and dysfunction in couple and family systems and not to reflect individual psychopathology. It assesses the degree to which a family or other ongoing relational unit meets the affective or instrumental needs of its members in the following areas: problem solving, organization, and emotional climate. An individual's GAF and GARF scores are likely to be the same, unless that individual has sufficiently individuated from his family of origin and developed psychologically and spiritually.

GARF scale ranges from 1 to 100 (lowest to highest). Families with GARF scores below 60 are associated with negative views of human nature, while scores above 80 are associated with positive views of human nature. Research indicates that scores below 60 represent midrange or lower functioning families (Beavers and Hampson, 1990). In such families human nature is considered evil, people cannot be trusted, and children need physical discipline and punishment to tame their "badness."

GARF is a clinician rated instrument in which the clinician rates the family or couples over all relational functioning in terms of problem solving, organization, and emotional climate. Parenthetically, GARF is reported on Axis V of the DSM-IV-TR alongside GAF.

God Image

God image refers to the way an individual views God. The image can vary from being loving and caring to stern and wrathful. There are various explanations as to how these images develop (Hoffman, 2005). Ana Marie Rizzuto (1979) demonstrated that children's images of God appeared to be linked to the way in which they perceived their parents, and that their attachment style influenced their experience of God later in life (Tisdale et al., 1997). Others found a link between God image and an individual's biological father, in that individuals project the characteristics of their fathers onto their images of God (Hood et al., 1996). Other factors appear to influence how the God image develops. For example, researchers have found that an adult client's God image can change as a result of psychotherapy (Cheston et al., 2003).

How is God image measured? The most common psychological measure is the God Image Scales, useful in research. The shorter version, God Image Inventory, is more applicable in clinical practice (Lawrence, 1997).

Illustration of Fr. Sisyphus Continued

Here is some additional information about Fr. Sisyphus. He and I worked together in psychotherapy for over one year. During the course of our sessions I was able to identify his anthropology via his God image, attachment style, and family functioning. From all three it was clear that he viewed human nature as bad and depraved. As therapy proceeded his God image shifted from harsh and unforgiving to compassionate and caring. He made progress in both therapy and concurrent spiritual direction. His rage, criticalness, and negativity also abated. Similarly, his views about human nature and personal change became more positive, views that were more consistent with a Catholic anthropology.

Changes in Anthropology

Two basic changes in one's anthropology are possible. The first involves a shift from an implicit to an explicit anthropology, while the second involves a shift in the content of one's anthropology, that is, view of human nature. These changes seldom result from reading, a homily, or advisement. They are most likely to occur as a result of transformational experiences fostered by psychotherapy, spiritual direction, or similar life changing circumstances.

The theological anthropology course in the seminary curriculum can be one of those life changing circumstances. A not uncommon experience is that seminarians respond to this course on both the cognitive and experiential levels. Besides fostering a shift from a previously implicit anthropology to a more explicit one, it can also foster a basic change in the seminarian's view of human nature. With classmates, formators, and a spiritual director, ongoing discussion and reflection on being made in the image of God and that all persons are a reflection of that image can lead to subtle (and not so subtle) changes in attitudes and actions. As the personal and professional implications of this reality begin to be internalized, a shift from a negative to a more positive view of human nature may begin to occur.

Unfortunately, this change does not take place in all seminarians. There are a number of reasons that include, among others, a lack of readiness and willingness to engage in the process of discussion and reflection, or opacity of character. For example, college students can take a similar course called psychology of human nature or philosophical psychology as part of a major or minor in psychology. However, taking and passing this course is unlikely to result in achieving personal changes or transformation. The reason is that most psychology students take this course for an academic requirement rather than as a soul searching or transformational experience. In contrast, in the context of a seminary formation program, seminarians who have the requisite readiness, willingness, and transparency of character are more likely to reflect on the meaning of the course content in their personal and professional lives, and are willing to dialogue and further reflect on this meaning with their spiritual director and other formators.

It should not be surprising that seminarians whose attitudes and actions reflect a negative view of human nature are likely to have insecure attachments, more negative images of God, and lower GAF and GARF scores than seminarians with more positive views of human nature. These seminarians are also not as likely to shift their anthropology during or following a theological anthropology course unless psychotherapy, spiritual direction, or another significant life event fosters the experience of spiritual transformation.

Concluding Note

Catholic anthropology extends the traditional view of anthropology to include what it means to be a person, the meaning of life, human nature, sin and brokenness, and restoration. Individuals' anthropology reflects their personality dynamics, although it may not be consistent with the Catholic vision. Because candidates' anthropology profoundly influences their attitudes, decisions, and actions, consulting psychologists, vocation directors, and seminary formators should consider its identification essential in the evaluation of candidates for seminary admission. It may be one of the most important factors in predicting how a future priest functions as a preacher, sacramental minister, spiritual director, and confessor. Parenthetically, in the past few years there has been renewed interest in Catholic anthropology among professionals, including the clinical training of psychologists (Brugger, 2008).

Notes

1. Identifying information has been changed to ensure privacy and confidentiality.

The Joys and Struggles of Priests across the Life Span in View of the Sexual Abuse Scandal

Gerard J. McGlone, SJ, and Fernando A. Ortiz

Introduction

Since the late 1960s, psychology has increasingly influenced priestly formation and priestly life. A few writers have attempted to look at clergy across the life span. Donald Goergen's book (1974) *The Sexual Celibate* immediately comes to mind, Donald Cozzens (2000) also wrote about these issues in his book *The Changing Face of the Priesthood*, and, of course, none more completely and expertly than our present colleague Len Sperry with his book *Sex, Priestly Ministry, and the Church* (2003). One key aspect mentioned in each of these books that needs further attention and care is the situational dynamics that are present in the clerical culture and in the church. It is evident, as will be seen in this chapter, that not taking these situational dynamics into consideration does not assist us as priests and as a church. The overwhelming evidence in the two John Jay reports, which will be discussed further in this chapter, points to situational, organizational, systemic, and personality based issues that warrant our time, attention, and understanding.

This chapter attempts to address some of these emerging issues and concerns in this fuller context. The focus here will be on the priests who have been recently ordained, priests in their middle years, and the current surge in the population of priests who are aging and facing retirement. This chapter is not meant to be as exhaustive as the books mentioned but it is intended to highlight some signs of hope and some emerging concerns. It will focus upon the issues of relationships, healthy sexuality, celibacy, affective maturity, and healthy aging. It critically reviews the research, including the recently released John Jay report on clergy sexual abuse, Steve Rossetti's survey (2011), and data on priests' happiness and satisfaction will be analyzed throughout this writing. Several strategies for increasing psychological spiritual health and well-being will also be described.

Today's Context

Few times in our church history seem so challenging and yet so full of opportunity. We see reports that priests are more than or at least as happy as anyone else in society (Rossetti, 2011). Indeed they are, in an individual sense. These data point out several features of the clergy today that warrant further analysis. They seem interesting and quite compelling. But the numbers of vocations are staying near record lows, so the question remains for most priests as to who will follow in their footsteps. For celibates, they ask a fundamental generative question—what or who will be left after we are gone? Loss and diminishment surround most clergy on a daily basis; they regularly accompany people in the dying and death process. But, with whom do they journey when loss and death is their own? Priests more and more often live in solitary, and sometimes isolated, work and living environments. They deal with the realities of sickness, death, ministering to the dying, burying the dead, comforting the sorrowful, grieving, and ministering to the sick quite well, maybe too well. These accumulated emotions often go unprocessed. They face the demands of a professional and pastoral lifestyle that forces them to face life's tragedies head-on. Loss and diminishment is part of the pastoral landscape. Yet, self-care and self-maintenance in this key area are often avoided or ignored. The pastoral environment or the work condition is not often healthy and life-giving. A major intervention at systemic levels is necessary in this regard. The inner life is neglected at its core. The inner journey of unprocessed grief and loss is most often not traveled.

Serious and effective pastoral, presbyteral, and strategic planning is necessary to address these complicated and important issues related to the overall well-being of priests and religious in the current pastoral environment. Clergy are asked to do more with fewer supports and people to help them do the pastoral tasks that are necessary in today's apostolate. Some are consolidating and closing parishes, while others are expanding with little priestly support. The size of the Catholic population is expanding with newer members, yet loss and consolidation are surrounding many orders and dioceses. The aging and diminishing population of clergy and religious seems to be challenging the church and her resources to figure out ways to first care for these incredible women and men, and secondly, how to staff parishes, seminaries, schools, and Catholic institutions, as never before. Various types of lay ministers, the emerging role and sheer number of permanent deacons, and the growing number of parishes without priests are challenging our old conceptions of ministry, clerical life, and the church (CARA, 2010). Each level of the pastoral scene is demanding new, critically adaptive, and different capacities for today's priests and religious.

They are working harder and harder to manage this time period and often without awareness of the enormous personal toll. Priests are trained well to enter the external pastoral landscape; few have been trained well to know how to go within, to care for and attend to *the inner man* in such a complex and demanding new landscape. They "priest" well; they often fail to "priest" themselves and each other. This is a serious and growing phenomenon.

A Preliminary Challenge

Before we discuss the issues throughout the priestly life span, we think it essential to talk about a challenge facing clergy and religious throughout the country. This challenge is to begin to address and overcome the ecclesial and presbyteral divisiveness—a key situational variable—that exists amongst and between clergy who are in the presbyterates and religious orders today. This issue is seen most often around varying and differing ecclesiologies and seems to manifest itself in several groupings: the "John Paul II (JPII)" priests on one end of the spectrum and the "Vatican II" priests on the other side of the spectrum. Many priests fall in between the two camps (Hoge and Wenger, 2003). The divisiveness is not helping matters and clearly is of our darker sides, if not outright sin. Saint Paul, as evident in his letters, clearly saw "divisiveness" as not being a sign of the Spirit and not of God. It needs to be named as such and addressed systemically and individually, or it will continue to bring the church and her priests down. It certainly goes against the priestly desire of Jesus that "they all may be one as you and I are one" (see John 17:21-22). It also may reveal an unhealthy way of perceiving ourselves and our reality.

Father Allan Figueroa Deck comments on this quite well: "We must be on our guard about a certain tendency in U.S. culture with its strong Nordic and Calvinist influences to get trapped as church leaders in the 'one-shoe-fits-all-size' mentality with its compulsion for dialectical, exclusivist and univocal thinking. Neither so-called conservative nor progressive/liberal responses are adequate for a church or parish seeking to evangelize. Those ideologically driven responses are generally too narrow, impractical and limited to one context rather than the wide gamut of circumstances that characterize a multicultural, multigenerational church" (Deck, 2009).

Father Deck continues, stating that "in the ongoing debate over the proper implementation of Vatican II, it is no secret that there has been an unhealthy polarization of thought. One group insists on dialogue with the modern world, openness and innovation, and another insists on a robust proclamation of the Christian message, the content of the faith and continuity with the tradition. May I suggest that the way forward has to do with a 'both/and' rather than an 'either/or' approach?" The eloquence and power of these statements speak for themselves.

It is our Catholic tradition to believe, think, and react in such an intellectually rigorous and relationally sound manner. The situational conflicts that we clearly see present in many dioceses and religious orders require conflict management skills that many of us practice in our parish communities and might need to utilize in our relationships with our fellow priests. These situational struggles and dynamics would not be seen in any individual battery of psychological tests or surveys. By way of analogy, I might be quite happy as a person, but that does not mean I like or am happy with my living situation, my marriage, my job, or, more appropriately, my vocation, which always exists in relationship, in a cultural and organizational dynamic and my relationship with an ecclesial institution. Connection, fraternity, and brotherhood are essential goals that any priest desires; new skills and bridge-building interventions might be necessary to heal this wounding polarization. In essence, it is a necessary and new way to "priest" each other.

The Early Years

Throughout the past several years, new programming for the newly ordained has emerged. This ministry is one of the greatest joys one can witness. These men are clearly men of God, talented, intelligent, multifaceted, and serious about their work for the church. Typically, the newly ordained demonstrate an incredible appeal to the people of God wherever they are of service. Their zeal and charisma is often quite apparent to young and old alike. This spirit-filled and graced time is always special and a time of enormous joy. The fruits of education and formation seem to be very real to them and to those whom they serve. The overwhelming majority of these men are doing great work and having a positive impact at a time when young vocations and the newly ordained are needed the most. Recent experiences and data also seem to indicate that the overwhelming majority adapt well from the house of formation or seminary life to these first years in priestly ministry.

Additionally, these times can be challenging in some important ways. First, data has existed for some time now that the first years after ordination can be critical for the priestly identity and formation of these men (Hoge, 2002). The first pastoral assignment and that first year form a pastoral "template" that remains with the man for most of his priestly and pastoral life. Extreme care, judgment, and sensitivity must be exercised by bishops, formators, fellow priests, and directors of personnel to see to it that the first assignment is with a good mentor, good worshiping community, good experience of presbyteral brotherhood, and good parish staff. This first template can and will have enormous influence in the ability of the young priest to become the healthiest priest of tomorrow.

Mentorship, supervision, and spiritual direction have also been proven to be extremely critical for the newly ordained. Oftentimes, dioceses and religious orders offer varied and specific programming designed for the ongoing formation of the newly ordained to encourage and support these efforts. It is born of necessity and can be both challenging and very different than in the later years of priestly service to the church. These programs and the inspiration often come out of the documents of the church, especially *Pastores Dabo Vobis*, written by Pope John Paul II in 1992. This unique vision in PDV, if captured by the newly ordained and all priests, can be transformative for the church, her people, and her priests.

However, new data across several dioceses suggests that some members of the newly ordained seem to be running into significant psychological and spiritual problems in the first years after ordination. Estimates show that 20 to 30 percent of the ordinand classes in the first five to ten years after ordination seem to experience significant distress or problematic behaviors. The issues range in order of prevalence from problems with vocational discernment issues to black-and-white thinking or rigidity, anger and conflict management problems, sexual harassment, and sexual misconduct with adults. What might be going on here?

Several observers have suggested two possibilities. First, there seems to be a "submarine-ing effect"—that these men are fine under the surface of seminary or formational life and suddenly only reveal who and what they are after ordination. The "ship" or man that surfaces is not recognizable by anyone, including himself. Second, these men have been problematic and formators have tried to stop them from being ordained, but they were ordained because of the "numbers" issues that are facing many dioceses and religious orders and they were thought to be problematic but yet salvageable. No solid research seems to suggest which conclusion might be more correct. We suggest that it might be both realities. These men are quite content with themselves but they do not function well in the current collaborative ecclesial environment. Their own harsh and sometimes rigid judgments of self tend to become projected onto their pastoral situations and relationships. Simply put, there seems to be an internal or inner affective immaturity that might be at the root cause of these problems.

The solution is not to add more courses to an already packed seminary curriculum and formation program. Also, psychological screening may not necessarily detect some of the major issues related to these individuals. Psychological assessment cannot predict everything about a particular person, especially when some of these men in formation are extremely guarded and continue to use strong psychological defense mechanisms. Three other solutions come quickly to mind: First, formation houses and seminaries might be served and could serve these men by incorporating more regular feedback from peers in the formation process that allows the men to hear and receive constructive feedback to learn essential communication and conflict management skills in the process. Second, incorporating more systematically developed feedback from the sites wherein they have regular and consistent pastoral ministry might allow the seminaries, formation houses, dioceses, and religious orders to better judge their readiness and capacities for ministerial and priestly life. Third, a relational health knowledge and competency or matrix might be necessary. Do we know how and with whom this person is friendly, are these friendships healthy and helpful, and does this man have one or two people with whom he talks and is authentically honest on a consistent basis? What, essentially, is the capacity for long-term, healthy, intimate, celibate friendships? Finally, addressing these three areas more effectively might help better manage these recent areas of concern. The arena that warrants attention and development seems to be an internal arena or competency that is better formed within a pastorally relevant context.

The Middle Years

At convocation after convocation, one sees these men of the church today. They are truly an amazing group. They are the "worker bees." They are often highly educated, dedicated, and inspiring to be around. Unlike many of their peers in America today, they are clearly not in this for the money. They exemplify some of the best gospel values and model an authentic witness to the paschal mystery that is both real and tangible. Their concerns often center on how to better serve within the massive demands of a situational and pastorally challenging and ever-changing apostolate. They are men of purpose who seek more understanding and more meaning in their lives. But, they as a group are not happy with the situation of the church today. This is quite clear. Each and every time that one speaks with them they voice similar and consistent themes that need serious attention, care, and healing.

The recent sexual abuse crisis has taken a toll upon them and their sense of trust, meaning, and purpose. They have trouble trusting the church and her leaders. They worry more about what this crisis has done to their people, their students, and their church. Many felt betrayed and abandoned by their bishops at Dallas in 2002, when they believe that the gospel of forgiveness was abandoned. They feel that they have been put "under the bus." Most especially, in light of the more recent troubles that have occurred in both Kansas City and Pittsburgh, they believe that a double standard exists in the church. The Dallas Charter applies to them but they ask a simple and direct question: Where is the charter for the bishops when they are faced with similar accusations? This essential lack of trust has many implications for these men. This sense of betrayal is still an open wound for many. Healing is still necessary.

As Rossetti (2011) rightly claims, these men love their priesthood, their people, and being priests; however, they do not have a sense that there is any plan and they do not trust the system to deal with the rapidly aging senior priests and the diminished numbers of young priests. They feel squeezed in the "middle" of all of these situational dynamics. They, like most men in America, have a sense of identity that is linked to their job or ministry and they often confuse *who they are* with the *role they fulfill*. This forms the undertow of more problems that hit these men at their core. They feel stuck and numb with all that is happening around them.

They do not spend enough time in prayer, or they do not pray regularly, and this is their greatest source of stress in hundreds of surveys from across the country. They feel like hypocrites. They experience a spiritual dissonance or disconnect because they represent someone or something every day and every week to hundreds or even thousands. They, like most married men in America, talk of the "love of their lives" to everyone they see and meet outside of their "home." When at home, they zone out, and they fail to spend time with their love, their beloved. They avoid the shame and embarrassment, at home, in silent solitude that often becomes unbearable loneliness. They feel more inadequate the moment they step onto the pulpit. They manage the hypocrisy and inadequacy like most American males. They too run from that feeling like most men, by working harder, or worse. Workaholism creates more isolation, which makes the priests more vulnerable to multiple forms of addictions, poor self-care, and even more possibilities of acting-out behaviors. The vicious circle often feels overwhelming and it can and does damage them. However, research clearly indicates that priests can and do step out of this circle and ask for help in appropriate, timely, and useful ways (McGlone, 2001; Rossetti, 2011).

Many priests and religious in the United States take advantage of healthy opportunities for relational well-being. Rossetti's study (2011) does allow us to make some conclusions about these men on this individual basis. The healthy religious or priest will typically have two to three friends with whom he can be authentically honest and fully himself. These priests and nonclerical friends alike keep him honest and hold him accountable to himself and to his celibate and healthy intimacy. This rootedness and honesty allow the celibate of today to flourish in ministry, in the priesthood, and in these complex pastoral situations.

Grace-Filled Aging

The current status of the clergy has been well-documented by many elsewhere for many years (CARA, 2010). Priests are rapidly aging and the numbers indicate that the next ten to fifteen years will be a tremendous transition for the church as these men retire and leave ministry permanently. This generation is an amazing group. The graciousness and the pure magnetism of these men is truly a gift that will be sorely missed by the people of God and her priests. They have staffed churches, parishes, schools, colleges, hospitals, and retreat houses, creating the amazing and respected reputation of the Catholic Church in America today. We owe this generation a debt of enormous gratitude.

Most of these men are aging well and gracefully. They have taken and do take their self-care seriously. They often exercise, have hobbies, and maintain friendships through various assignments and stages in their religious and priestly life. The ones who have done this well have accepted their not "doing" anything anymore and accepted the loss of status and privilege with both dignity and graceful resignation. They prepared for this advent in aging by not clinging to their ministry and positions. They had their finances in order and their plans were set in place when they were asked or asked themselves to retire. Notice the ability to plan and control that which was inevitable, listening to their bodies enough and to what life was telling them and how much this process led to the actual graced-filled ability to age well and graciously. These are men of prayer and men of relationship who were able to enjoy their worshiping communities with whom they had success while not clinging to them or the "need" to work till they dropped.

However, there is significant recent research that is suggesting that a sizable percentage of these men may be more prone to aging poorly in the present time frame and in the years ahead. There seem to be poorly diagnosed or missed forms of depression. This form of geriatric depression is often masked by a consistent and pervasive ruminative style that is expressed in a persistent negativity. It shows itself toward others or themselves and activities that they used to enjoy. It seems to be expressed in an inability to stop their running thoughts from constantly going over details in their head—that is, rumination—which often paralyzes these men. A lack of physical care and poor eating habits coupled with poor hygiene and poor patterns of exercise manifest in high blood pressure, high rates of diabetes, and poor health diagnoses. This collection of behaviors often coalesces into an isolated, lonely lifestyle. These men need consistent and often multiple levels of intervention to begin to have a decent quality of life in their final years as priests.

Finally, they are leaving their ministry and priestly life just as the church is beginning to manage the fuller effects of what the abuse scandal has done to the church and to them as priests. Let us begin to understand what we now know.

The John Jay Study

The first caveat when we look at this data is that when one sees or hears stories about abuse and abusers, there often seems to be little sympathy, little understanding, and little tolerance. As members of a treatment community, our bias and belief reside in the efficacy of treatment and in the possibility of forgiveness. Such beliefs do not explain away nor do they ever mean to condone any crime or sin. In treatment of sex offenders, one often hears the saying, "There is no cure, but these conditions are manageable." This current analysis is an attempt at understanding a complex and perplexing societal and ecclesial problem (McGlone, 2011). Secondly, the rise in our society of elements that see sex offenders as subhuman or even lepers is evident in various stories in the media (e.g., *Miami Herald*, Feb. 26, 2010).

The frenzy both after the 2002 crisis and in the current crisis in other parts of the world has served us in many ways in the field of child maltreatment but it also has had some significant downsides (Finkelhor, 2003). It seems to be both a public policy disaster and an inhumane event when convicted sex offenders cannot find any residence other than a tent under a highway bridge. If we know in the field that stress can be a situational trigger for some offenders to reoffend, it seems both logical and prudent to decrease stress, not increase it through punitive and politically popular residency sanctions against them.

Finally and similarly, in the church there have been several amazing developments since the Dallas Charter in June 2002. Enormous strides have been made to keep the church and her children safer; hundreds of thousands have been trained in child protection and safety; the research supported by the USCCB is extraordinary and singular as a faith community in its transparency and possible effects in our society (Terry and Ackerman, 2008). These are but a few of the many accomplishments. As a faith community, we can be quite proud of these accomplishments and they are yielding some significant and measurable gains. Much still needs to be done, however, as the data suggests. These are, and should be, helping the field of child protection and maltreatment enormously, but, at what price? If we do not model forgiveness in our church and faith community, what do we abandon and what have we lost? One cannot help but recall the late Cardinal Avery Dulles's lament, if not warning, at the same Dallas meeting when he predicted that this Dallas Charter could irrevocably damage the priest-bishop relationship. One wonders if he was right. Is it not time to reconsider the charter's zero-tolerance policy, now that we know that 98 percent of clerical sex offenders are not pedophiles after all (Terry, 2010)? Can't we figure out a way to be both forgiving and accountable? Most solid psychologically based research points to the mental health benefits of forgiveness. Our tradition has a long sacred deposit of faith that now makes scientific sense! Can we at least pose the question? We believe that it is time.

Additionally, sexual abuse of children by members of the Roman Catholic clergy and religious is an enormously complex problem in today's society. The more recent news that has spread across Europe and elsewhere in the world certainly tells a different story than the one that the news reports and pundits uttered in the early part of the twenty-first century. Now it clearly is not "an American problem." We see this in the numerous news stories in Australia, Ireland, England, Germany, Austria, Switzerland, Belgium, and Italy.

Understanding the Problem

One of the first and the most important developments since Dallas deals with a more full descriptive picture of the nature and scope of the problem that contextualizes treatment today (Tallon and Terry, 2008). Cynthia Calkins Mercado, Jennifer Tallon, and Margaret Smith (2008) have allowed us to view the full dimensions of the issues in light of the John Jay College of Criminal Justice Study and the effect of the Dallas Charter's zero-tolerance mandates. Concretely, it continues to inform treatment and direct discharge planning. This one study has confirmed what the treatment centers and the treating psychologists have known for some time: there is an enormous heterogeneity within this clerical population. This heterogeneity still demands and demanded a varied and far more nuanced response to a very complex and challenging clinical reality (Loftus and Camargo, 1993). This data confirms that the "one-size-fits-all" treatment approach simply does not work and clearly is not appropriate with this clerical population. Additionally, the yearly audits since the charter in 2002 and the USCCB response to the problem have had some positive effects that need additional discussion and analysis.

The John Jay study (as it has become known) has given us enormous data that is both descriptive and useful. It estimates essential prevalence and incidence data about this problem between the years 1950 and 2002. The study is a tribute to the research team at the John Jay College and the USCCB for sponsoring it. It also describes the reality facing treatment providers. Researchers seem to estimate that about 4.2 percent of the priest population (1950–2002) in those years were sexual offenders. Religious brothers and priests made up about 2.7 percent. The reason for this significant discrepancy is still unknown at this time. The data seems to also suggest that these men tend to be divided into various types of clerical sex offenders and these seem to fit into three main groupings. The first group and the vast majority, about 85 percent, are nondiagnosable or, for the purposes of this chapter, are the "undifferentiated" clerical sex offenders. They are not easily diagnosed with a paraphilic or sexual disorder and typically had one victim or incident. If no disorder fits them, what are they? The second grouping makes up the remainder and is about 10 percent of the study. These men would best be categorized as ephebophiles, or those men attracted to adolescents. The third and final group, the pedophile group, was about 2.2 percent of the total group. Additionally, these men, about 150 of them, accounted for about 30 percent of the victims and clearly had a diagnosable sexual disorder. In these cases, with better screening, these men could have been prevented from abusing children (Terry and Ackerman, 2008; Terry, 2010). As discussed earlier, their victims—about 80 percent—were typically adolescent males.

Latest Prevalence

This data places the new ten-year rate of abuse by clergy in the church at around 0.4–0.5 percent, which is little known and seldom cited by anyone. This is quite a decrease from the original study statistics cited above and the overall prevalence rate in society (1–3 percent). It is quite obvious in the recent data released each year from the USCCB that there are fewer and fewer cases of clerical sexual abuse in the US Catholic Church being reported. If this data is to be taken seriously, the overall current prevalence rates seem to be lingering around 0.4 to 0.5 percent of all religious and priests in the United States (CARA, 2007, 2008, 2009). Two issues quickly emerge. First, the recent data from CARA suggests that half of all these new cases of reported sexual abuse were performed by international clergy. Additionally, the figures clearly indicate that the more recent surge of international clergy (about 8,000–12,000), now estimated to be about 15 percent of the total number of priests in the United States, needs to be examined far more closely and seriously. This is a source of concern. Unlike the typical seminarian in the United States, and for many reasons, most of these clergy never have any psychological screening evaluations (McGlone, Ortiz, and Karney, 2010).

Types of Offenders

For several years, the clerical and lay offenders have been divided into two general types: situational and preferential (Finkelhor and associates, 1986). Within these groupings or typologies one often sees co-varying or co-occurring disorders of a sexual and nonsexual nature. Treatment would follow from what type of offender was diagnosed and if there are any comorbid conditions. The situational, or "opportunistic," offender typically had more environmentally based triggers and therefore similar treatment solutions, that is, grieving the loss of a parent (particularly the loss of the mother), dealing with burnout, management of situational stress and anger, managing naïve sexual knowledge, poor sexual boundaries, and immature sexual development. These offenders—the clear majority of all clerical offenders—were also more generally amenable and open to treatment and typically had very few victims or one victim. The opportunistic offender seems more fixated and more emotionally like his victims, more self-focused or self-centered, more dependent or needy in his interpersonal relationships, and more driven by his sexual urges toward children. Providers often thought them to be narcissistically disordered but research has yet to support that theory. There has been some support for more dependent-like features in these more serial type offenders (McGlone, 2001). These men typically had many more victims, were sometimes not open to treatment, and were more convinced that their offending behavior was consensual and helpful to their victims.

While making no excuses for Roman Catholic clerical sex offenders, we can observe that child sexual abuse is a widespread problem. Existing research data suggest that about 80 percent of all sexual abuse of children in the United States occurs within families. Heterosexual married men are the usual perpetrators (Finkelhor, 1984; Gonsiorek, 1995; Terry and Ackerman, 2008). Clerical child sexual abuse is found in other religious denominations as well. For example, consider recent articles in the *New York Times*, such as "Data Shed Light on Child Sexual Abuse by Protestant Clergy" (Associated Press, 2007). This article focuses on three companies that provide malpractice insurance to a majority of Protestant churches. These companies reported "they typically receive upwards of 260 reports a year of children younger than 18 being sexually abused by members of the clergy, church staff members, volunteers or congregants." In "Preachers Accused of Sins, and Crimes" Jim Avila, Bonnie Van Gilder, and Matt Lopez, on April 13, 2007 (ABC News, 20/20), detailed a six-month investigation by a television news program in the United States. They "found Protestant ministers, supposed men of God from every denomination, sexually abusing the children who trusted them. The investigation uncovered 'preacher predators' in every corner of the country" (Avila, Van Gilder, and Lopez, 2007). Philip Jenkins, author of *Pedophiles and Priests*, found no evidence that the incidence of child molestation committed by Roman Catholic priests was any greater than within other Christian and non-Christian denominations (Jenkins, 1996).

We might also look at child molestation in other institutions that serve children. Charol Shakeshaft (2004), a Hofstra University professor, under contract with the US Department of Education, conducted a reanalysis of data from a major study funded by the American Association of University Women (AAUW) in 2000. The sample was drawn from a list of 80,000 schools to create a stratified two-stage sample design of 2,065 eighth- to eleventh-grade students. Researchers administered surveys in schools to 1,559 male and female public school students in grades eight to eleven (ages 13–16 or 17); in addition, 505 public school eighth- to eleventh-grade students completed online surveys, for a total of 2,064 respondents. The sample included representative subpopulations of Latino/a, white, and African descent students. The findings can be generalized to all public school students in eighth to eleventh grades at a 95 percent confidence level with a margin of error of plus or minus 4 percentage points. A flaw of the study is that it asked only about *unwanted* sexual encounters, despite the fact that the students were legally underage. The study is also difficult to compare to existing data on clergy because the AAUW survey asked about both physical contact and noncontact events, such as sexual innuendo, and it asked about sexual events with peers (other students) as well as with adult educators. More important, the rates computed are percentages of *victims*, not perpetrators. Looking at the full sample, 9.6 percent of the original 2,064, or 247, reported that they had been targets of educator abuse (contact and/ or noncontact). Roughly four times as many respondents were targets of contact or noncontact abuse from other students. From the AAUW data we cannot estimate the number or percent of *educators* engaged in the abuse.

In her discussion, Shakeshaft also implicates school districts for using the same strategy as American bishops and dioceses, in transferring their "problem teachers" from one school to another without regard to their transgressions. The only other secular child-service organization in the United States to research the problem of sexual abuse by adults was the Boy Scouts of America in the 1990s. From media reports we know there was a problem of child sexual abuse with some Boy Scout volunteers. We still do not know the rates of abuse because these corporate data remain proprietary, that is, not released for public consumption (Terry and Ackerman, 2008).

The rates for all types of child sexual abuse in the United States are fairly consistent and staggering, one in four (25 percent) females before the age of 21 and one in six males (16 percent) before the age of 21 have reported being subjected to sexually abusive behaviors (Terry and Ackerman, 2008). Yet these sensational estimates have not sufficiently forwarded the cause of child protection in the United States (Finkelhor, 2003; Vieth, 2003). Further, sexual abuse is the least prevalent of all the forms of violence against children in most societies as well as in the United States (Finkelhor, 2003). Rates of neglect, physical abuse, and emotional abuse of children far exceed rates of sexual abuse.

Organizational Dynamics

The first key aspect in understanding this problem of clerical sexual abuse is that this issue is embedded in an ecclesiastical cultural environment. Situational factors have enormous power and influence upon the individuals in the "abuse event." Certain individuals—the clear majority of priests, sometimes estimated at about 95 percent—are able to relate normally and healthfully to children within the ecclesiastic environment, but others cannot. Clerical child sexual abuse comes from this ecclesiastical setting and takes place within a relationship of power, trust, and dominance.

Clearly, some priests have misused their role to such an extent that a victim's concept and very experience, if not the full reality, of the "sacred" is sacrificed and, in some cases, destroyed permanently. On the other hand, some victims of abuse—both familial and clerical—appear to the casual observer to live seemingly normal lives. The resiliency of victims or survivors is as varied as their experiences. This being said, this experience, harm, and pain must never escape attention. The pain and hurt suffered by thousands of children matters, and must be the clarion call to understand this unique abuse of power. This chapter is an attempt to understand a serious, horrible problem. It should not be construed to be an attempt to justify any aberrant and destructive behavior.

Prevalence and Incidence

Reliable statistical figures for sex offenders among Catholic clergy (priests and brothers) in the United States are extremely difficult to ascertain (see table 11.1). The Center for Applied Research in the Apostolate (CARA) at Georgetown University estimates the current total number of priests to be about 42,000. It estimates that 57 percent of these priests are diocesan with the remaining being religious order priests and brothers. Some researchers estimated that from 0.2 to 4.0 percent (Jenkins, 1996; McGlone, 2003), or between 84 and 1,680, of priests were child sexual abusers. Other researchers estimate numbers as high as 2,000 to 3,000 priests, or, using the midpoint of 2,500, 5.3 percent of the current clerical population (Angelica, 1993; Berry, 1992; Sipe, 1995; Plante, 1999).

After the sexual abuse crisis hit in January 2002, the United States Conference of Catholic Bishops (USCCB) commissioned researchers at the John Jay College (JJC) of Criminal Justice of the City University of New York (CUNY) to do a fifty-two-year (1950–2002) retrospective study of this problem. Significantly, 98 percent of the dioceses and almost 78 percent of all religious orders participated in this research. The John Jay College of Criminal Justice study (henceforth the JJC study), led by principal investigator Karen J. Terry, has thrown significant new light on many dimensions of the problem (Terry and Ackerman, 2008; Terry, 2010). The JJC study estimated an overall prevalence rate of abuse of minors perpetrated by Catholic clergy at about 4.2 percent (3 to 6 percent). The figures given here reflect the percent distribution of the overall findings. Key to this interpretation is that 88 percent of the sexual offenders in the JJC study do *not* fit any DSM categories that we currently utilize for diagnosis.

Table 11.1. Prevalence data from sample estimates, on sexual contacts of Catholic clergy

Researchers	Pedophiles	Ephebophiles	Pedophiles + Ephebophiles	Sexually Active with Consenting Adults†
Loftus and Camargo (1992)	2.7%	8.4%	11.1%	27.8%
Connors (1994)	0.2–0.3%	5–8%	5.2–8.3%	Not reported
Sipe (1990, 1995)	2%	4%	6%	40–50%
Jenkins (1996)	0.3%	2–4%	2.3–4.3%	Not reported
John Jay College (2006)			4.5%	Not reported
MIDPOINTS	2%	5–8%	6%	36.4%

† Sexually active with adults refers to a priest who is engaged genitally with a consenting adult in a nonpastoral setting. This is an attempt to avoid confusion with sexual harassment cases involving adult employees under a priest's supervision.

Interestingly, the JJC study found a diocesan clergy prevalence rate of about 4.2 percent (3.0–6.0 percent) but the corresponding prevalence rate was reported to be around 2.7 percent (1–3 percent) for members of male religious orders (priests and brothers). The probable prevalence rates fall between the numbers in parenthesis. The reasons for the disparity between these two groups would be extremely important and are still unexplored at this time (Terry and Ackerman, 2008; Terry, 2010). This discrepancy warrants critical attention and future research. One possibility might be that religious order priests traditionally live in communities of members of the order, and thus may have more social support than diocesan priests, who often live alone or with one other priest.

Some question the percentages and numbers of the JJC study. Specifically, some think these studies underreport the problem (Angelica, 1993; Berry, 1992; Burkett and Bruni, 1993; Economus, 1996; Sipe, 1995). About 80 percent of these offenders had acted out with adolescent males, and thus are classified as *same-sex ephebophiles*, an observation that is often underreported (Connors, 1994; Jenkins, 1996; Loftus, 1999; Plante, 1999; Terry,

2010). This observation is important for targeted prevention. If we know, as we now do, that adolescents are most at risk, then we can warn them, their schools, their parish communities, and their parents as to how to prevent this abuse from occurring in the future.

Margaret Smith and her colleagues, Andres Rengifo and Brenda Vollman (2008), and the JJC study data are perplexing in reporting that 88 percent of clerical child sexual abusers do not seem to fit neatly into any single diagnostic category, that is, they have multiple diagnoses. The inability to distinguish clear types of sexual offenders prevents the public, clinicians, researchers, and, therefore, most Catholics from fully understanding the complexity of the problem (Cimbolic and Cartor, 2006; Golden, 2002; Haugaard, 2000; Plante, 2010). This also makes prevention strategies hard to design. Terry (and Ackerman, 2008; 2010) and her colleagues of the USCCB research also contend that the majority of the clerical offenders (57 percent) who had only one victim do not easily fit into *any* diagnostic category. These observations raise important questions. Should we have a "one-size-fits-all" response in our handling of offenders in the zero-tolerance policy? Is the risk the same for all clerical offenders? Some writers have suggested that the target of intervention should be the clerical culture rather than clerics. They castigate the inherent lack of honesty in the "secret lives" of the clerics who are sexually acting out (Sipe, 2010). Still others see the main problem as stunted psychosexual development or affective immaturity of clerics (Plante, 2010).

The estimated number of alleged victims in the fifty-two-year period of the John Jay study was about 10,667 and the estimated number of alleged abusers was around 4,362. About 8,533 (80 percent) of these allegations were substantiated; about 10 percent were examined and not substantiated. The remaining 10 percent of cases could not be determined (substantiated or not substantiated) because of death of one or both of the individuals involved. The report estimates that only 5–9 percent of these cases were ever adjudicated in a secular court of law. This seems to be due to several factors: (1) the unique shame and power differential in the clerical abuse cycle, (2) antiquated laws, (3) the variations in the criminal statutes of limitations in states, and (4) the longer delays in reports of abuse from male victims. According to the JJC study, the rates of victims per clerical offender ranged from 56 percent with just one victim to about 3 percent (about 149 priests) with large numbers of victims. This latter group accounted for over 27 percent of the total victims during the study time frame. Each of these latter men had about ten or more victims; these offenders accounted for over 2,960 victims. Three-quarters of these men were diocesan pastors (Tallon and Terry, 2008). These same authors point out that better screening could have prevented this most severe abuse from happening.

More recent analyses of the JJC data also help in clarifying the necessary distinctions within these groups (Cartor, Cimbolic, and Tallon, 2008; Cimbolic and Cartor, 2006). Additional data analyses place the subgroupings of "ephebophiles" in four distinct categories (Cimbolic and Cartor, 2006; Cartor, Cimbolic, and Tallon, 2008). The four subgroupings proposed for ephebophiles are (1) individuals who are attracted to adolescent males, (2) individuals who are attracted to adolescent females, (3) individuals who are attracted to both adolescent males and adolescent females, and (4) those who seem to be nondiscriminating in choice of victims—male or female, child or adolescent. It is the contention of the JJC researchers that the same-sex abuse cases are not attributable to homosexual tendencies per se but to other personal difficulties (Terry, 2010).

More on the John Jay Study

The JJC study has helped us enormously. Little has been known about sexually offending priests and religious because of many factors, not the least of which had been the Catholic Church's unwillingness and/or inability to sponsor or lead objective research on abusive clerics (Loftus, 1999; Plante, 1999; 2002). However, these attitudes dramatically changed after 2002, leading to the detailed findings of the JJC study. The support of the USCCB for the latest attempts to look at this issue in more detail is commendable and unlike any other church or faith denomination in the United States (Plante, 2010; Terry, 2010). Access to subjects had been a primary stumbling block in previous research and is still so in any current research project (Loftus, 1999; Terry, 2010). Jenkins (1996), and more recently Thomas Plante (1999, 2002) and Donald Cozzens (2000), detailed the complexities of the social situation within which the church is attempting to respond. These accounts are often depictions of unintentional and, in some cases, intentional neglect and ignorance on the part of church leaders. More often than not, they are vivid descriptions of the divergent political agendas entangled with the problem of clerical sexual abuse (Jenkins, 1996; Plante, 2002, 2010).

It becomes essential to depict the historical roots of the problem and to have a clear classification as to the phenomena being critiqued, namely, clearly distinguishing between pedophiles and ephebophiles (Cimbolic and Cartor, 2006; Connors, 1994; Jenkins, 1996; Loftus and Camargo, 1992; Plante, 1999, 2002, 2010), and between those cases with males versus females as victims/objects choices. In the last part of this chapter, the fuller context within which this abuse takes place will be explored. But, it is also senseless to vilify the media when they have helped the church and our society come to grips with a phenomenon that would not have been addressed had it not been for their efforts (Smith, Rengifo, and Vollman, 2008).

The Importance of Location

In real estate marketing, location is everything. So too location is key in the understanding and possible prevention of clerical sexual abuse. We assume that sexual abuse is at least in part a situational event, namely, there exist factors within both the perpetrator and the victim that combine or coalesce into this nightmarish event. Then it would make sense that researchers would want to know where that abuse occurred and whether that location was significant. Several key pieces of data suggest that this is indeed the case in regard to clerical sexual abuse (Terry and Ackerman, 2008; Tallon and Terry, 2008). The JJC study found that there seemed to be no part of the United States that was untouched by this problem. Rural or city, small or large parishes, and small or large dioceses were equally affected by this problem. In effect, there seemed to be a system-wide failure, response, and pattern (Terry and Ackerman, 2008). In general, because the sexual abuse occurred in private, in most cases parish residences or rectories, priests' or religious order houses were where the abuse took place. Abuse also happened in church buildings (17 percent), in parents' homes (13 percent), in vacation homes of the clerics (10 percent), or in parish or church sponsored schools (10 percent). The true predatory pedophile most often offended in the victim's own home (Tallon and Terry, 2008). This one bit of information concerning location might be quite key in regard to more effective prevention strategies and policies. Monitoring, education, and reducing situational triggers about these times and interactions with minors can become key to prevention efforts (Terry and Ackerman, 2008). Simply put, reducing the opportunity for being alone with a minor in a private location reduces risk (Tallon and Terry, 2008).

Grooming behaviors for these clerical offenders were fairly consistent with and similar to lay sexual offenders (Tallon and Terry, 2008). The data does not suggest a significant trend here. When clerical sexual offenders used gifts and enticements, they used them the same way any offender uses them to entice the child into this event. Some would use socializing with the family as one way to gain access to the child. Most did not use threatening behaviors.

The data strongly suggest that most of the clerical offenders were not homogenous—they were "generalists," not "specialists," in their offending. Compared to lay offenders, clerics had a later onset for their behaviors, typically not until after ordination. The mean age for offending behaviors was between thirty-five and thirty-seven years of age. Since these behaviors showed a heterogeneity of expression, the situational factors become even more critical to analyze and use for assessment and for more effective prevention programming (Terry and Ackerman, 2008; Tallon and Terry, 2008).

There were some similarities and differences in the criminal-like behaviors of the clerical offender. For some, a criminal is a criminal (Piquero et al., 2008). There was a set of behaviors and actions that replicated what lay criminals do. There was deceit, significant physical perpetration, and planning. Unlike the typical criminal offender in society, the clerical offenders differed in terms of their age at offending behavior, the types of offending behaviors, and their recidivism rates. Most started at a later age than the typical offender and they seemed to wait until after ordination. They showed a much lower rate of reoffense than the typical offender. The duration of offending behavior was also less for the clerical offender than for the lay sexual offender.

A clerical abuser of children sometimes has a history of being sexually abused. In the John Jay 2006 supplemental report, single-incident clerics are less likely to have a recorded history of abuse (physical/sexual abuse and substance abuse) than clerics with more than one incident. The group of single-incident clerics included 4.2 percent who had suffered physical or sexual abuse as children, compared to 8.8 percent for clerics with multiple incidents. It should be noted that these rates are well below rates for male lay victims of sexual abuse *only* (one in six males before the age of twenty-one, or 16.6 percent) (Terry and Ackerman, 2008). For those who were abused, the question becomes, how does this man integrate or not integrate this fact into his sexuality, celibate capacity, and sexual fantasies or attractions? Overall the JJC study found a rate of 9 percent with a history of being sexually abused for the clerical sexual offenders. Other studies have found that priest nonoffenders have higher rates of being sexually abused as children, yet against children (McGlone, 2001). To suggest that anyone who has a history of being sexually abused should be excluded from consideration for admittance to the priesthood seems rash and ill-advised. There is little evidence to support an assumption of predictability such as in the myth of a "victim to victimizer" so commonly believed by many (Cannon, 2001). It seems prudent to question what significance this event has in the person's sexual identity, but the data do not support use of a childhood history of sexual abuse as an exclusionary criteria for candidacy to religious life and priesthood.

Finally, time becomes an important variable to discuss. It is important to place this current crisis within certain key time frames of when the abuse occurred and what time frames seem significant for both the victims and the clerical sexual offenders, and the crisis itself. Overall, like most sexual abuse in society, the sexual abuse rates in the church seem to be trending downward (Terry, 2010; Finkelhor and Jones, 2004). There is speculation that prevention efforts both in society and in the church community are having a positive and measurable effect (Terry, 2010).

Unlike reporting of sexual abuse in society, the data suggest that the clear majority of sexual abuse in the church was reported some twenty-five to thirty years after the event happened. The role of the cleric and the majority of victims being male seem to be the main variables for this trend. There also seem to be two major times when most abuse was reported—in the early '90s (the first sexual abuse crisis hit in 1992) and in the year right after the Dallas Charter in 2002. There seems to be a significant trend in the abuse incidents occurring in the '70s and the '80s. However, simply looking at a trend line does not help in understanding the fact that over 70 percent of all abuse happened before 1970 (Terry, 2010). There are significant years in the data, as in 1970, when almost 10 percent of all the ordinands in the United States were known to have committed sexual offenses against minors. Thomas Plante and Kathleen McChesney (2011) have edited a new book that highlights the very latest in all of these issues.

How has this impacted priests' aging and retiring at this time in the history of the church in the United States? This is a necessary and critical question that must influence their final years and one that needs to be researched in these months and years ahead. No data exists to answer this question at this time. It is, however, a question with which priests of every age group must grapple in their personal and pastoral understanding of themselves and their priesthood. It is the inner journey within the current ecclesial situation.

12

Reflections on the Inner Life of Priests

Toward Excellence in Pastoral Ministry:
Psychological Assessment and Integrated Formation

Katarina Schuth, OSF

The development of "the inner life of priests" is a complex process that begins long before ordination. The values and personality traits, the attitudes and skills required for excellent pastoral ministry are instilled at a foundational level during childhood, but the years of seminary formation are pivotal in shaping priests who will serve as whole, holy, and competent pastors. All four areas of formation—human, spiritual, intellectual, and pastoral—play a role in fostering qualities that will lead to ministerial excellence. Maximum growth can take place in these areas when formators have a keen awareness of their own psychological makeup and can apply that understanding to the formation of seminarians. As the chapters of this book attest, the relationship between the inner life of priests and its outer expression is close. The formation of the inner life of seminarians will considerably affect the external shape of their future ministry. Thus, this brief reflection focuses on two fundamental concepts—Catholic anthropology and core values—both underpinning good formational practices that ultimately affect pastoral ministry.

Katarina Schuth, OSF, holds the Endowed Chair for the Social Scientific Study of Religion at St. Paul Seminary School of Divinity, University of St. Thomas, St. Paul, Minnesota.

The first concept, Catholic anthropology, is taken up in several chapters and addresses "the emotional, mental, moral, relational, and spiritual health of the human person." It concerns "the origins and purpose of human persons as well as the place of sin, suffering, personal effort, grace, and healing" (Sperry). In this view, human nature is essentially good, but affected by original sin, representing a realistic and essentially positive view of life. Individuals do fail and fall, but through grace and effort they overcome evil and rise again. A contrary Freudian view suggests that human nature is basically bad and that hope for personal and spiritual transformation is simply an illusion. The result is "a sense of spiritual futility inconsistent with a Catholic anthropology." Since the position a seminarian favors will affect his ministerial relationships, it is essential to emphasize and reinforce the idea that the negative view of human nature is not in accordance with Catholic teaching.

Practically speaking, the effects of one's beliefs and attitudes about the human person are evident in many aspects of pastoral ministry. If one's view is that human beings are basically bad, or at least deficient and unable to change, the negative attitude will express itself in ministerial relationships. It is well documented, for example, that many newly ordained priests find it difficult to collaborate with laypeople. While the usual explanation given is their desire to fully exercise their authority and maintain control, it seems likely that their behaviors also are related to their perception of the human condition: lay ministers are not to be trusted, they are not dedicated or spiritual enough, and so they are unable to deliver adequate pastoral services. This attitude can carry over to the content of homilies and the character of the sacrament of reconciliation. The negative view stresses sin and judgment and a stern image of God, while the positive view portrays a caring and compassionate God who understands weakness, and gives grace to overcome sinfulness.

In teaching college-age students, one of their major complaints about the church relates to the negative approach of religious education classes and homilies. One student wrote, "The tactics used were what I would call scare tactics, that we would go to hell if we missed Mass, rather than teaching us that Jesus really cares about us." They long for words of encouragement that give them a sense of hope for the future. The possibility that the absence of a well-developed Catholic anthropology is responsible for these attitudes and behaviors seems very real. The potential to transform such attitudes during formation likewise seems possible and necessary.

A second concept related to psychological understandings that flow into pastoral ministry is related to core values. Integration of all areas of formation contributes to the development of the basic approach a seminarian will take in all his behaviors, which reflect his inner life, the "core" or essence of who he is. One of the tasks of formation is to assist the future priest in forming core values that reflect the life of Christ, the virtues and attitudes related in the gospels. The Program of Priestly Formation identifies some of these qualities: honesty, humility, emotionality, extraversion, agreeableness, conscientiousness, and openness. One of the chapters of this book helpfully defines and offers evaluative questions to guide formation personnel in their work with seminarians around virtue ethics. On the positive side, the core values one is looking for in a person are affective maturity with deep relational capacities, a prudent and discerning man, open to God's design and free from self-preoccupation. On the contrary, "core values of clerical culture have been identified as privilege, entitlement, separateness, and status."

Being able to discern the values that are indeed "core" takes careful observation, psychological understanding, and spiritual insight. Formation personnel are aware of how much behaviors of seminarians can shift when an authority figure is observing. Recounting numerous interactions I have had with seminary faculty who do not vote on the continuation of a seminarian and ultimately on whether or not he should be ordained, they report that the behaviors they encounter with some seminarians are much more negative than the priests who do have a vote. It leads one to be aware of the values and attitudes that are truly "core" to the person and those that are for external observation only, but are not part of their inner life. Situational factors, as well as individual and organizational dynamics, all contribute to the way a person will act, so it is important to perceive what the behaviors actually signify.

Taking full advantage of the fruits of psychological assessment and becoming more astute in using in formation what psychology can contribute will immensely improve outcomes in human, spiritual, intellectual, and pastoral formation. Development of a sound Catholic anthropology will assist seminarians in forming thoroughly Christlike core values and will ensure that the inner life of priests will be rich and full and capable of sustaining inspiring pastoral ministry.

"A Bridge, Not an Obstacle"
Human Formation for a Healthy and Holy Priesthood:
The Legacy of Pope John Paul II

Monsignor Jeremiah J. McCarthy

In 1992, Pope John Paul II authored his landmark encyclical on priestly formation, *Pastores Dabo Vobis* (I Will Give You Shepherds, hereafter PDV). The pope, building on the wise scholastic principle *gratia perficit naturam* ("grace perfects, or brings nature to its completion"), affirmed that the holistic formation of priests builds upon a solid, human foundation. In other words, future priests must be healthy, human persons, with sound interpersonal skills and the ability to relate to other people with affective maturity.

Affective maturity is the fruit of a well-formed personality. One who is affectively mature integrates thinking with feeling, the head with the heart. Another way of expressing this capacity is emotional intelligence. In making this affirmation central to priestly training, the pope is invoking an incarnational, Catholic anthropology. Because Jesus dared to become one of us, our humanity is blessed, an instrument of grace. Paragraph 22 of the Second Vatican Council document Pastoral Constitution on the Church in the Modern World beautifully captures this Catholic anthropology:

> For, by his incarnation, he, the Son of God, has in a certain way united himself with each individual. He worked with human hands, he thought with a human mind. He acted with a human will, and with a human heart he loved. Born of the Virgin Mary, he has truly been made one of us, like to us in all things except sin.

In the normative document that guides the training of priests in the United States, The Program of Priestly Formation, fifth edition (PPF hereafter), formation activities in the seminary endeavor to integrate four distinctive dimensions or "pillars": human, spiritual, intellectual, and pastoral. The PPF highlights the priority of human formation to anchor the achievement of the other dimensions. The PPF explicitly grounds its understanding of human formation based upon Pope John Paul's encyclical:

Msgr. Jeremiah J. McCarthy is executive director of the National Catholic Educational Association (NCEA) Seminary Department.

The basic principle of human formation is to be found in *Pastores dabo vobis*, no. 43: the human personality of the priest is to be a bridge and not an obstacle for others in their meeting with Jesus Christ the Redeemer of the human race. As the humanity of the Word made flesh was the *instrumentum salutis* ["instrument of salvation"], so the humanity of the priest is instrumental in mediating the redemptive gifts of Christ to people today. As *Pastores dabo vobis* also emphasizes, human formation is the "necessary foundation" of priestly formation. (75)

The text of the PPF (76) then proceeds to identify ten key skills that should characterize a priest who exemplifies authentic human formation:

- *A free person*: a person who is free *to be* who he is in God's design . . .

- *A person of solid moral character with a finely developed moral conscience, a man open to and capable of conversion . . .*

- *A prudent and discerning man . . .*

- *A man of communion*: a person who has real and deep relational capacities . . .

- *A good communicator. . .*

- *A person of affective maturity*: someone whose life of feelings is in balance and integrated into thought and values . . . .

- *A man who respects, cares for, and has vigilance over his body . . .*

- *A man who relates well with others, free of overt prejudice and willing to work with people of diverse cultural backgrounds*: a man capable of wholesome relations with women and men as relatives, friends, colleagues, staff members, and teachers, and as encountered in areas of apostolic work

- *A good steward of material possessions . . .*

- *A man who can take on the role of a public person . . .*

The PPF argues that human formation

comes together in a particular way in the domain of human sexuality, and this is especially true for those who are preparing for a life of celibacy. The various dimensions of being a human person—the physical, the psychological, and the spiritual—converge in affective maturity, which includes human sexuality. (77)

Since it is incumbent that the humanity of the priest serve, in the words of the pope, as a "bridge and not an obstacle" to the proclamation of the gospel, it is no surprise that priestly formation programs must pay particular attention to solid formation in sexuality and the skills to live a life of celibate chastity with integrity, joy, and a peaceful integration of feeling and thinking.

Insights from the human sciences, especially psychology, contribute to our understanding of what constitutes healthy human formation. As the articles in the NCEA publication *Seminary Journal* make clear, the psychological sciences assist bishops, vocation directors, and seminary faculties to gain insight into a candidate's innate capacities and skills to participate in the seminary formation program. Experts in psychology provide invaluable help in the screening and admission of candidates. The screening process is valuable not only to identify problematic candidates who should not be admitted, but, more important, to help the candidate understand his gifts and talents and to enable the seminary staff to develop a plan of formation so that he can strengthen these gifts and overcome weaknesses that would impede his future effectiveness as an ordained minister.

Human formation refers to the interpersonal skills and capacities necessary for any candidate for the priesthood. These capacities, including psychological health, are essential for spiritual, intellectual, and pastoral formation to be successful. If a candidate is lacking or otherwise profoundly wounded with respect to these fundamental human capacities, no amount of prayer or spiritual direction is going to change the picture, and it is an abuse of the seminary formation program to assume that such changes can occur. In some cases, candidates may benefit from follow-up work with a counselor and the PPF provides support for these kinds of initiatives (PPF, 80). However, if a candidate requires serious, long-term therapy, the candidate should withdraw from the seminary program until he has resolved his issues (ibid.).

Clearly, solid human formation is critical to the psychosexual maturity that is essential for helping seminarians to live a life of celibate chastity joyfully and peacefully. Seminaries, following the direction of Pope John Paul II and the PPF, have developed excellent programs of formation in celibate chastity that contribute to the integration of the spiritual, moral, and psychological wisdom of the church's teaching on human sexuality. This topic, alone, is worth an extended essay in its own right. However, I would like to focus on an aspect of human formation that is of particular importance if priestly ministry is not only to survive but also to thrive in the future.

In PDV, Pope John Paul, under the category of affective maturity, highlights the importance of the ability to relate to others:

> Of special importance is the capacity to relate to others. This is truly fundamental for a person who is called to be responsible for a community and to be a "man of communion." This demands that the priest not be arrogant, or quarrelsome, but affable, hospitable, sincere in his words and heart, prudent and discreet, generous and ready to serve, capable of opening himself to clear and brotherly relationships and of encouraging the same in others, and quick to understand, forgive and console (cf. 1 Tm. 3:1-5; Ti. 1:7-9). (43; n. 125)

As I reflect on this passage in light of my many years engaged in the formation of seminarians, I am reminded of the wisdom of a great priest, the late Msgr. Philip Murnion of the Archdiocese of New York. Msgr. Murnion, for years, ran the National Pastoral Life Center that sought to strengthen the work of priests and laity by emphasizing the need to affirm each other's gifts and to work together collaboratively. As he often used to say, "Priesthood is not a license for private practice."

Msgr. Murnion gave voice to the great insight of the Second Vatican Council that reaffirms the church's understanding that the ordained priesthood and the priesthood of the baptized faithful, while they differ in essence and not just degree, are, however, "interrelated":

> Though they differ essentially and not only in degree, the common priesthood of the faithful and the ministerial or hierarchical priesthood are none the less interrelated; each in its own way shares in the one priesthood of Christ. (Dogmatic Constitution on the Church, 10)

Priestly identity, therefore, far from being threatened by collaboration with the baptized faithful, is strengthened by this mutual engagement. The recovery of the importance of human formation in today's seminary benefits the health of the entire church. If I may invoke a biological metaphor to amplify on this point, in the animal kingdom, biologists differentiate between creatures with an exoskeleton and those with an endoskeleton. Beetles and tortoises are examples of animals with a hardened carapace, an external skeletal structure or exoskeleton. Larger animals, including humans and other mammals, have an internal skeleton or endoskeleton.

For those creatures with an endoskeleton there is room for adaptability and growth in ways not possible for those possessing a rigid, inflexible exoskeleton. I believe that Pope John Paul II has helped us to see that formation for priesthood cannot be understood as acquiring a role or identity that one assumes as an exoskeleton or suit of armor. Priestly identity, especially the ability to relate to others, must be developed from the inside out as an endoskeleton that enables the priest to be the selfless servant of others, in particular, the baptized faithful.

To put it another way, a program of solid, human formation in the seminary is about personal integrity, accountability, and responsibility. A program that attends seriously to observable, demonstrable behavioral indicators of personal, moral, and spiritual maturity contributes to the holistic vision of the PPF, a vision that integrates the four pillars of formation.

The sacrament of orders is an ecclesial sacrament. It exists for the good of the church, to make sure that Christ's eucharistic mission to feed and to gather all persons endures to the end of time. Mature, healthy, well-trained priests are essential if we are to realize the brilliant ministerial vision of the church proclaimed by the Second Vatican Council. In view of the interrelated character of the ordained priesthood and the priesthood of the baptized faithful, the flowering of lay ministry is a gift to be celebrated. It is a magnificent blessing that does not diminish the role of the ordained, but accentuates the need for ordained leadership so that the fullness of the church may be realized. Creating a climate in which the gifts of all of the baptized and those of the ordained are respected in relationships of mutuality and care is the surest antidote against the harm done to the Body of Christ by elitism and clericalism. Priesthood is God's great and good gift, but it is God's great and good gift for the sake of the church, for the sake of God's holy people.

By way of conclusion, the PPF affirms the importance of psychology to support the screening, admission, health, and ongoing formation of seminarians and priests. Human formation is the foundational pillar for the training of priests. Ensuring that the priest's humanity is a "bridge and not an obstacle," in the wonderful phrase of Pope John Paul II, is an enduring legacy that is being implemented in seminary formation programs across the country. It is a legacy that will repay dividends for the flourishing of the church, a gift for which all of us who love the priesthood are deeply grateful.

The Inner Life: Being Healthy and Holy

Jan Slattery

Writing this reflection as an employee of the church as well as a practicing Catholic, mother, and grandmother, it has become quite apparent that clergy need to pay attention to their inner life. These times in our church demand this attentive focus and sensitivity. In addition, mutual, honest, and fraternal discussions and a keen awareness of why they chose priestly life are demanded in these times. My focus and attention will be on several points. First, my own experience working with both clergy and the church has been and remains a great gift and blessing. The vast majority of priests, deacons, and lay ministers and church officials "get it." This will never make the front pages of the *New York Times* or of the *Chicago Tribune* or be the "breaking news" of CNN. Our tradition was, is, and will always be one of being a child's advocate and as a place where the little ones can come to the Lord. The church's tradition is one of being a sacred and safe place.

More recently, the sad facts of the current crisis and worldwide scandal ought not diminish nor darken this fact; however, in many people's minds and hearts—believers and nonbelievers alike—it does. This fact cannot be ignored but perhaps in some strange and often painful way this precise place and time is ours to choose. The current situation is ours to which we must respond. What can we do with it? These dynamics are often not pretty and they certainly are not comfortable to manage, understand, and discuss. Additionally, the efforts of hundreds of safe environment coordinators and of the victim assistance coordinators are the untold success stories of the current crisis. The thousands of teachers, parish employees, and volunteers know about how to work toward prevention of child abuse and neglect in all of its forms. This is a cold hard fact that will never be a front-page story nor appreciated in its fuller implications for society at large. The current situation can be viewed as either a horrible tragedy or a blessing. Perhaps, it is both. Solid theology seems to direct us in this regard. It is this part of the inner life—basic awareness—that is central to acknowledge and to develop.

Second, the priests and brothers who have harmed children seem to share one key aspect of their "inner life" in common. They have most often seen their behaviors and actions as unproblematic. The problem is, they do not

Jan Slattery is director of the Archdiocese of Chicago's Office for the Protection of Children and Youth.

think they have a problem! This central aspect of these men is an interior dimension of who they are. They seem *not* to be able to reflect, discern, and understand the seriousness of what they have done and what impact their actions have had upon the church, the people of God, their victims, the victims' families, and the observers of their actions in society. The broad scope and the impact of their actions is so deep and so vast that it is often hard for any one of us to grasp but it is strikingly absent in most of the alleged clerical offenders. This inner capacity seems to be of interest to researchers but is most important in the initial and ongoing assessment of candidates to the seminaries and religious life, men in formation, and men in ongoing formation programs for clergy. These facts, as seen throughout this book and in the lived experiences of so many of us, must be transformed into concrete means of change. No organization can prevent all abuse from ever occurring again, but this one detail must be examined more deeply and more intently at every stage of formation, if we are to assist in the ongoing prevention of abuse.

Third, central in the inner life of priests is an ability to be aware of "who you are," how you influence others and are influenced by others. It is the ability to relate. Some call it the ability to "get along." This ability is based on an inner sense of relating well to self, others, and God. It first develops internally but shows itself externally. Again, most clergy are able to relate well and manage this aspect of themselves quite well. However, we now see problematic behaviors with clergy and even church workers in different and more challenging ways. Now, it seems that men from other countries, the more lonely and isolated clergy, the more naively heroic young church personnel, and some of the newly ordained clergy seem to be afflicted with an inability to relate well and healthfully with and to others. The dominant problems seem to be mostly grouped in the following categories:

1. Poor management of conflict
2. Poor personal boundaries
3. An inability to collaborate with others
4. Sexual misconduct with adults
5. Anger management problems

These recent years—post-Dallas—seem to highlight relational deficits that are all too common in both the laity and clergy. The inability to relate well to others—both children and adults—in a healthier manner is both striking and troublesome. But the solution seems to be psychological testing and interviews assessing the capacity to relate effectively. Such observations may require mentoring or supervision that hopefully will lead to healthier pastoral behavior. Concrete observation, mentorship, and supervision of these men and women—which could be incorporated into seminary training, ongoing formation programs for the newly ordained, the orientation program for priests from various cultures, and the new pastoral assignments for the young adult lay employees—will be our best form of prevention in this problem area.

Intercultural Competence and the Baptismal Call of All the Faithful

Allan Figueroa Deck, SJ

More people today are on the move, migrating across international borders, than ever before in the history of the human race. Among them are significant numbers of priests, men and women religious, and prospective candidates for the priesthood and religious life. The pastoral contexts for today's Catholic parishes, schools, and organizations reveal an ever-growing cultural, racial, and ethnic diversity. Seminaries, theological centers, and houses of religious formation are increasingly characterized by the encounter of diverse cultures. Almost 30 percent of the clergy and seminarians in the United States were born outside the country or are first-generation children of immigrants.

In this situation it is crucial that the nature of interculturality—intercultural communications and relations—be explicitly and intentionally explored. Taking diversity for granted, presuming that the myriad, delicate issues around cultural attitudes, preferences, behaviors, and ways of thinking are irrelevant and/or will simply resolve themselves is not a heads-up approach to facilitating the profound process of "giving and receiving," of mutual encounter, that is typical of intercultural relations at their best. In parishes, schools, and Catholic organizations throughout the United States as well as in seminaries and houses of formation, it is necessary to get serious about the very real blessings and challenges produced by the growing encounter of diverse cultures in most ecclesial settings today.

While there exists a great deal of goodwill around the question of diversity and multiculturalism on the part of church leaders and the faithful, there is usually not a great deal of real familiarity with the details about culture in its deepest anthropological meaning nor about the special conditions created in community settings when diverse cultures begin to rub shoulders and interact.

In other words, what does one need to know? How does one interpret information about cultures other than one's own? What attitudes are more constructive for responding to these situations? What can one practically

Allan Figueroa Deck, SJ, is executive director of the USCCB Secretariat of Cultural Diversity in the Church.

do to promote mutuality and reconciliation among all? What is intercultural competence really about? How does one become "proficient" in this area?

The US bishops' Committee on Cultural Diversity in the Church has produced five Guidelines for Intercultural Competence that provide a place to begin, an introduction to the attitudes, knowledge, and skills appropriate for intercultural engagement. The bishops insist on the need to ground the guidelines in a vision rooted in theology and in the church's contemporary magisterium and not merely in the secular wisdom of multiculturalism. They provide a simple educational tool in the form of a five-module workshop—one module for each of the guidelines—titled Building Intercultural Competence for Ministers. Here are the guidelines:

- Frame issues of diversity theologically in terms of the Church's identity and mission to evangelize

- Seek an understanding of culture and how it works

- Develop intercultural communications skills in pastoral settings

- Expand one's knowledge of the obstacles that impede effective intercultural relations

- Foster ecclesial integration rather than assimilation in Church settings, with a spirituality of reconciliation and mission

In the case of the assessment of candidates for the priesthood and religious life, what are the variations in attitudes and practices toward assessment itself from culture to culture? The failure to ask this question about cross-cultural exchanges of this nature leads to lack of information, misinformation, or distortion that negatively impacts recruitment and admission programs. Cross-cultural awareness is a key factor as well in the appropriate vetting of international priests and religious, or "missionaries" as they rightly may be called, for service outside their countries of origin.

Intercultural awareness and competence is a basic requirement for all Catholics who wish to follow Jesus Christ in the life of missionary discipleship to which all the baptized are called. The focus on competencies affects everyone, not just the international seminarian, priest, deacon, religious, or lay pastoral agent, but also their local US counterparts. Indeed, Catholics generally need to get serious about cultures, especially modern, secular culture, and about how the Gospel engages cultures, since this is the central point of Pope Benedict XVI's call for a new evangelization. Catechesis cannot proceed effectively if it prescinds from insight into cultures. Pope Benedict XVI, building on the legacy of his predecessors, Popes Paul VI and John Paul II, is encouraging church leaders of every kind to engage cultures on behalf of the Gospel message and repropose the faith among peoples for whom it has become "old hat" or irrelevant. To successfully do that requires intercultural capacity to engage and transform a people's most deeply cherished symbols, rituals, and narratives in the light of the Christian revelation. Consequently, proficiency in working with cultures and with intercultural contexts is not only a practical necessity for intelligently assessing, admitting, forming, and educating prospective candidates for ecclesial leadership. It is a requirement for effectiveness of ministry across the board. Intercultural competence gives us the tools to make faith come alive, to make it engaging, palpable, concrete, and exciting for the diverse cultural groups that make up the church in the United States today.

References

Ainsworth, M., and Bowlby, J. (1965). *Child Care and the Growth of Love*. London: Penguin Books.

Allen, J., and Dana, R. H. (2004). "Methodological Issues in Cross-Cultural and Multi-cultural Rorschach Research." *Journal of Personality Assessment* 82, 189–206.

American Psychiatric Association (2000). *Diagnostic and Statistical Manual of Mental Disorders, Fourth Edition, Text Revision*, DSM-IV-TR. Washington, DC.

Angelica, J. C. (1993). *Moral Emergency: Breaking the Cycle of Child Sexual Abuse*. Kansas City, MO: Sheed & Ward.

Associated Press (2007). "Data Shed Light on Child Sexual Abuse by Protestant Clergy." *New York Times* (June 16).

Avila, J., Van Gilder, B., and Lopez, M. (2007). "Preachers Accused of Sins, and Crimes." ABC News, 20/20. New York.

Badcock, Gary (1998). *The Way of Life: A Theology of Christian Vocation*. Grand Rapids: William B. Erdmans.

Batsis, T. (1993). "Roman Catholic Vocation Directors' Attitudes Regarding Psychological Assessment of Seminary and Religious Order Applicants." *Consulting Psychology Journal* 45 (3), 25–30.

Baumeister, R., and Exline, J. (1999). "Virtue, Personality, and Social Relations: Self-Control as the Moral Muscle." *Journal of Personality* 67 (6), 1165–94.

Baumeister, R., and Tierney, J. (2011). *Willpower: Rediscovering the Greatest Human Strength*. New York: Penguin Press.

Baumeister, R. F., Vohs, K. D., and Tice, D. M. (2007). "Strength Model of Self-Control." *Current Directions in Psychological Science* 16, 351–55.

Beavers, W. R., and Hampson, R. (1990). *Successful Families: Assessment and Intervention*. New York: Norton.

Beck, R., and McDonald, A. (2004). "Attachment to God: The Attachment to God Inventory, Tests of Working Model Correspondence, and an Exploration of Faith Group Differences." *Journal of Psychology and Theology* 32, 92–103.

Bellah, R., Madsen, R., Sullivan, W., Swidler, L., and Tipton, S. (1985). *Habits of the Heart: Individualism and Commitment in American Life.* New York: Harper & Row.

Berry, J. (1992). *Lead Us Not into Temptation: Catholic Priests and the Sexual Abuse of Children.* New York: Doubleday.

Betancourt, J., Green, J., and Carrillo, E. (2002). *Cultural Competence in Health Care: Emerging Frameworks and Practical Approaches.* New York: Commonwealth Fund.

Bier, W., ed. (1970). *Psychological Testing for Ministerial Selection.* New York: Fordham University Press.

Billett, S. (2011). *Vocational Education: Purposes, Traditions and Prospects.* Dordrecht, Netherlands: Springer.

Bolton, H. E. (1921). *The Spanish Borderlands: A Chronicle of Old Florida and the Southwest.* Foreword by Albert L. Hurtado. 1st ed., 1921. Albuquerque: University of New Mexico Press, 1996.

Brugger, E. C. (2008). "Anthropological Foundations for Clinical Psychology: A Proposal." *Journal of Psychology and Theology* 36 (1), 15.

Brugger, E. C. (2009). "Psychology and Christian Anthropology." *Edification: Journal of the Society for Christian Psychology* 3 (1), 5–18.

Bruner, J., and Taguiri, R. (1954). "Person Perception." In G. Lindzey (ed.), *Handbook of Social Psychology*, vol. 2. Reading, MA: Addison Wesley.

Burkett, E., and Bruni, F. (1993). *A Gospel of Shame: Children, Sexual Abuse, and the Catholic Church.* New York: Viking.

Cannon, M. (2001). "Cycle of Child Abuse: Links between Being a Victim and Becoming a Perpetrator." *British Journal of Psychiatry* 179, 459–96.

Cartor, T., Cimbolic, M., and Tallon, M. (2008). "Differentiating Pedophilia from Ephebophilia in Cleric Offenders." *Sexual Addiction and Compulsivity* 15 (4), 311–19.

Catechism of the Catholic Church (1994). Vatican City: Libreria Editrice Vaticana.

Center for Applied Research in the Apostolate (CARA) (2007; 2008; 2009; 2010). Annual Report. Washington, DC: Georgetown University.

Center for Applied Research in the Apostolate (CARA) (2011a). "Frequently Requested Church Statistics." http://cara.georgetown.edu/CARAServices/requestedchurchstats.html. Accessed September 5, 2011.

Center for Applied Research in the Apostolate (CARA) (2011b). "The Class of 2011: Survey of Ordinands to the Priesthood." A Report to the Secretariat of Clergy, Consecrated Life & Vocations. http://www.usccb.org/beliefs-and-teachings/vocations/ordination-class/upload/ordination-class-2011-report.pdf. Accessed September 5, 2011.

Cervantes, R. C., Padilla, A. M., and Salgado de Snyder, N. (1991). "The Hispanic Stress Inventory: A Culturally Relevant Approach to Psychosocial Assessment." *Psychological Assessment* 3 (3), 438–47.

Chamberlain, S. (2005). "Recognizing and Responding to Cultural Differences in the Education of Culturally and Linguistically Diverse Learners." *Intervention in School and Clinic* 40 (4), 195–211.

Cheston, S., Piedmont, R., Eanes, B., and Lavin, L. (2003). "Changes in Clients' Images of God over the Course of Outpatient Therapy." *Counseling and Values* 47, 96–108.

Cimbolic, M., and Cartor, T. (2006). "Looking at Ephebophilia through the Lens of Priest Sexual Abuse." *Sexual Addiction and Compulsivity: The Journal of Treatment and Prevention* 13 (4), 347–59.

Commons, M., and Richards, F. (2003). "Four Postformal Stages." In J. Demick and C. Andreoletti (eds.), *Handbook of Adult Development*, 199–219. New York: Kluwer Academic/Plenum.

Conference of Major Superiors of Men (1983). In Solidarity and Service: Reflections on the Problem of Clericalism in the Church. Washington, DC.

Connors, C. (1994). "Keynote Address to National Catholic Council on Alcoholism." Washington, DC: St. Luke's Institute.

Cooper, A. (1998). "Further Developments in the Clinical Diagnosis of Narcissistic Personality Disorder." In E. F. Ronningstam (ed.), *Disorders of Narcissism: Diagnostic, Clinical, and Empirical Implications*, 53–74. Washington, DC: American Psychiatric Press.

Costello, T. (2007). "Integrating Formative Roles." In A. Maanenti, S. Guarinelli, and H. Zollner (eds.), *Formation and the Person*, 242. Leuven: Peeters.

Cozzens, D. B. (2000). *The Changing Face of the Priesthood: A Reflection on the Priest's Crisis of Soul*. Collegeville, MN: Liturgical Press.

Crowell, J. A., and Treboux, D. (1995). "A Review of Adult Attachment Measures: Implications for Theory and Research." *Social Development* 4, 294–327.

Cuéllar, I., Arnold, B., and Maldonado, R. (1995). "Acculturation Rating Scale for Mexican Americans-II: A Revision of the Original ARSMA Scale." *Hispanic Journal of Behavioral Sciences* 17 (3), 275–304.

Dana, R. H. (1995a). "Impact of the Use of Standard Psychological Assessment on the Diagnosis and Treatment of Ethnic Minorities." In J. F. Aponte, R. Y. Rivers, and J. Wohl (eds.), *Psychological Interventions and Cultural Diversity*, 57–73. Boston: Allyn and Bacon.

Dana, R. H. (1995b). "Culturally Competent MMPI Assessment of Hispanic Populations." *Hispanic Journal of Behavioral Sciences* 17, 305–19.

Dana, R. H. (1996). "Culturally Competent Assessment Practice in the United States." *Journal of Personality Assessment*, 66, 472–87.

Dana, R. H. (1998). *Understanding Cultural Identity in Intervention and Assessment*. Thousand Oaks, CA: Sage.

Dana, R. H. (2005). *Multicultural Assessment: Principles, Applications, and Examples*. Mahwah, NJ: L. Erlbaum Associates.

Darley, J., and Batson, D. (1973). "From Jerusalem to Jericho: A Study of Situational and Dispositional Variables in Helping Behavior." *Journal of Personality and Social Psychology* 27, 100–108.

Deck, A. F. (2009). "Critical Issues for an Evangelizing Parish." National Federation of Priests Councils, Keynote Address (NFPC). San Antonio, TX.

Dik, B., Duffy, R., and Eldridge, B. (2009). "Calling and Vocation in Career Counseling: Recommendations for Promoting Meaningful Work." *Professional Psychology: Research and Practice* 40, 625–32.

Dorfman, W., and Hersen, M. (2001). *Understanding Psychological Assessment.* New York: Kluwer Academic/Plenum Publishers.

Economus, T. (1996). Panel presentation at the LINK-UP September conference. Chicago, IL.

Erikson, Erik. *Childhood and Society.* New York: W. W. Norton, 1950.

Falkenhain, M. A., Duckro, P. N., Hughes, H. M., Rossetti, S. J., and Gfeller, J. D. (1999). "Cluster Analysis of Child Sexual Offenders: A Validation with Roman Catholic Priests and Brothers." *Sexual Addiction and Compulsivity* 6 (4), 317–36.

Fava, G. (1999). "Well-Being Therapy." *Psychotherapy and Psychosomatics* 68, 171–78.

Fernandez, K., Boccaccini, M. T., and Noland, R. M. (2007). "Professionally Responsible Test Selection for Spanish-Speaking Clients: A Four-Step Approach for Identifying and Selecting Translated Tests." *Professional Psychology: Research and Practice* 38, 363–74.

Finkelhor, D. (1984). *Child Sexual Abuse: New Theory and Research.* New York: Free Press.

Finkelhor, D. (2003). "The Legacy of the Clergy Sexual Abuse Scandal." *Child Abuse and Neglect* 27, 1225–29.

Finkelhor, D., and associates (1986). *The Sourcebook on Child Sexual Abuse.* Newbury Park, CA: Sage.

Finkelhor, D., and Jones, M. (2004). "Explanations for the Decline in Sexual Abuse Cases." Department of Juvenile Justice, Department of Justice. Washington, DC: US Government.

George, F. (2010). *The Difference God Makes: A Catholic Vision of Faith, Communion, and Culture.* New York: Crossroads.

Giordan, G. (2007). *Vocation and Social Context.* Leiden: Brill.

Goh, M. (2005). "Cultural Competence and Master Therapists: An Inextricable Relationship." *Journal of Mental Health Counseling* 27, 71–81.

Golden, O. (2002). "The Federal Response to Child Abuse and Neglect." *American Psychologist* 5 (9), 1050–53.

Goleman, D. (2006). *Emotional Intelligence: Why It Can Matter More Than IQ.* 10th Anniversary Ed. New York: Random House.

Goleman, D. (2007). Social Intelligence: The New Science of Human Relationships. New York: Random House.

Gonsiorek, J. C., ed. (1995). *Breach of Trust: Sexual Exploitation by Health Care Professionals and Clergy.* Thousand Oaks, CA: Sage.

Groth-Marnat, G. (2009). *Handbook of Psychological Assessment.* Hoboken, NJ: Wiley.

Haugaard, J. J. (2000). "The Challenge of Defining Child Sexual Abuse." *American Psychologist* 55 (9), 1036–39.

Hennessy, J. (1994). "Psychological Testing in Vocational Selection." In Robert Wister (ed.), *Psychology, Counseling and the Seminarian,* 116–23. Washington, DC: National Catholic Educational Association, Seminary Department.

Hoffman, L. (2005). "A Developmental Perspective on the God Image." In R. Cox, B. Ervin-Cox, and L. Hoffman (eds.), *Spirituality and Psychological Health,* 129–47. Colorado Springs: Colorado School of Professional Psychology Press.

Hoge, D. R. (2002). *The First Five Years of the Priesthood: A Study of Newly Ordained Catholic Priests.* Collegeville, MN: Liturgical Press.

Hoge, D. R., and Okure, A. (2006). *International Priests in America: Challenges and Opportunities.* Collegeville, MN: Liturgical Press.

Hoge, D. R., and Wenger, J. E. (2003). *Evolving Visions of the Priesthood: Changes from Vatican II to the Turn of the New Century.* Collegeville, MN: Liturgical Press.

Hood, R. W. Jr., Spilka, B., Hunsberger, B., and Gorsuch, R. (1996). *The Psychology of Religion: An Empirical Approach.* 2nd ed. New York: Guilford Press.

Ippolito, J., Latcovich, M., and Malyn-Smith, J. (2008). *In Fulfillment of Their Mission: The Duties and Tasks of a Roman Catholic Priest: An Assessment Project.* Arlington, VA: National Catholic Education Association.

Jenkins, P. (1996). *Pedophiles and Priests: Anatomy of a Contemporary Crisis.* New York: Oxford University Press.

John Jay College (principal investigator and author) (2004). The Nature and Scope of the Problem of Sexual Abuse of Minors by Catholic Priests and Deacons in the United States, 1950–2000. Washington, DC: United States Catholic Conference of Bishops (USCCB). http://www.usccb.org/issues-and-action/child-and-youth-protection/reports-and-research.cfm.

John Jay College (principal investigator and author) (2006). The Nature and Scope of the Problem of Sexual Abuse of Minors by Catholic Priests and Deacons in the United States, supplementary data analysis. Washington, DC: United States Catholic Conference of Bishops (USCCB).

John Paul II (1992). *Pastores Dabo Vobis.* Boston: Saint Paul Books and Media.

Johnson, J., Lenartowicz, T., and Apud, S. (2006). "Cross-Cultural Competence in International Business: Toward a Definition and a Model." *Journal of International Business Studies* 37, 525–43.

Jones, E. E., and Thorne, A. (1987). "Rediscovery of the Subject: Intercultural Approaches to Clinical Assessment." *Journal of Consulting and Clinical Psychology* 55 (4), 488–95.

Kann, L., Telijohann, S. L., and Wooley, S. L. (2007). "Health Education: Results from the School Health Policies and Programs Study 2006." *Journal of School Health* 77 (8), 408–34.

Kaslow, N. (2004). "Competencies in Professional Psychology." *American Psychologist* 59, 774–81.

Kelley, C. (1995). *Cross-Cultural Adaptability Inventory.* North Brunswick, NJ: National Computer Systems.

Kennedy, E., and Heckler, V. (1972). The Catholic Priest in the United States: Psychological Investigations. Washington, DC: United States Catholic Conference.

Kinra, Asha K. (2008). *Guidance and Counselling.* New Delhi, India: Pearson Higher Education.

Kouzes, J., and Posner, B. (2007). *Leadership Practices Inventory.* 3rd ed. San Francisco: Pfieffer.

Lasch, C. (1979/1991). *The Culture of Narcissism.* New York: W.W. Norton.

Lawrence, R. T. (1997). "Measuring the Image of God: The God Image Inventory and the God Image Scales." *The Journal of Psychology and Theology* 25, 214–26.

Lee, K., and Ashton, M. (2010). *The HEXACO Personality Inventory—Revised: A Measure of the Six Major Dimensions of Personality.* http://hexaco.org/index .html.

Loftus, J. A. (1999). "Sexuality in Priesthood: *Noli Me Tangere.*" In T. G. Plante (ed.), *Bless Me Father For I Have Sinned: Perspectives on Sexual Abuse by Roman Catholic Priests*, 7–20. Westport, CT: Praeger.

Loftus, J. A., and Camargo, R. J. (1992). "Child Sexual Abuse among Troubled Clergy: A Descriptive Summary." Resources in Education (ERIC Document Reproduction Services No. ED 354-420). Greensboro, NC: ERIC/CASS University of North Carolina.

Loftus, J. A., and Camargo, R. J. (1993). "Treating the Clergy." *Annals of Sex Research* 6, 287–303.

Lu, F. G., Lim, R. F., and Mezzich, J. E. (1994). "Issues in the Assessment and Diagnosis of Culturally Diverse Individuals." In J. Oldham & M. Riba (eds.), *Review of Psychiatry*, vol. 14. Washington, DC: American Psychiatric Press.

Main, M., and Solomon, J. (1990). "Procedures for Identifying Infants as Disorganized/Disoriented during the Ainsworth Strange Situation." In M. Greenberg, D. Cicchetti, and E. Cummings (eds.), *Attachment in the Preschool Years*, 121–60. Chicago: University of Chicago Press.

Malgady, R. G. (1996). "The Question of Cultural Bias in Assessment of Diagnosis of Ethnic Minority Clients: Let's Reject the Null Hypothesis." *Professional Psychology: Research and Practice* 27, 73–77.

Masterson, J. (1993). *The Emerging Self: A Developmental Self & Object Relations Approach to the Treatment of the Closet Narcissistic Disorder of the Self.* New York: Brunner/Mazel.

Mayer, J., Salovey, P., and Caruso, D. (2008). "Emotional Intelligence: New Ability or Eclectic Traits." *American Psychologist* 63, 503–17.

McClone, K. (2009). "Intimacy and Healthy Affective Maturity: Guidelines for Formation." *Human Development* 30 (4), 5–13.

McGlone, G. J. (2001). "Sexually Offending and Non-Offending Roman Catholic Clergy: Characterization and Analysis." Unpublished dissertation. Ann Arbor, MI: UMI Publications.

McGlone, G. J. (2003). "Prevalence and Incidence of Roman Catholic Clergy Sex Offenders." *Sexual Addiction and Compulsivity* 10, 111–21.

McGlone, G. J. (2011). "Understanding the Clerical Sex Offender: A Review of the Research." In B. Geary and J. Greer (eds.), *The Dark Night of the Church's Soul.* Suffolk: Kevin Mayhew Publications.

McGlone, G. J., Ortiz, F. A., and Karney, R. J. (2010). "A Survey of Psychological Assessment Practices in the Screening and Admission Process of Candidates to the Priesthood in the U.S. Catholic Church." *Professional Psychology: Research and Practice* 41 (6), 526–32.

McGlone, G. J., Ortiz, F. A., and Viglione, D. J. (2009). "Cause for Hope and Concern: A Commentary on the Vatican Statement Guidelines for the Use of Psychology in the Admission and Formation of Candidates for the Priesthood." *Human Development* 30, 12–20.

McGlone, G. J., and Viglione, D. J. (2003). "The Rorschach Protocols of Non-Offending Roman Catholic Clergy: A New Template?" Paper Presentation. Society of Personality Assessment Annual Conference. San Francisco: SPA.

Meloy, J. (1986). "Narcissistic Psychopathology and the Clergy." *Pastoral Psychology* 35, 50–55.

Mercado, C., Tallon, J., and Smith, M. (2008). "Persistent Sexual Abusers in the Catholic Church: An Examination of Characteristics and Offense Patterns." *Criminal Justice and Behavior* 35, 629–42.

Miller-Jones, D. (1989). "Culture and Testing." *American Psychologist* 44 (2), 360–66.

Moore, T. (1936). "Insanity in Priests and Religious: I: The Rate of Insanity in Priests and Religious." *American Ecclesiastical Review* 95, 601–13.

Myerson-O'Neill, M. (1968). "The Bases of Clinical Inference." *Journal of Clinical Psychology* 24 (3) 366–72.

National Catholic Education Association (NCEA) (2010). "Psychological Assessment: The Testing and Screening of Candidates for Admission to the Priesthood in the U.S. Catholic Church: A Survey Study Conducted by the NCEA Seminary Department." Arlington, VA.

Niebuhr, G. (2000). "Vietnamese Immigrants Swell Catholic Clergy: Growing Influence on a Changing Church." *New York Times* (April 24).

Odell, C. (2010). "Together Is Better! 300 Catholic Leaders Share Stories, Hopes at Diversity Conference." May 12. *National Catholic Reporter.* http://ncronline .org/news/faith-parish/together-better. Accessed August 29, 2011.

Offit, A. (1977/1981). *The Sexual Self.* Philadelphia: Lippincott.

Oldham, J. M., and Riba, M. B. (eds.) (1995). "Issues in the Assessment and Diagnosis of Culturally Diverse Individuals." *American Psychiatric Press Review of Psychiatry* 14, 477–510.

O'Meara, T. (1999). *Theology of Ministry.* Rev. ed. New York: Paulist Press.

Ortiz, F., and McGlone, G. (2010). "Seminary Formators and Psychologists: A Collaboration Model." *Seminary Journal* 16 (1), 53–59.

Paniagua, F. (2005). *Assessing and Treating Culturally Diverse Clients: A Practical Guide.* 3rd ed. Thousand Oaks, CA: Sage.

Pedersen, P. (1988). *Handbook for Developing Multicultural Awareness.* Washington, DC: American Association for Counseling and Development.

Piquero, A., Piquero, N., Terry, K. J., and Youstin, T. (2008). "Uncollaring the Criminal: Understanding Criminal Careers of Criminal Clerics." *Criminal Justice and Behavior* 35, 583–99.

Plante, T. G. (ed.) (1999). *Bless Me Father for I Have Sinned: Perspectives on Sexual Abuse Committed by Roman Catholic Priests.* Westport, CT: Praeger.

Plante, T. G. (2002). "A Study of Priest Sexual Offenders." Paper presentation. Family Research Laboratory Annual Conference. Portsmouth, NH: University of New Hampshire.

Plante, T. G. (2010). "Understanding the Sexual Abuse of Roman Catholic Clergy." University of Santa Clara web site.

Plante, T. G., and Boccaccini, M. (1998). "A Proposed Psychological Assessment Protocol for Applicants to Religious Life in the Roman Catholic Church." *Pastoral Psychology* 46, 363–72.

Plante, T. G., and McChesney, K., eds. (2011). *Sexual Abuse in the Catholic Church: A Decade of Crisis, 2002–2012.* Santa Barbara, CA: Praeger.

Ramirez, S. Z., Wassef, A., Paniagua, F. A., and Linskey, A. O. (1996). "Mental Health Providers' Perceptions of Cultural Variables in Evaluating Ethnically Diverse Clients." *Professional Psychology: Research and Practice* 27, 284–88.

Ridley, C. R., Li, L. C., and Hill, C. L. (1998). "Multicultural Assessment: Reexamination, Reconceptualization, and Practical Application." *The Counseling Psychologist* 26 (6), 939–47.

Rizzuto, A. M. (1979). *The Birth of the Living God: A Psychoanalytic Study.* Chicago: University of Chicago Press.

Rolheiser, R. (2002). "On Carrying the Sexual Abuse Scandal Biblically." The Henry Somerville Lecture in Christianity and Communications. http://www .ronrolheiser.com/articles.

Rollack, D., Terrel, M. D. (1996). "Multicultural Issues in Assessment: Toward an Inclusive Model." In J. L. DeLucia-Waack (ed.), *Multicultural Counseling Competencies: Implications for Training and Practice*, 113–53. Alexandria, VA: Association for Counselor Education and Supervision.

Ronningstam, E. (2011). "Narcissistic Personality Disorder in DSM V: In Support of Retaining a Significant Diagnosis." *Journal of Personality Disorders* 25, 248–59.

Ross, L. (1977). "The Intuitive Psychologist and His Shortcomings: Distortions in the Attribution Process." In L. Berkowitz (ed.), *Advances in Experimental Social Psychology*, 173–220. Vol. 10. New York: Academic Press.

Rossetti, S. (2011). *Why Priests Are Happy*. South Bend, IN: Ave Maria Press.

Sandoval, J., Frisby, C. L., Geisinger, K. F., Scheunemean, J. D., and Grenier, J. R. (1998). *Test Interpretation and Diversity: Achieving Equity in Assessment*. Washington, DC: American Psychological Association.

Schuth, K. (1999). *Seminaries, Theologates, and the Future of Church Ministry: An Analysis of Trends and Transitions*. Collegeville, MN: Liturgical Press.

Schuth, K. (2006). *Priestly Ministry in Multiple Parishes*. Collegeville, MN: Liturgical Press.

Schuurman, J. D. (2003). *Vocation: Discerning Our Callings in Life*. Grand Rapids: William B. Eerdmans.

Seligman, M., Steen, T., Park, N., and Peterson, C. (2005). "Positive Psychology Progress: Empirical Validation of Interventions." *American Psychologist* 60, 410–21.

Shakeshaft, C. (2004). "Educator Sexual Misconduct: Synthesis of the Existing Literature." US Department of Education. Washington, DC: US Government.

Sipe, A. W. R. (1990). *A Secret World: Sexuality and the Search for Celibacy*. New York: Brunner/Mazel.

Sipe, A. W. R. (1995). *Sex, Priest, and Power: Anatomy of a Crisis*. New York: Brunner/Mazel.

Sipe, A. W. R. (1999). "The Problem of Prevention in Clergy Sexual Abuse." In T. G. Plante (ed.), *Bless Me Father For I Have Sinned: Perspectives on Sexual Abuse Committed by Roman Catholic Priests*, 111–34. Westport, CT: Praeger.

Sipe, A. W. R. (2010). "When Is a Crisis a Crisis: The Current Crisis of Sexuality in the Catholic Church." *National Catholic Reporter* (July 10).

Smith, M., Rengifo, A., and Vollman, B. (2008). "Trajectories of Abuse and Disclosure: Child Sexual Abuse by Catholic Priests." *Criminal Justice and Behavior* 35, 570–82.

Sperry, L. (2002). *Transforming Self and Community: Revisioning Pastoral Counseling and Spiritual Direction*. Collegeville, MN: Liturgical Press.

Sperry, L. (2003). *Sex, Priestly Ministry, and the Church*. Collegeville, MN: Liturgical Press.

Sperry, L. (2005). "Psychopathic Personality: An Absolute Contraindication for Ordination to the Priesthood." *Seminary Journal* 11, 64–70.

Sperry, L. (2009a). "Christian Anthropology of Healing: A Biopsychospiritual Perspective." In D. Shoeninger, K. Fung, L. Lussier, B. Lay, and R. Caccese (eds.), *Christian Anthropology: The Nature of the Human Person, Human Brokenness, and Healing*. McLean, VA: Xulon Press.

Sperry, L. (2009b). "Ethics and the Role of Christian Anthropology in Christian Healthcare Practice." *Journal of Christian Healing* 25 (2), 52–54.

Sperry, L. (2010a). *Core Competencies in Counseling and Psychotherapy*. New York: Routledge.

Sperry, L. (2010b). "Culture, Personality, Health, and Family Dynamics: Cultural Competence in the Selection of Culturally-Sensitive Treatments." *The Family Journal* 18, 316–20.

Sperry, L. (2010c). "Psychotherapy Sensitive to Spiritual Issues: A Post-Materialist Psychology Perspective and Developmental Approach." *Psychology of Religion and Spirituality* 2, 46–56.

Sperry, L. (2011a). "Culturally, Clinically, and Ethically Competent Practice with Individuals and Families Dealing with Medical Conditions." *The Family Journal* 19, 212–16.

Sperry, L. (2011b). "Evaluating Clinical Cases Using Clinical, Ethical, Spiritual, and Contextual-Cultural Competence Criteria: Part I." *Journal of Christian Healing*.

Sperry, L. (2011c). "Evaluating Clinical Cases Using Clinical, Ethical, Spiritual, and Contextual-Cultural Competence Criteria: Part II." *Journal of Christian Healing*.

Sperry, L., and Shafranske, E. (eds.) (2005). *Spiritually Oriented Psychotherapy*. Washington, DC: American Psychological Association.

Sue, D. W., and Sue, D. (2003). *Counseling the Culturally Diverse: Theory and Practice*. 4th ed. New York: John Wiley.

Sue, S. (1996). "Measurement, Testing, and Ethnic Bias: Can Solutions Be Found?" In G. R. Sodowsky and J. C. Impara (eds.), *Multicultural Assessment in Counseling and Clinical Psychology*, 7–36. Lincoln, NE: Buros Institute of Mental Measurements.

Sundberg, N. D., and Gonzales, L. R. (1981). "Cross-Cultural and Cross-Ethnic Assessment: Overview and Issues." In P. McReynolds (ed.), *Advances in Psychological Assessment*, 460–541. Vol. 5. San Francisco: Jossey-Bass.

Tallon, J., and Terry, K. J. (2008). "Analyzing Paraphilic Activity, Specialization, and Generalization in Priests Who Sexually Abused Minors." *Criminal Justice and Behavior* 35, 615–28.

Tang, T., Sutarso, T., Davis, G., Dolinski, D., Ibrahim, A., and Wagner, S. (2008). "To Help or Not to Help? The Good Samaritan Effect and the Love of Money on Helping Behaviors." *Journal of Business Ethics* 82, 865–87.

Terry, K. J. (2010). Update and Report to the USCCB Meeting in Baltimore (November). Washington, DC: USCCB.

Terry, K. J., and Ackerman, A. (2008). "Child Sexual Abuse in the Catholic Church: How Situational Crime Prevention Strategies Can Help Create Safe Environments." *Criminal Justice and Behavior* 35, 643–57.

Thies, J. (2010). "Cultural Competence: An Ongoing Quest." *Health Progress* (July–August), 11–14.

Tischler, L., Biberman, J., and McKeage, R. (2002). "Linking Emotional Intelligence, Spirituality and Workplace Performance: Definitions, Models and Ideas for Research." *Journal of Managerial Psychology* 17, 203–18.

Tisdale, T. C., Key, T. L., Edwards, K. J., Brokaw, B. E., Kemperman, S. R., and Cloud, H. (1997). "Impact of God Image and Personal Adjustment, and Correlations of the God Image to Personal Adjustment and Object Relations Development." *Journal of Psychology and Theology* 5, 227–39.

Twenge, J., and Campbell, W. (2010). *The Narcissism Epidemic: Living in the Age of Entitlement.* New York: Free Press.

United States Catholic Conference of Bishops (USCCB) (2006). Program of Priestly Formation. 5th ed. Washington, DC: USCCB.

United States Catholic Conference of Bishops (USCCB) (2010). Report of the Implementation of the Dallas Charter and the John Jay Study. Washington, DC: USCCB.

Van de Vijver, F. J. R., and Leung, K. (2001). "Personality in Cultural Context: Methodological Issues." *Journal of Personality* 69, 1007–31.

Vatican Congregation for Catholic Education (2008). Guidelines for the Use of Psychology in the Admission and Formation of Candidates for the Priesthood. http://www.vatican.va/roman_curia/congregations/ccatheduc/documents/rc_con_ccatheduc_doc_20080628_orientamenti_en.html.

Vieth, V. (2003). *Keeping the Faith: A Call for Collaboration between Faith Based Communities and Child Protection Communities.* Alexandria, VA: APRI.

Westermeyer, J. (1987). "Cultural Factors in Clinical Assessment." *Journal of Consulting and Clinical Psychology* 55, 471–78.

Wrzesniewski, A., McCaukley, C., Rozin, P., and Schwartz, B. (1997). "Jobs, Careers, and Callings: People's Relations to Their Work." *Journal of Research in Personality* 31, 21–33.

Authors and Contributors

Gerard J. McGlone, SJ, PhD, is executive director at Saint John Vianney Center in Downingtown, Pennsylvania. A nationally known expert and presenter, he has authored many articles, chapters, and books, including *Creating Safe and Sacred Places* (Saint Mary's Press, 2003), and two nationally acclaimed prevention programs: "The Instruments of Hope and Healing" and "Critical Conversations."

Len Sperry, MD, PhD, is a professor at Florida Atlantic University and at the Medical College of Wisconsin. He consults to dioceses and religious orders and is on ten editorial boards, including *Psychology of Religion and Spirituality*. Among his six hundred plus publications are the award-winning *Transforming Self and Community: Revisioning Pastoral Counseling and Spiritual Direction* (Liturgical Press, 2002); *Sex, Priestly Ministry, and the Church* (Liturgical Press, 2003); and *Spirituality in Clinical Practice* (2nd ed., Routledge, 2011).

The Most Reverend J. Michael Miller, CSB, has been archbishop of Vancouver since 2009, and was named coadjutor in 2007 by Pope Benedict XVI. Previously, he was secretary of the Vatican's Congregation for Catholic Education and vice president of the Pontifical Work of Priestly Vocations.

Fernando A. Ortiz, PhD, a consultant with the Saint John Vianney Center in Downingtown, Pennsylvania, is a licensed psychologist and the director of the Counseling Center at Gonzaga University in Spokane, Washington. His areas of research and practice include personality assessment and multicultural psychology. He works closely with Catholic dioceses and seminary personnel, providing consultation and training on the psychological treatment and screening of candidates to the priesthood.

Index of Names

Index of Subjects